# Hiking
# Yellowstone
## National Park

Published in cooperation
with Trails Illustrated Maps

Bill Schneider

FALCON®

Helena, Montana

**A FALCON GUIDE®**

Falcon® Publishing is continually expanding its list of recreational guidebooks. All books include detailed descriptions, accurate maps, and all the information necessary for enjoyable trips. You can order extra copies of this book and get information and prices for other Falcon guidebooks by writing Falcon, P.O. Box 1718, Helena, MT 59624 or calling toll-free 1-800-582-2665. Also, please ask for a free copy of our current catalog. Visit our website at www.FalconOutdoors.com or contact us by e-mail at falcon@falcon.com.

Photographs by the author.
Cover photo by Jeff and Alexa Henry.

Library of Congress Cataloging-in-Publication Data

Schneider, Bill.
   Hiking Yellowstone National Park / Bill Schneider.
       p.  cm.
   "Published in cooperation with Trails Illustrated Maps."
   ISBN 1-56044-564-5 (pbk.)
   1. Hiking—Yellowstone National Park—Guidebooks.   2. Backpacking—Yellowstone National Park—Guidebooks.   3. Trails—Yellowstone National Park—Guidebooks.   4. Yellowstone National Park—Guidebooks. I. Title.
GV199.42.Y45S346   1997
796.51'09787'52—dc21                                                    97-13908
                                                                                            CIP

## CAUTION

Outdoor recreational activities are by their very nature potentially hazardous. All participants in such activities must assume the responsibility for their own actions and safety. The information contained in this guidebook cannot replace sound judgment and good decision–making skills, which help reduce risk exposure, nor does the scope of this book allow for disclosure of all the potential hazards and risks involved in such activities.

Learn as much as possible about the outdoor recreational activities in which you participate, prepare for the unexpected, and be cautious. The reward will be a safer and more enjoyable experience.

♻ Text pages printed on recycled paper.

*"There is just one hope of repulsing the tyrannical amibition of civiliation to conquer every inch of the whole earth. That hope is the organization of spirited people who will fight for the freedom and preservation of wilderness."*

Bob Marshall

# CONTENTS

# CONTENTS

# CONTENTS

# CONTENTS

# ACKNOWLEDGMENTS

*Special thanks to the National Park Service for their cooperation in getting this book researched and reviewed for accuracy.*

Yellowstone is a huge place with an immense trails system and many special regulations to go with it. Getting everything right was not an easy task, and actually, it would have been an impossible task without the close cooperation of the National Park Service in the writing and review of this book.

The NPS spent many hours in planning and going over every word of the manuscript. This took time, of course, but the end result should be worth it. This book contains the most accurate and updated information available on the trails of Yellowstone—thanks of course to the NPS. If anybody has the impression rangers are there to make your life difficult, I can assure you that the opposite is true.

Tom Olliff of the Backcountry Office deserves special thanks for his help in coordinating the entire project from start to finish. However, the following rangers helped with the review—Brian Chan, Anne Marie Chytra, Colette Daigle-Berg, Bonnie Gafney, Les Inafuku, Mark Marshall, Dave Phillips, Mike Ross, and George Sechrist.

I must also thank the rangers I ran into out on the trails. I didn't get your names, but thanks for enduring my lengthy lists of questions.

Hiking over 800 miles of trails in one summer was quite the assignment, and my hiking partners had to survive a killer schedule (and bears, bugs, bison, big river fords, and other hazards) to get it covered. They are Carrie Bowen, Derek Sondregger, and the rest of the Schneider family (Marnie, Heidi, Greg and Russ). Also, Falcon employees Randall Green and Ric Bourie hiked the Mallard Lake Trail and helped write that hike description.

As always, the staff at Falcon Press Publishing had to put up with distractions and help in many ways. Special thanks to Randall Green, our guidebook editor, and Tony Moore who did the maps and charts, Sarah Synder who did the copy editing, and Janet Bukantis and Darlene Jatkowski who did the page layout.

## Yellowstone National Park Overview

# Getting to the Bechler River Ranger Station

# LEGEND

| | | | |
|---|---|---|---|
| Interstate | 00 | Picnic Area | |
| U.S. Highway | 00  000 | Campground | |
| State or County Road | 00  000 | Backcountry Camp | |
| Interstate Highway | ⟹ | Bridge | |
| Paved Road | ⟹ | Cabins/Buildings | ■ |
| Gravel Road | ⟹ | Ranger Station | |
| Unimproved Road | =======⟹ | Peak/Elevation | 9,782 ft. |
| Trailhead/Parking | ◯  Ⓟ | Falls | |
| Main Trail | ~~~~ | Pass/Saddle | )( |
| Secondary Trail | ~~~~ | Overlook/Point of Interest | ▢ |
| River/Creek | ⌒ | | |
| Lake | ⬭ | Continental Divide | |
| Spring | ⟳ | Map Orientation | N |
| Geyser/Hot Spring | ☼  ☼ | | |
| Forest/Wilderness Boundary | – – – – · | Scale | Miles  0  1  2 |
| State Boundary | MONTANA ▬ ▪ ▬ ▪ ▬ WYOMING | | |

X

# PREFACE: WHAT IT'S REALLY LIKE TO HIKE IN YELLOWSTONE

Hiking in Yellowstone is unlike any other place on Earth.

In Yellowstone, you can be alone. The park suffers the bad reputation of being overcrowded, but that is rarely the case on backcountry trails. While thousands drive around the Old Faithful area trying to find the bathroom, you can hike all day in the backcountry without seeing another person.

In Yellowstone, you can hike to some of the best fishing in the world. And the trout you catch have never seen a hatchery or eaten a marshmallow.

In Yellowstone, you can hike through perhaps the richest remaining wildlife sanctuary in the lower 48 states.

In Yellowstone, you can hike every step with the shadow of the great bear. In fact, it's impossible to hike in Yellowstone without thinking of the majestic grizzly bear. If you're anxious to see a grizzly, you'll be up early and late glassing the slopes. If you're ingrained with fear of the bear, you'll be noisily hiking in the heat of the day, watching the trail ahead and at night tossing sleeplessly in your tent convincing yourself that each night sound is a bear approaching.

In Yellowstone, you can come around a bend in the trail and be eyeball to eyeball with a 2,000-pound bison. At this point, of course, you beat a hasty retreat off the trail. Bison never yield to hikers.

In Yellowstone, you can hike through thermal areas—and not just on boardwalks in heavily used, roadside geyser basins. You can also spend hours carefully exploring backcountry thermal areas. Some thermal areas aren't even marked on maps. Mother Nature is in high gear in Yellowstone. New thermal areas spring up every year, and others cool off and go away. So you never know what will be around the next bend in the trail.

In Yellowstone, you can see so many waterfalls. Because the unique geology of the park has caused sudden uplifts, Yellowstone has more waterfalls than any other national park.

In Yellowstone, you can hear the drawn-out howl of the wolf, recently returned to its rightful place in the natural system of America's first national park. The master predator's song is like frosting on the cake for your night in the Yellowstone wilderness.

In Yellowstone, you can hike along the most beautiful streams. Some are large, like the Yellowstone or Snake, or small, like the Nez Perce or Fan, but all are untamed and natural—textbook examples of what a watercourse is supposed to look like without rip-rap or dams or bridges or channel straightening.

In Yellowstone, you have to really try hard to not have a memorable hike.

*Hiking the Black Canyon of the Yellowstone.*

*The Bighorn Pass Trail through Panther Creek, a good example of the openness of the terrain found in much of Yellowstone.*

# INTRODUCTION: BEARS, BISON, AND BUGS...

Here are a few things you might want to know about hiking in Yellowstone.

**Bears:** Unlike many parks and wilderness areas, you can't just go anywhere anytime. Yellowstone is managed for natural regulation in general and for the preservation of large predators, like grizzly bears and wolves. In some areas of the park, bear management affects hiking. Some areas are closed permanently, for part of the season, or have limited hours. In addition, any hazardous situation that develops often brings temporary trail closures that protect both bears and people.

**Bison:** The abundant wildlife of Yellowstone adds a spectacular element to the hiking experience, but when you see bison on or near the trail, do not be nonchalant. Bison look tame, slow, and docile, but the opposite is true in all cases. Always give bison a wide berth.

**Bugs:** The mosquito populations of Yellowstone are infamous. In June and July and even occasionally in August, the clouds of mosquitoes seem like they could block out the sun, so come prepared with plenty of repellent and netting. You can also wait until August or September when most mosquitoes die off.

**Prime season:** The best time to hike Yellowstone is August and September—for several reasons. First, hungry mosquitoes await hikers in June and July. Second, Yellowstone gets hundreds of inches of snow annually, and you can't hike high-altitude trails until mid-July. Some low-altitude areas (most notably the Bechler) stay wet and marshy into July. (In early July, Bechler Meadows can be a large lake, one or two feet deep!) Third, high water in Yellowstone streams can make fords dangerous until mid-July or later. And fourth, bear management regulations restrict entry and camping into some areas until July 1 or July 15.

**Downfall:** The fires of 1988 heavily burned much of Yellowstone, and now hikers are experiencing "the morning after." From a positive viewpoint, hikers can see the wonderful regeneration of a forest in many places. From a negative viewpoint, however, hikers can expect to climb over many downed snags left by the fire. Millions of burned trees will fall down in the next few years in Yellowstone, and probably a million or two will fall over trails. It's basically impossible for the Park Service trail crews to keep up with this, so expect to be climbing over a few logs on many trails in Yellowstone.

**Fords:** Many trails in Yellowstone involve fording large rivers. If this isn't on your agenda, be sure to research your hike in advance to make sure it doesn't involve a ford. Refer to the safety chapter in this book for information on fording rivers more safely and for a list of trails that have fords over large streams.

**Weather:** It can snow any day of the year in Yellowstone, so always be prepared for it. Normal weather patterns (if there is such a thing) in the

*Taking a break on the way to Heart Lake.*

*Fishing Thorofare Creek.*

summer create clear mornings with thundershowers (or "rollers" as they're called locally) in the mid-afternoon, followed by a clear, coolish evening. This means early morning hikers usually enjoy better weather, and they more often get their tents set up before it rains.

**Sharing:** Hikers don't have the trails of Yellowstone to themselves. They share those trails with a growing number of backcountry horsemen. If you meet a stock party on the trail, yield by moving off the trail on the uphill side and quietly let the stock animals pass.

**Getting to the trailhead:** If you have to drive long distances in Yellowstone, plan on about twice the normal driving time. This is especially true if you go through the Hayden Valley between Canyon and Fishing Bridge. You also save time by getting up early and driving to the trailhead before most tourists leave camp and clog the roads.

**Research pays:** Try to plan your trip (and alternatives to it) before you get to Yellowstone. This saves valuable time—and you want to spend that time hiking instead of driving around or waiting in traffic jams, right? Have a back-up plan. Bear management, fires, high water, road construction, and other factors can change things, and you want to have an alternative plan.

# PLANNING YOUR TRIP

It's amazing how pleasant and stress-free your hiking trip to Yellowstone can be when it's well planned. The following information should help you plan your trip.

## GETTING TO YELLOWSTONE

Yellowstone National Park crosses the boundary of three states—Idaho, Montana, and Wyoming, and unlike most national parks, Yellowstone has five entrance stations. You can drive to the park from these five gateway communities—Red Lodge, Gardiner, and West Yellowstone (all in Montana), or Cody and Jackson (in Wyoming). In addition, you can enter the park at the Bechler River Ranger Station in the far southwestern corner of the park, accessed from Ashton, Idaho. Expect to pay a fee to enter the park, but at least this money now actually goes to the park instead of the U.S. Treasury.

The roads to the park are well-maintained, but only two-lanes, and often crowded with traffic, including slow-moving vehicles. If you drive during mid-day, don't be in a hurry.

You can fly into small airports at Jackson, Wyoming, or West Yellowstone, Montana, but most park visitors fly into larger airports at Salt Lake City, Utah; Billings, or Bozeman, Montana; or Idaho Falls, Idaho.

The roads in the park are heavily used and always need repair, but they are all easily passable with any two-wheel-drive vehicle. The park speed limit is 45 mph (and strictly enforced), but in many cases, traffic moves much slower.

## GETTING A BACKCOUNTRY PERMIT

In Yellowstone, you must have a permit for all overnight use of the backcountry. If you use the advance reservation system, expect to pay a small fee for that permit. However, you can still walk into a vistior center without a reservation and get a free backcountry permit.

In 1996, the park installed a new computerized reservation system. This replaced a cumbersome system where hikers had to wait in line for permits and often couldn't get their preferred site. With the new system, you can usually get the campsites you want—as long as you start planning long in advance.

You really need a Backcountry Trip Planner, which explains the process of getting a permit. Get one by calling or writing:

Backcountry Office
P.O. Box 168
Yellowstone National Park, WY 82190
(307) 344-2160 or (307) 344-2163

The reservation system is relatively new, so some policies might change, but for now, the NPS has established the following policies:

*Hiking the Yellowstone River Picnic Area Trail and observing a natural fire in Hellroaring Creek in 1996. Fires can change your plans, so have a back-up plan.*

- Reservations are made on a first-come, first-served basis, beginning April 1 each year.

- You can call for help or advice, but phone reservations won't be accepted. Reservations must be submitted by mail or in person.

- Reservation requests must be on the Trip Planning Worksheet that comes with the Backcountry Trip Planner.

- A fee (currently $15) is charged for each trip. If you return to a road and go back into the backcountry at a second trailhead, that's another trip—and another fee.

- You can pay with cash, personal check, travelers check, or money order. At this point, credit cards are not accepted. The fee is nonrefundable.

- A confirmation notice will be sent out. This is not a permit, but you can exchange it for your official permit when you get to the park.

- Get your permit in person at a ranger station not more than 48 hours in advance of the first day of your trip, but no later than 10 a.m. the first day of your trip. If you miss this deadline, your permit will be released to other backcountry users.

- If the NPS has to close a trail or campsite for resource protection or safety reasons, the Backcountry Office will try to help you plan a similar trip.

- You can pick up permits at the following locations in the park:

Bechler Ranger Station
Canyon Ranger Station/Visitor Center
Mammoth Ranger Station/Visitor Center
Old Faithful Ranger Station
Tower Ranger Station
West Entrance Ranger Station
Grant Village Ranger Station
Lake Ranger Station
South Entrance Station

If possible, plan on getting your permit from one of the main locations listed above. In some cases, you can also get permits at the following locations, but the rangers stationed here have other responsibilities and may not be available when you get there.

East Entrance Ranger Station
Northeast Entrance Ranger Station
Bridge Bay Ranger Station

## BACKCOUNTRY CAMPSITES

If you're like most hikers coming to Yellowstone, you want more information about the campsites. You want to know if it has a good view, how far you have to carry water, how sheltered it is, if there is firewood around, etc. However, unless you're lucky enough to know somebody who has been at a campsite or find a backcountry ranger before you get your permit, that campsite will only be numbers on a map. Specific information on campsites is difficult to get.

Backcountry rangers in Yellowstone are, of course, familiar with the campsites, but they're usually in the backcountry, not at the visitor center giving out permits. NPS personnel stationed at the visitor centers commonly do not have specific information on campsites or trail conditions.

For the most part, the NPS has done a superb job of locating campsites in Yellowstone, so there aren't many bad choices. Nonetheless, some campsites are definitely better than others. If you plan to carry a big pack 10 miles into a mountain lake with several designated campsites, you really want a nice one, right? That's why we checked out every campsite while researching this guidebook and hiking the trails of Yellowstone. We've included a few details on every backcountry campsite in four sections following the trail descriptions for that corner of the park.

We rated the campsites with five-star (5★) campsite being the best and one star (1★) the worst. These ratings are, of course, subjective. When you go there, you might have a higher or lower opinion of the campsite. In most cases, we were at these campsites only once, so weather conditions on that

*Soaking in a great view over Beaverdam Creek at the north end of the Thorofare.*

day could sway our opinion. Also, a campsite might be under water with swarms of mosquitoes in June and July but dry and bug-free in August and September. The rating system is certainly not scientific, but it should give you some useful guidelines for selecting your evening accommodations.

Before you reserve a campsite, make sure you've checked the restrictions. Many campsites don't allow campfires, and others are closed until late in the season to protect fragile wildlife resources or for safety considerations.

As listed in the handout from the backcountry office, the NPS has split Yellowstone's campsites into four categories: hiker-only, stock-party-only, boater-access-only, and mixed which can be reserved by backpackers, boaters, or backcountry horsemen. This book only includes information on hiker-only or mixed campsites.

Numerous campsites in Yellowstone have obviously used tent sites too close to the food area or bear pole. For bear safety considerations, use another tent site at least 100 feet away from the food area or bear pole.

All campsites in Yellowstone are supposed to have bear poles. While hiking the park, we found a few without bear poles. Although this is usually a temporary problem, be prepared to improvise. Also, the bear pole is not always easy to find, so look carefully around before you assume there isn't one at your campsite. In some cases, a hard-to-see cable has been strung between two trees to serve as a food storage device.

Don't assume that all campsites are easy to find or have a noticeable trailside sign. These signs sometimes get knocked down or stolen. Keep the topo map out. When you get close to the campsite, watch carefully for it, so you don't have to backtrack to find it. In addition, ask the ranger giving you the permit for specific instructions to the campsite and mark the exact location on your topo map.

The park also has some off-trail campsites varying from 200 yards to a mile from the trail. These campsites are not always easy to find, and some do not have maintained spur trails. Again, ask about this when getting your permit.

One last note on campsites: The NPS is in the process of moving campsites located too close to trails. Bears use trails at night as travel corridors, so camping near a trail increases the chance of an encounter. This means some of the information listed in the campsite rating sections of this book might be outdated when you get your permit. When getting your permit, ask the ranger if the site has been moved.

## FOR MORE INFORMATION

For a great summary of basic facts on visiting Yellowstone, call the main park number and ask for a free copy of *Yellowstone Today*, a newspaper published by The Yellowstone Association. You can also get a copy at the entrance station when you enter the park. The paper contains a list of commercial services available in the park, updates on park road construction, lists of events and guided tours, campgrounds, medical and emergency services and facilities, area museums, special exhibits, and lots more useful information. *Yellowstone Today* will answer most of your questions about park services.

Because of budget cuts, the NPS is sometimes unable to keep up with all visitor inquiries, so please be patient when trying to get your questions answered. There are many books and other publications on Yellowstone that provide a wealth of excellent information, and this is often a better way to get information than calling the NPS directly. Many of these publications are available from The Yellowstone Association.

Contact the NPS at this address and phone number:
National Park Service
Park Headquarters
P.O. Box 168
Yellowstone National Park, WY 82190
(307) 344-7381

Contact The Yellowstone Association at this address and phone number:
The Yellowstone Association
P.O. Box 117
Yellowstone National Park, WY 82190
(307) 344-2296

TW Recreational Services handles commercial lodging in the park. If you need accommodations in the park, use this address and phone number:
TW Recreational services
P.O. Box 165
Yellowstone National Park, WY 82190
(307) 344-5324

---

## EMERGENCY MEDICAL SERVICES

In case of an emergency, call 911, just like the big city. However, because of the remote location, the park has limited medical facilities. You can find "comprehensive medical care in a wilderness setting" at three clinics (set up by the West Park Hospital in Cody, Wyoming) at Lake, Mammoth, and Old Faithful.

# YELLOWSTONE TRAIL FINDER

|  | EASY | MODERATE | DIFFICULT |
|---|---|---|---|
| **Backcountry Lakes** | Ice Lake | Heart Lake | Heart Lake Loop |
|  | Cascade Lake | Crevice Lake | Heart Lake to Snake |
|  | Trout Lake | Mallard Lake | River |
|  | Lost Lake | Falls River Basin | Heart Lake and the Two |
|  | Ribbon Lake | Bechler Short Loop | Ocean |
|  | Grizzly Lake | Lewis River | Yellowstone Lake to |
|  | Clear Lake Loop | Turbid Lake | Heart Lake |
|  | Riddle Lake | Wrangler Lake | Thorofare and South |
|  | Beula Lake | Grebe Lake | Boundary |
|  | Robinson Lake | Cache Lake | Thorofare and Two |
|  | Harlequin Lake | Cygnet Lakes | Ocean Plateau |
|  |  | Chain of Lakes | Summit Lake |
|  |  |  | Crescent Lake |
|  |  |  | Buffalo Lake |
|  |  |  | Fern Lake |
|  |  |  | Wapiti Lake |
|  |  |  | Sportsman Lake |
|  |  |  | Gallatin Skyline |
|  |  |  | Mary Mountain Trail |
|  |  |  | Shoshone Lake |
| **Waterfalls** | Wraith Falls | Osprey Falls | Black Canyon of the |
|  | Mystic Falls |  | Yellowstone |
|  | Fairy Falls |  | Union Falls |
|  | Tower Fall |  | Bechler River |
|  | Brink of the Lower |  | Buffalo Lake |
|  | Falls |  |  |
|  | Uncle Tom's Trail |  |  |
|  | Little Gibbon Falls |  |  |
|  | Ice Lake |  |  |
|  | Natural Bridge |  |  |
|  | Canyon Rim (North |  |  |
|  | and South) |  |  |

# YELLOWSTONE TRAIL FINDER

| | EASY | MODERATE | DIFFICULT |
|---|---|---|---|
| **Alpine Country** Ridges, passes, and plateaus | | Mount Washburn Thunderer | Sky Rim Gallatin Skyline Sportsman Lake Crescent Lake Big Horn Peak Specimen Ridge Republic Pass Dunraven Pass to Canyon Pitchstone Plateau Fawn Pass Bighorn Pass Thorofare and South Boundary Trail Two Ocean Loop Heart Lake and Two Ocean Plateau Bliss Pass |
| **Along Streams** | Boiling River Fan Creek Upper Gallatin River Lone Star Geyser Yellowstone Picnic Area Bacon Rind Creek | Sevenmile Hole Pebble Creek Rescue Creek Lava Creek Canyon Bechler Short Loop Solfatara Creek Tower Creek Garnet Hill Lewis Channel Bechler Meadows Nez Perce Creek Alum Creek Gneiss Creek | Bechler River Black Canyon of the Yellowstone Lamar River Mist Creek Pass Sportsman Lake Fairy Creek Heart Lake and Snake River Snake River Loop Thorofare and South Boundary Trail Thorofare and Two Ocean Plateau Heart Lake and Two Ocean Plateau Fern Lake Slough Creek Falls River Basin Bull Mountain Loop Mary Mountain Trail |

# YELLOWSTONE TRAIL FINDER

|  | EASY | MODERATE | DIFFICULT |
|---|---|---|---|
| **Thermal Areas** | Upper Geyser Basin<br>Sentinal Meadows<br>Lone Star Geyser<br>Artists Paintpots<br>Clear Lake Loop<br>The Hoodoos | Monument Geyser<br>Basin<br>Wahb Springs<br>Heart Lake<br>Sevenmile Hole<br>Turbid Lake | Wapiti Lake<br>Fern Lake<br>Snake River Loop<br>Heart Lake Loop<br>Dunraven Pass to Canyon<br>Heart Lake and the<br>Snake River<br>Fairy Creek<br>Republic Pass<br>Shoshone Lake<br>Pitchstone Plateau |
| **Really Flat Trails with No Hills** | Bacon Rind Creek<br>Boiling River<br>Cascade Lake<br>Canyon Rim (North<br>and South)<br>Ribbon Lake<br>Clear Lake Loop<br>Riddle Lake<br>Ice Lake<br>Storm Point<br>Sentinel Meadows<br>Upper Geyser Basin<br>Lone Star Geyser<br>Fairy Falls<br>Mystic Falls<br>Robinson Lake<br>Artists Paintpots<br>Beula Lake<br>Harlequin Lake | Fan Creek<br>Upper Gallatin River<br>Grebe Lake<br>Cygnet Lakes<br>Alum Creek<br>Nez Perce Creek<br>Bechler Short Loop<br>Wrangler Lake<br>Gneiss Creek<br>Lewis Channel | Chain of Lakes<br>Yellowstone Lake to<br>Heart Lake<br>Bechler Meadows |
| **Base Camp Option** | Hellroaring Creek<br>Grebe Lake<br>Bechler Short Loop | Shoshone Lake<br>Heart Lake<br>Bechler Meadows | Crescent Lake<br>Fern Lake<br>Wapiti Lake<br>Bull Mountain Loop<br>Pitchstone Plateau |
| **Mountain Tops** |  | Mount Washburn<br>Observation Peak<br>Purple Mountain<br>Avalanche Peak<br>Bunsen Peak<br>Divide Mountain | Electric Peak<br>Big Horn Peak<br>Mount Holmes<br>Mount Sheridan<br>Dunraven Pass to Canyon<br>Specimen Ridge |

11

# YELLOWSTONE TRAIL FINDER

|  | EASY | MODERATE | DIFFICULT |
|---|---|---|---|
| **Overnight Backpacking Trips** | Grizzly Lake<br>Ice Lake<br>Upper Gallatin River<br>Fan Creek<br>Ribbon Lake<br>Hellroaring Creek<br>Cascade Lake<br>Clear Lake Loop<br>Sentinel Meadows<br>Beula Lake<br>Robinson Lake | Gneiss Creek<br>Rescue Creek<br>Crevice Lake<br>Chain of Lakes<br>Mallard Lake<br>Wahb Springs<br>Sevenmile Hole<br>Wrangler Lake<br>Pebble Creek<br>Slough Creek<br>Agate Creek<br>Lamar River<br>Bechler Short Loop<br>Observation Peak<br>Shoshone Lake<br>Lewis Channel Loop<br>Union Falls<br>Bechler Meadows<br>Heart Lake<br>Grebe Lake<br>Lava Creek Canyon | Sky Rim<br>Sportsman Lake<br>Crescent Lake<br>The Gallatin SkyLine<br>Mount Holmes<br>Black Canyon of the<br>    Yellowstone<br>Republic Pass<br>Bliss Pass<br>Bull Mountain Loop<br>Dunraven Pass to<br>    Canyon<br>Mist Creek Pass<br>Wapiti Lake<br>Summit Lake<br>Fairy Creek<br>Pitchstone Plateau<br>Bechler River<br>Falls River Basin<br>Buffalo Lake<br>Heart Lake Loop<br>Snake River Loop<br>Two Ocean Loop<br>The Thorofare and<br>    South Boundary Trail<br>Yellowstone Lake to<br>    Heart Lake<br>Two Ocean Plateau and<br>    Heart Lake<br>Heart Lake to Snake<br>    River |
| **Trails To Avoid if You Don't Want To See Lots of Horses** |  | Fan Creek<br>Garnet Hill<br>Cascade Lake (from<br>    Cascade Creek<br>    Trailhead)<br>Upper Gallatin River<br>Wahb Springs | Sportsman Lake<br>Fawn Pass<br>Bighorn Pass<br>Lamar River<br>Thorofare and the<br>    South Boundary Trail |

# YELLOWSTONE TRAIL FINDER

| | EASY | MODERATE | DIFFICULT |
|---|---|---|---|
| **Trails To Avoid if You Don't Like Fording Big Rivers** | | Upper Gallatin River<br>Wrangler Lake | Bighorn Pass<br>Specimen Ridge<br>Black Canyon of the<br>    Yellowstone<br>Mist Creek Pass<br>Hayden Valley<br>Thorofare and South<br>    Boundary Trail<br>Two Ocean Loop<br>Yellowstone Lake to<br>    Heart Lake<br>Heart Lake and the Two<br>    Ocean Plateau<br>Heart Lake Loop<br>Heart Lake to Snake<br>    River<br>Snake River Loop<br>Shoshone Lake<br>Bechler River<br>Union Falls<br>Falls River Basin<br>Bechler Meadows<br>Buffalo Lake |
| **Trails To Avoid if You Don't Want To See Lots of People** | Boiling River<br>Trout Lake<br>Tower Fall<br>Canyon Rim (North<br>    and South)<br>Uncle Tom's Trail<br>Brink of Lower Falls<br>Pelican Creek<br>    Nature Trail<br>Storm Point<br>Natural Bridge<br>Upper Geyser Basin<br>Mystic Falls<br>Fairy Falls<br>Cascade Lake | Bunsen Peak<br>Mount Washburn<br>Cascade Lake<br>Sevenmile Hole<br>Elephant Back<br>    Mountain<br>Heart Lake<br>Lone Star Geyser | Slough Creek<br>Lamar River |

# USING THIS GUIDEBOOK

To use this book effectively, please note the following items.

## TYPE OF TRAILS

Suggested hikes have been split into the following categories:

**Loop:** Starts and finishes at the same trailhead, with no (or very little) retracing of your steps. Sometimes the definition of loop is stretched to include "lollipops" and trips that involve a short walk on a road at the end of the hike to get back to your vehicle.

**Shuttle:** A point-to-point trip that requires two vehicles (one left at the other end of the trail) or a pre-arranged pick up at a designated time and place. One good way to manage the logistical problems of shuttles is to arrange for another party to start at the other end of the trail. The two parties meet at a pre-determined point and then trade keys. When finished, they drive each other's vehicles home.

**Out-and-back:** Traveling to a specific destination, then retracing your steps back to the trailhead.

**Base camp:** A point-to-point hike where you spend several nights at the same campsite, using the extra days for fishing, relaxing, or day hiking.

## RATINGS

To help you plan your trip, trails are rated as to difficulty. However, difficulty ratings for trails serve as a general guide only, not the final word. What is difficult to one hiker may be easy to the next. In this guidebook, difficulty ratings consider both how long and how strenuous the route is. Here are general definitions of the ratings.

**Easy:** Suitable for any hiker, including children or elderly persons, without serious elevation gain, hazardous sections, or places where the trail is faint.

**Moderate:** Suitable for hikers who have some experience and at least an average fitness level. Probably not suitable for children or the elderly unless they have an above-average level of fitness. The hike may have some short sections where the trail is difficult to follow, and often includes some hills.

**Difficult:** Suitable for experienced hikers with above-average fitness level, often with sections of the trail that are difficult to follow or even some off-trail sections that could require knowledge of route-finding with topo map and compass, sometimes with serious elevation gain, and possibly some hazardous conditions.

## DISTANCES

In this guidebook, most distances came from NPS signs and brochures, but some trail mileage was estimated. Since it's so difficult and time

*Some trails in Yellowstone such as this one in Lynx Creek on the South Boundary Trail go through burned areas with numerous downed trees.*

consuming to precisely measure trails, most distances listed in any guidebook, on trail signs, and in park brochures are usually somebody's estimate. Keep in mind that distance is often less important than difficulty. A rocky, 2-mile, uphill trail can take longer and require more effort than 4 miles on a well-contoured trail on flat terrain. The moral of this story is don't get too excited if the distance is slightly off.

## MAPS

The maps in this book serve as a general guide only. You definitely should take a better map with you on your hike. The maps in this guidebook do not have enough detail or do not cover enough territory.

There are a variety of maps for Yellowstone, but in preparing this book, we used Trails Illustrated Maps or the USGS quads. You can get both maps at park visitor centers or sport stores around the park. You can order Trails Illustrated Maps from Falcon (see ordering information in back of this book). You can usually special order any USGS quad from your local sport store, or you can order them directly from the USGS at the following address:

Map Distribution
U.S. Geological Survey
Box 25286, Federal Center
Denver, CO 80225

# USGS TOPOGRAPHIC MAPS

## Index to USGS 7.5 Minute Quadrangles

| | | | |
|---|---|---|---|
| 1 | Big Horn Peak | 41 | Jack Straw Basin |
| 2 | Sportsman Lake | 42 | Buffalo Meadows |
| 3 | Electric Peak | 43 | Lower Geyser Basin |
| 4 | Gardiner | 44 | Mary Lake |
| 5 | Ash Mountain | 45 | Beach Lake |
| 6 | Specimen Creek | 46 | Lake |
| 7 | Hummingbird Creek | 47 | Lake Butte |
| 8 | Roundhead Butte | 48 | Mount Chittenden |
| 9 | Cutoff Mountain | 49 | Cathedral Peak |
| 10 | Cooke City | 50 | Pahaska |
| 11 | Divide Lake | 51 | Buffalo Lake NE |
| 12 | Joseph Peak | 52 | Summit Lake |
| 13 | Quadrant Mountain | 53 | Old Faithful |
| 14 | Mammoth | 54 | Craig Pass |
| 15 | Blacktail Deer Creek | 55 | West Thumb |
| 16 | Tower Junction | 56 | Dot Island |
| 17 | Lamar Canyon | 57 | Frank Island |
| 18 | Mount Hornaday | 58 | Sylvan Lake |
| 19 | Abiathar Peak | 59 | Plentycoups Peak |
| 20 | Pilot Peak | 60 | Eagle Creek |
| 21 | Richards Creek | 61 | Buffalo Lake |
| 22 | Three Rivers Peak | 62 | Trischman Knob |
| 23 | Mount Holmes | 63 | Shoshone Geyser Basin |
| 24 | Obsidian Cliff | 64 | Lewis Falls |
| 25 | Cook Peak | 65 | Mount Sheridan |
| 26 | Mount Washburn | 66 | Heart Lake |
| 27 | Amethyst Mountain | 67 | Alder Lake |
| 28 | Opal Creek | 68 | Trail Lake |
| 29 | Wahb Springs | 69 | Eagle Peak |
| 30 | Canoe Lake | 70 | Pinnacle Mountain |
| 31 | West Yellowstone | 71 | Bechler Falls |
| 32 | Mount Jackson | 72 | Cave Falls |
| 33 | Madison Junction | 73 | Grassy Lake Reservoir |
| 34 | Norris Junction | 74 | Lewis Canyon |
| 35 | Crystal Falls | 75 | Snake Hot Springs |
| 36 | Canyon Village | 76 | Mount Hancock |
| 37 | White Lake | 77 | Crooked Creek |
| 38 | Pelican Cone | 78 | Badger Creek |
| 39 | Little Saddle Mountain | 79 | The Trident |
| 40 | Pollux Peak | 80 | Open Creek |

16

# USGS TOPOGRAPHIC MAPS

## ELEVATION CHARTS

Many—but not all—hike descriptions include elevation charts. These charts don't give a detailed picture of elevation gain and loss on a hike, but they give you a general idea of how much climbing or descending you face on a trail. Hikes without elevation charts are either very short hikes or hikes without significant elevation gain or loss.

## SHARING

Everybody hopes to have a wilderness all to themselves, but that rarely happens. Instead, we have to share the trails of Yellowstone with other hikers and, more than most national parks, backcountry horseman, including large stock parties led by an outfitter.

If you meet a stock party on the trail, move off the trail on the uphill side and quietly let the stock animals pass. It's too difficult (and sometimes dangerous) for the stock animals to yield. Hikers should always yield to horses.

*Hikers share the trails with horses in Yellowstone, even in remote areas like this spot near the summit of Mount Sheridan.*

## BACKCOUNTRY REGULATIONS

Backcountry use regulations aren't intended to complicate your life. They help preserve the natural landscape and protect park visitors. The following backcountry use regulations are distributed to hikers when they get their permits.

In Yellowstone, you must:

- Have a permit for all overnight use of the backcountry.

- Camp in designated campsites.

- Build campfires in established fire rings and only at campsites where campfires are allowed.

- Suspend food at least 10 feet above the ground and 4 feet horizontally from a post or tree.

- Carry out all trash. If you can pack it in, you can pack it out.

- Have a valid park fishing permit if you're fishing the waters of Yellowstone. Children 11 years or younger do not need permits.

In Yellowstone, you must **not**:

- Feed, touch, tease, frighten, or intentionally disturb wildlife.

- Take pets into the backcountry.

- Possess or operate a motorized vehicle, bicycle, wheeled vehicle, or cart in any undeveloped area or on any backcountry trail.

- Dispose of human waste within 100 feet of any water source, or campsite, or within sight of a trail.

- Toss, throw, or roll rocks or other items inside caves, into valleys, canyons, or caverns, down hillsides, or into thermal features.

- Possess, destroy, injure, deface, remove, dig, or disturb from its natural state any plant, rock, animal, mineral, cultural, or archaeological resource.

- Violate a closure, designation, use, or activity restriction or condition, schedule or visiting hours, or public use limit.

- Use or possess weapons, traps, or nets.

## RATING THE HILLS

In the process of publishing dozens of hiking guides, Falcon Press Publishing has been trying to come up with a rating system to help hikers determine how difficult those "big hills" really are. Such a system would help hikers decide how far they wanted to hike that day or even whether they wanted to take that trail at all. In the past, our guidebook authors have described hills to the best of their ability, but subjectively. What is a big hill to one hiker might be a slight upgrade to the next.

Also, it isn't only going up that matters. Some hikers hate going down steep hills and the knee problems that go with descending with a big pack. These "weak-kneed" hikers might want to avoid Category 1 and Category H hills.

With the publication of this guidebook, Falcon is trying a new system to qualitatively rate hills. This new system combines the elevation gain and the length of that section of trail with a complicated mathematical formula to come up with a numerical hill-rating similar to the system used by cyclists. The system only works for climbs of 0.5 mile or longer, not short, steep hills.

Here is a rough description of the categories, listed from easiest to hardest.

**Category 5:** A slight upgrade.

**Category 4:** Usually within the capabilities of any hiker.

**Category 3:** A well-conditioned hiker might describe a Category 3 climb as "gradual," but a poorly conditioned hiker might complain about the steepness. It's definitely not steep enough to deter you from hiking the trail, but these climbs will slow you down.

**Category 2:** Most hikers would consider these "big hills," steep enough, in some cases, to make hikers choose an alternative trail, but not the real lung-busting, calf-stretching hills.

**Category 1:** These are among the steepest hills in the park. If you have heart or breathing problems, or simply dislike climbing big hills, you might look for an alternative trail.

**Category H:** These are hills that make you wonder if the person who laid out the trail was on drugs. Any trail with a Category H hill is steeper than any trail should be. (Incidentally, "H" stands for "Horrible.")

The climbs in Yellowstone are rated according to the following chart. Some climbs are rated in the hike descriptions of this book, but if not included (or to use this formula in other hiking areas), get the mileage and elevation gain off the topo map and look them up on this chart.

# FALCON HILL RATING CHART

| ELEVATION GAIN (in feet) | DISTANCE (in miles) | | | | | | | | | | | |
|---|---|---|---|---|---|---|---|---|---|---|---|---|
| | 0.5 | 1.0 | 1.5 | 2.0 | 2.5 | 3.0 | 3.5 | 4.0 | 4.5 | 5.0 | 5.5 | 6.0 |
| 200 | 4.2 | 5.0 | 5.4 | 5.5 | 5.6 | 5.6 | 5.7 | 5.7 | 5.7 | 5.7 | 5.7 | 5.7 |
| 300 | 3.3 | 4.5 | 4.9 | 5.2 | 5.3 | 5.4 | 5.5 | 5.5 | 5.5 | 5.5 | 5.6 | 5.6 |
| 400 | 1.8 | 4.0 | 4.5 | 4.8 | 5.1 | 5.2 | 5.3 | 5.3 | 5.4 | 5.4 | 5.4 | 5.4 |
| 500 | 1.0 | 3.5 | 4.2 | 4.5 | 4.7 | 5.0 | 5.1 | 5.2 | 5.2 | 5.2 | 5.3 | 5.3 |
| 600 | H | 3.0 | 3.8 | 4.2 | 4.4 | 4.6 | 4.9 | 4.9 | 5.0 | 5.1 | 5.1 | 5.1 |
| 700 | H | 2.5 | 3.4 | 3.9 | 4.2 | 4.3 | 4.5 | 4.8 | 4.9 | 4.9 | 4.9 | 5.0 |
| 800 | H | 1.4 | 3.1 | 3.6 | 3.9 | 4.1 | 4.2 | 4.3 | 4.7 | 4.7 | 4.8 | 4.9 |
| 900 | H | H | 2.7 | 3.3 | 3.6 | 3.9 | 4.0 | 4.1 | 4.2 | 4.6 | 4.7 | 4.7 |
| 1,000 | H | H | 2.3 | 2.9 | 3.4 | 3.6 | 3.8 | 3.9 | 4.0 | 4.1 | 4.5 | 4.6 |
| 1,100 | H | H | 1.9 | 2.7 | 3.1 | 3.4 | 3.6 | 3.7 | 3.8 | 3.9 | 3.9 | 4.5 |
| 1,200 | H | H | H | 2.4 | 2.8 | 3.1 | 3.4 | 3.5 | 3.6 | 3.7 | 3.8 | 3.9 |
| 1,300 | H | H | H | 2.1 | 2.6 | 2.9 | 3.2 | 3.3 | 3.5 | 3.5 | 3.6 | 3.7 |
| 1,400 | H | H | H | 1.8 | 2.3 | 2.7 | 2.9 | 3.1 | 3.3 | 3.4 | 3.5 | 3.5 |
| 1,500 | H | H | H | 1.6 | 2.1 | 2.4 | 2.7 | 2.9 | 3.1 | 3.2 | 3.3 | 3.3 |
| 1,600 | H | H | H | H | 1.9 | 2.2 | 2.3 | 2.7 | 2.9 | 2.9 | 3.1 | 3.2 |
| 1,700 | H | H | H | H | 1.7 | 1.9 | 2.3 | 2.5 | 2.7 | 2.8 | 2.9 | 3.0 |
| 1,800 | H | H | H | H | 1.5 | 1.8 | 2.0 | 2.3 | 2.5 | 2.6 | 2.7 | 2.8 |
| 1,900 | H | H | H | H | 1.3 | 1.7 | 1.9 | 2.1 | 2.3 | 2.4 | 2.6 | 2.6 |
| 2,000 | H | H | H | H | H | 1.5 | 1.7 | 1.9 | 2.1 | 2.2 | 2.4 | 2.5 |
| 2,100 | H | H | H | H | H | 1.3 | 1.6 | 1.8 | 1.9 | 2.0 | 2.2 | 2.3 |
| 2,200 | H | H | H | H | H | 1.2 | 1.4 | 1.6 | 1.8 | 1.9 | 1.9 | 2.1 |
| 2,300 | H | H | H | H | H | 1.0 | 1.3 | 1.5 | 1.7 | 1.8 | 1.9 | 1.9 |
| 2,400 | H | H | H | H | H | H | 1.2 | 1.4 | 1.5 | 1.6 | 1.8 | 1.8 |
| 2,500 | H | H | H | H | H | H | 1.0 | 1.2 | 1.4 | 1.5 | 1.6 | 1.7 |
| 2,600 | H | H | H | H | H | H | H | 1.1 | 1.3 | 1.4 | 1.5 | 1.6 |
| 2,700 | H | H | H | H | H | H | H | H | 1.1 | 1.3 | 1.4 | 1.5 |
| 2,800 | H | H | H | H | H | H | H | H | H | 1.1 | 1.3 | 1.4 |
| 2,900 | H | H | H | H | H | H | H | H | H | 1.0 | 1.2 | 1.3 |
| 3,000 | H | H | H | H | H | H | H | H | H | H | 1.0 | 1.1 |

# THE AUTHOR'S FAVORITES

| | | |
|---|---|---|
| **For Photography** | Sky Rim<br>Gallatin Skyline<br>Sportsman Lake<br>Specimen Ridge<br>Mount Holmes | Canyon Rim (North and South)<br>Mount Sheridan<br>Mount Washburn<br>Bechler River |
| **For Fishing** | Lamar River<br>Trout Lake<br>Slough Creek<br>Chain of Lakes<br>Bechler River | Lewis Channel<br>Shoshone Lake<br>Heart Lake Loop<br>Thorofare and South Boundary Trail<br>Yellowstone Lake to Heart Lake |
| **For High-Altitude Scenery** | Electric Peak<br>Mount Holmes<br>Mount Sheridan | Avalanche Peak<br>Gallatin Skyline<br>Sky Rim |
| **For Wildlife** | Gneiss Creek<br>Fawn Pass<br>Alum Creek<br>Specimen Ridge | Slough Creek<br>Hayden Valley<br>Mary Mountain |
| **For Wildflowers** | Pebble Creek<br>Specimen Ridge<br>Mount Washburn | Hayden Valley<br>Bechler Meadows |
| **For an Easy Day Hike** | Upper Geyser Basin<br>Tower Fall<br>Boiling River<br>Storm Point<br>Cascade Lake<br>Beula Lake | Canyon Rim (North and South)<br>Mystic Falls<br>Riddle Lake<br>Yellowstone River Picnic Area<br>Mount Washburn |
| **For a Moderate Day Hike** | Fan Creek<br>Beaver Ponds<br>Clear Lake Loop<br>Osprey Falls<br>Wahb Springs | Upper Gallatin River<br>Sevenmile Hole<br>Cache Lake<br>Nez Perce Creek<br>Bechler Short Loop |

# THE AUTHOR'S FAVORITES

| | | |
|---|---|---|
| **For a Long, Hard Day Hike** | Sky Rim<br>Fawn Pass<br>Bighorn Pass<br>Mount Holmes<br>Pitchstone Plateau<br>Big Horn Peak | Black Canyon of the Yellowstone<br>Dunraven Pass to Canyon<br>Mary Mountain<br>Hayden Valley<br>Union Falls<br>Specimen Ridge |
| **For the First Night in the Wilderness** | Cascade Lake<br>Grizzly Lake<br>Ice Lake | Mallard Lake<br>Shoshone Lake<br>Hellroaring Creek |
| **For a Moderate Overnighter** | Rescue Creek<br>Sevenmile Hole<br>Heart Lake<br>Crevice Lake | Grebe Lake<br>Bechler Meadows<br>Bechler Short Loop |
| **For a True Wilderness Adventure** | Fern Lake<br>Gallatin Skyline<br>Snake River Loop<br>Bechler River<br>Two Ocean Loop | Heart Lake and Two Ocean Plateau<br>Sportsman Lake<br>Thorofare and South Boundary Trail<br>Yellowstone Lake to Heart Lake |
| **For Thermal Areas** | Upper Geyser Basin<br>Shoshone Lake<br>Wahb Springs | Lone Star Geyser<br>Heart Lake<br>Sentinel Meadows |
| **For a Good Chance of Seeing a Bear** | Slough Creek<br>Hayden Valley<br>Fawn Pass<br>Bighorn Pass | Mary Mountain<br>Dunraven Pass to Canyon<br>Thorofare and South Boundary Trail |
| **For a Really Flat Trail** | Fan Creek<br>Upper Gallatin River<br>Cascade Lake<br>Chain of Lakes<br>Upper Geyser Basin | Riddle Lake<br>Nez Perce Creek<br>Lone Star Geyser<br>Bechler Meadows<br>Yellowstone Lake to Heart Lake |
| **For Base Camp Options** | Crescent Lake<br>Heart Lake | Fern Lake<br>Bechler Meadows |

# LEAVE NO TRACE

Going into a national park such as Yellowstone is like visiting a famous museum. You obviously do not want to leave your mark on an art treasure in the museum. If everybody going through the museum left one little mark, the piece of art would be quickly destroyed—and of what value is a big building full of trashed art? The same goes for a pristine wilderness such as Yellowstone, which is as magnificent as any masterpiece by any artist. If we all left just one little mark on the landscape, the wilderness would soon be despoiled.

A wilderness can accommodate human use as long as everybody behaves. But a few thoughtless or uninformed visitors can ruin it for everybody who follows. All wilderness users have a responsibility to know and follow the rules of no trace camping. An important source of these guidelines, including the most updated research, can be found in the book *Leave No Trace*. (Ordering information in the back of this book.)

Nowadays most wilderness users want to walk softly, but some aren't aware that they have poor manners. Often their actions are dictated by the outdated habits of a past generation of campers who cut green boughs for evening shelters, built campfires with fire rings, and dug trenches around tents. In the 1950s, these "camping rules" may have been acceptable. But they leave long-lasting scars, and today such behavior is absolutely unacceptable. The wilderness is shrinking, and the number of users is mushrooming. More and more camping areas show unsightly signs of heavy use.

Consequently, a new code of ethics is growing out of the necessity of coping with the unending waves of people who want a perfect wilderness experience. Today, we all must leave no clues that we have gone before. Canoeists can look behind the canoe and see no trace of their passing. Hikers, mountain bikers, and four-wheelers should have the same goal. Enjoy the wildness, but leave no trace of your visit.

---

**THREE FALCON PRINCIPLES OF LEAVE NO TRACE**

- Leave with everything you brought in.

- Leave no sign of your visit.

- Leave the landscape as you found it.

---

Most of us know better than to litter—in or out of the wilderness. Be sure you leave nothing, regardless of how small it is, along the trail or at the campsite. This means you should pack out everything, including orange peels, flip tops, cigarette butts, and gum wrappers. Also, pick up any trash that others leave behind.

Follow the main trail. Avoid cutting switchbacks and walking on vegetation beside the trail.

*The Petrified Forest on Specimen Ridge. Be sure to leave petrified wood, even small pieces, exactly where you found it.*

Don't pick up "souvenirs," such as rocks, antlers, or wildflowers. The next person wants to see them, too, and collecting such souvenirs violates park regulations.

Avoid making loud noises that may disturb others. Remember, sound travels easily to the other side of the lake. Be courteous.

Carry a lightweight trowel to bury human waste 6-8 inches deep and pack out used toilet paper. Keep human waste at least 300 feet from any water source.

Finally, and perhaps most importantly, strictly follow the pack-in/pack-out rule. If you carry something into the backcountry, consume it or carry it out.

Leave no trace—and put your ear to the ground in the wilderness and listen carefully. Thousands of people coming behind you are thanking you for your courtesy and good sense.

# MAKE IT A SAFE TRIP

The Boy Scouts of America have been guided for decades by what is perhaps the single best piece of safety advice—Be Prepared! For starters, this means carrying survival and first-aid materials, proper clothing, compass, and topographic map—and knowing how to use them.

Perhaps the second-best piece of safety advice is to tell somebody where you're going and when you plan to return. Pilots must file flight plans before every trip, and anybody venturing into a blank spot on the map should do the same. File your "flight plan" with a friend or relative before taking off.

Close behind your flight plan and being prepared with proper equipment is physical conditioning. Being fit not only makes wilderness travel more fun, it makes it safer. To whet your appetite for more knowledge of wilderness safety and preparedness, here are a few more tips.

- Check the weather forecast. Be careful not to get caught at high altitude by a bad storm or along a stream in a flash flood. Watch cloud formations closely, so you don't get stranded on a ridgeline during a lightning storm. Avoid traveling during prolonged periods of cold weather.

- Avoid traveling alone in the wilderness.

- Keep your party together.

- In Yellowstone, be extremely careful around thermal areas. In some cases, a thin crust can break and cause a severe burn, or death.

*Hikers in Alum Creek, getting dangerously close to bison. Make a wide detour around any bison you meet on the trails of Yellowstone.*

- Study basic survival and first aid before leaving home.

- Don't eat wild plants unless you have positively identified them.

- Before you leave for the trailhead, find out as much as you can about the route, especially the potential hazards.

- Don't exhaust yourself or other members of your party by traveling too far or too fast. Let the slowest person set the pace.

- Don't wait until you're confused to look at your maps. Follow them as you go along, from the moment you start moving up the trail, so you have a continual fix on your location.

- If you get lost, don't panic. Sit down and relax for a few minutes while you carefully check your topo map and take a reading with your compass. Confidently plan your next move. It's often smart to retrace your steps until you find familiar ground, even if you think it might lengthen your trip. Lots of people get temporarily lost in the wilderness and survive—usually by calmly and rationally dealing with the situation.

- Stay clear of all wild animals.

- Take a first-aid kit that includes, at a minimum, the following items: sewing needle, snake-bite kit, aspirin, antibacterial ointment, two antiseptic swabs, two butterfly bandages, adhesive tape, four adhesive strips, four gauze pads, two triangular bandages, codeine tablets, two inflatable splints, Moleskin or Second Skin for blisters, one roll 3-inch gauze, CPR shield, rubber gloves, and lightweight first-aid instructions.

- Take a survival kit that includes, at a minimum, the following items: compass, whistle, matches in a waterproof container, cigarette lighter, candle, signal mirror, flashlight, fire starter, aluminum foil, water purification tablets, space blanket, and flare.

Last but not least, don't forget that the best defense against unexpected hazards is knowledge. Read up on the latest in wilderness safety information in the recently published *Wild Country Companion*. Check the back of this guidebook for ordering information.

---

## YOU MIGHT NEVER KNOW WHAT HIT YOU

The high altitude topography of Yellowstone is prone to sudden thunderstorms, especially in July and August. If you get caught by a lightning storm, take special precautions. Remember,

- Lightning can travel far ahead of the storm, so be sure to take cover before the storm hits.

- Don't try to make it back to your vehicle. It isn't worth the risk. Instead, seek shelter even if it's only a short way back to the trailhead. Lightning storms usually don't last long, and from a safe vantage point, you might enjoy the sights and sounds.

- Be especially careful not to get caught on a mountaintop or exposed ridge; under large, solitary trees; in the open; or near standing water.

- Seek shelter in a low-lying area, ideally in a dense stand of small, uniformly sized trees.

- Stay away from anything that might attract lightning, such as metal tent poles, graphite fishing rods, or pack frames.

- Get in a crouch position and place both feet firmly on the ground.

- If you have a pack (without a metal frame) or a sleeping pad with you, put your feet on it for extra insulation against shock.

- Don't walk or huddle together. Instead, stay 50 feet apart, so if somebody gets hit by lightning, others in your party can give first aid.

- If you're in a tent, stay there, in your sleeping bag with your feet on your sleeping pad.

---

### THE SILENT KILLER

Be aware of the danger of hypothermia—a condition in which the body's internal temperature drops below normal. It can lead to mental and physical collapse and death.

Hypothermia is caused by exposure to cold and is aggravated by wetness, wind, and exhaustion. The moment you begin to lose heat faster than your body produces it, you're suffering from exposure. Your body starts involuntary exercise, such as shivering, to stay warm and makes involuntary adjustments to preserve normal temperature in vital organs, restricting bloodflow in the extremities. Both responses drain your energy reserves. The only way to stop the drain is to reduce the degree of exposure.

With full-blown hypothermia, as energy reserves are exhausted, cold reaches the brain, depriving you of good judgment and reasoning power. You won't be aware that this is happening. You lose control of your hands. Your internal temperature slides downward. Without treatment, this slide leads to stupor, collapse, and death.

To defend against hypothermia, stay dry. When clothes get wet, they lose about 90 percent of their insulating value. Wool loses relatively less heat; cotton, down, and some synthetics lose more. Choose rain clothes that cover the head, neck, body, and legs and provide good protection against wind-driven rain. Most hypothermia cases develop in air temperatures between 30 and 50 degrees Fahrenheit, but hypothermia can develop in warmer temperatures.

If your party is exposed to wind, cold, and wet, think hypothermia. Watch yourself and others for these symptoms: uncontrollable fits of shivering; vague, slow, slurred speech; memory lapses; incoherence; immobile, fumbling hands; frequent stumbling or a lurching gait; drowsiness (to sleep is to die); apparent exhaustion; and inability to get up after a rest. When a member of your party has hypothermia, he or she may deny any problem. Believe the symptoms, not the victim. Even mild symptoms demand treatment, as follows:

- Get the victim out of the wind and rain.

- Strip off all wet clothes.

- If the victim is only mildly impaired, give him or her warm drinks. Then get the victim in warm clothes and a warm sleeping bag. Place well-wrapped water bottles filled with heated water close to the victim.

- If the victim is badly impaired, attempt to keep him or her awake. Put the victim in a sleeping bag with another person—both naked. If you have a double bag, put two warm people in with the victim.

## FORDING RIVERS

Perhaps more than in most national parks, the trails in Yellowstone involve fords of major streams like the Lamar, Bechler, Falls, Gallatin, and Yellowstone rivers. When done correctly and carefully, crossing a big river can be safe, but you must know your limits.

The most important advice is be smart. There are cases where you simply should turn back. Even if only one member of your party (such as a child) might not be able to follow larger, stronger members, you might not want to try a risky ford. Never be embarrassed by being too cautious.

One key to safely fording rivers is confidence. If you aren't a strong swimmer, you should be. This not only allows you to safely get across a river that is a little deeper and stronger than you thought, but it gives you the confidence to avoid panic. Just like getting lost, panic can easily make the situation worse.

Another way to build confidence is to practice. Find a warm-water river near your home and carefully practice crossing it both with a pack and without one. You can also start with a smaller stream and work up to a major river. After you've become a strong swimmer, get used to swimming in the current.

When you get to the ford, carefully assess the situation. Don't automatically cross at the point where the trail comes to the stream and head on a straight line for the marker on the other side. A mountain river can reform itself every spring during high run-off, so a ford that was safe last year might be too deep this year. Study upstream and downstream and look for a place where the stream widens and the water is not over waist deep on the shortest member of your party. The tail end of an island is usually a good place, as is a long riffle. The inside of a meander sometimes makes a safe ford, but in other cases a long shallow section can be followed by a short, deep section next to the outside of the bend where the current picks up speed and carves out a deep channel.

*Fording streams can get risky in Yellowstone. Use extreme caution.*

Before starting any serious ford, make sure your matches, camera, billfold, clothes, sleeping bag, and perhaps other items you must keep dry are in watertight bags.

In Yellowstone, most streams are cold, so have dry clothes ready for you when you get to the other side to minimize the risk of hypothermia. This is especially true on a cold, rainy day.

Minimize the amount of time you spend in the water, but don't rush across. Instead, go slowly and deliberately, taking one step at a time, being careful to get each foot securely planted before lifting the other foot. Take a 45 degree angle instead of going straight across, following a riffle line if possible.

Don't try a ford with bare feet. Wear hiking boots without the socks, sneakers or tightly strapped sandals.

Stay sideways with the current. Turning upstream or downstream greatly increases the force of the current.

In some cases, two or three people can cross together, locking forearms with the strongest person on the upstream side.

If you have a choice, ford in the early morning when the stream isn't as deep. In the mountains, the cool evening temperatures slow snow melt and reduce the water flow into the rivers.

On small streams, a sturdy walking stick used on the upstream side for balance helps prevent a fall, but in a major river with a fast current, a walking stick offers little help.

Loosen the belt and straps on your pack. If you fall or get washed downstream, a water-logged pack can anchor you to the bottom (followed shortly by death), so you must be able to easily get out of your pack. Actually, for a short period, your pack might actually help you become buoyant and float across a deep channel, but in a minute or two, it could become an anchor.

If you're 6'4" and a strong swimmer, you might feel secure crossing a big river, but you might have children or vertically challenged hikers in your party. In this case, the strongest person can cross first and string a line across the river to aid those who follow. This line (with the help of a carbiner) can also be used to float packs across instead of taking a chance of a water-logged pack dragging you under. (If you knew about the ford in advance, you could pack along a lightweight rubber raft or inner tube for this purpose.) Depending on size and strength, you might also want to carry children.

Be prepared for the worst. Sometimes circumstances can arise where you simply must cross instead of going back, even though the ford looks dangerous. Also, you can underestimate the depth of the channel or strength of the current, especially after a thunderstorm when a muddy river hides its true depth. In these cases, whether you like it or not, you might be swimming.

It's certainly recommended to avoid these situations, but if it happens, be prepared. The first rule is don't panic. The second rule is do not try to swim directly across. Instead, pick a long angle and gradually cross to the other side, taking as much as a 100 yards or more to finally get across. If your pack starts to drag you down, get out of it immediately, even if you have to abandon it. If you lose control and get washed downstream, go feet first, so you don't hit your head on rocks or logs.

And finally, be sure to report any dangerous ford to a ranger as soon as you finish your trip.

## Hikes with Serious Fords

| | |
|---|---|
| Upper Gallatin River | Heart Lake and the Two Ocean Plateau |
| Bighorn Pass | Heart Lake Loop |
| Specimen Ridge | Heart Lake to Snake River |
| Black Canyon of the Yellowstone | Snake River Loop |
| Mist Creek Pass | Shoshone Lake |
| Wrangler Lake | Bechler River |
| Hayden Valley | Union Falls |
| Thorofare and South Boundary Trail | Falls River Basin |
| Two Ocean Loop | Bechler Meadows |
| Yellowstone Lake to Heart Lake | Buffalo Lake |

# BE BEAR AWARE

The first step of any hike in bear country is an attitude adjustment. Nothing guarantees total safety. Hiking in bear country like Yellowstone adds a small additional risk to your trip. However, that risk can be greatly minimized by adhering to this age-old piece of advice—be prepared. And being prepared doesn't only mean having the right equipment. It also means having the right information. Knowledge is your best defense.

You can—and should—thoroughly enjoy your trip to bear country. Don't let the fear of bears ruin your vacation. This fear can accompany you every step of the way. It can be constantly lurking in the back of your mind, preventing you from enjoying the wildest and most beautiful places left on Earth. And even worse, some bear experts think bears might actually be able to sense your fear.

Being prepared and being knowledgeable gives you confidence. It allows you to fight back the fear that can burden you throughout your stay in bear country. You won't—nor should you—forget about bears and the basic rules of safety, but proper preparation allows you to keep the fear of bears at bay and let enjoyment rule the day.

And on top of that, do we really want to be totally safe? If we did, we probably would never go hiking in

*In Yellowstone, bears often get higher priority than hikers, so be prepared for special regulations and closures that might affect your hiking plans.*

the wilderness—bears or no bears. We certainly wouldn't, at much greater risk, drive  hundreds of miles to get to the trailhead. Perhaps a tinge of danger adds a desired element to our wilderness trip.

## HIKING IN BEAR COUNTRY

Nobody likes surprises, and bears dislike them, too. The majority of bear maulings occur when a hiker surprises a bear. Therefore, it's vital to do everything possible to avoid these surprise meetings. Perhaps the best way is to know the five-part system. If you follow these five rules, the chance of encountering a bear on the trail sink to the slimmest possible margin.

- Be alert.

- Go in a large group and stay together.

- Stay on the trail.

- Hike in the middle of the day.

- Make loud noise.

**No substitute for alertness:** As you hike, watch ahead and to the sides. Don't fall into the all-too-common and particularly nasty habit of fixating on the trail 10 feet ahead. It's especially easy to do this when dragging a heavy pack up a long hill or when carefully watching your step on a heavily eroded trail.

Using your knowledge of bear habitat and habits, be especially alert in areas most likely to be frequented by bears such as avalanche chutes, berry patches, along streams, through stands of whitebark pine, etc.

Watch carefully for bear sign and be especially watchful (and noisy) if you see any. If you see a track or a scat, but it doesn't look fresh, pretend it's fresh. This area is obviously frequented by bears.

**Watch the wind:** The wind can be a friend or foe. The strength and direction of the wind can make a significant difference in your chances of an encounter with a bear. When the wind is blowing at your back, your smell travels ahead of you alerting any bear that might be on or near the trail ahead. Conversely, when the wind blows in your face, your chances of a surprise meeting with a bear increase, so make more noise and be more alert.

A strong wind can also be noisy and limit a bear's ability to hear you coming. If a bear can't smell **or** hear you coming, the chances of an encounter greatly increase, so watch the wind.

**Safety in numbers:** There have been very few instances where a large group has had an encounter with a bear. On the other hand, a large percentage of hikers mauled by bears were hiking alone. Large groups naturally make more noise and put out more smell and probably appear more threatening to bears. In addition, if you're hiking alone and get injured, there is nobody to go for help. For these reasons, rangers in Yellowstone recommend parties of four or more hikers when going into bear country.

If the large party splits up, it becomes two small groups, and the advantage is lost, so stay together. If you're on a family hike, keep the kids from running ahead. If you're in a large group, keep the stronger members from going ahead or weaker members from lagging behind. The best way to prevent this natural separation is to ask one the slowest members of the group to lead. This keeps everybody together.

**Stay on the trail:** Although bears use trails, they don't often use them during mid-day when hikers commonly use them. Through generations of associating trails with people, bears probably expect to find hikers on trails, especially during mid-day.

Contrarily, bears probably don't expect to find hikers off trails. Bears rarely settle down in a day bed right along a heavily used trail. However, if you wander around in thickets off the trail, you are more likely to stumble into an occupied day bed or cross paths with a traveling bear.

**Sleeping late:** Bears—and most other wildlife—usually aren't active during the middle of a day, especially on a hot summer day. Wild animals are most active around dawn and dusk. Therefore, hiking early in the morning or late afternoon increases your chances of seeing wildlife, including bears. Likewise, hiking during mid-day on a hot August day greatly reduces the chance of an encounter.

**Sounds:** Perhaps the best way to avoid a surprise meeting with a bear is to make sure the bear knows you're coming, so make lots of noise. Some experts think metallic noise is superior to human voices, which can be muffled by natural conditions, but the important issue is making lots of noise, regardless of what kind of noise.

**Running:** Many avid runners like to get off paved roads and running tracks and onto backcountry trails. But running on trails in bear country can be seriously hazardous to your health.

**Leave the night to the bears:** Like running on trails, hiking at night can be very risky. Bears are more active after dark, and you can't see them until it's too late. If you get caught at night, be sure to make lots of noise, and remember that bears commonly travel on hiking trails at night.

**You can be dead meat, too:** If you see or smell a carcass of a dead animal when hiking, immediately vacate the area. Don't let your curiosity keep you near the carcass a second longer than necessary. Bears commonly hang around a carcass, guarding it and feeding on it for days until it's completely consumed. Your presence could easily be interpreted as a threat to the bear's food supply, and a vicious attack could be imminent.

If you see a carcass ahead of you on the trail, don't go any closer. Instead, abandon your hike and return to the trailhead. If the carcass is between you and the trailhead, take a very long detour around it, upwind from the carcass, making lots of noise along the way. Be sure to report the carcass to the local ranger. This might prompt a temporary trail closure or special warnings and prevent injury to other hikers. Rangers will, in some cases, go in and drag the carcass away from the trail.

**Cute, cuddly, and lethal:** If you see a bear cub, don't go one inch closer to it. It might seem abandoned, but it most likely is not. Mother bear is probably very close, and female bears fiercely defend their young.

**It doesn't do you any good in your pack:** If you brought a repellent such as pepper spray, don't bury it in your pack. Keep it as accessible as possible. Most pepper spray comes in a holster or somehow conveniently attaches to your belt or pack. Such protection won't do you any good if you can't have it ready to fire in one or two seconds. Before hitting the trail, read the directions carefully and test fire the spray.

**Regulations:** Nobody likes rules and regulations. However, national parks have a few that you must follow. These rules aren't meant to take the freedom out of your trip. They are meant to help bring you back safely.

When you get a backcountry camping permit in Yellowstone, you get a brochure with a list of these rules—and get to see a video, too. Be sure to take a few minutes to read the brochure and the notices posted on the information board at the trailhead.

**But I didn't see any bears:** Now, you know how to be safe. Walk up the trail constantly clanging two metal pans together. It works every time. You won't see a bear, but you'll hate your "wilderness experience." You left the city to get away from loud noise.

Yes, you can be very safe, but how safe do you want to be and still be able to enjoy your trip? It's a balancing act. First, be knowledgeable and then decide how far you want to go. Everybody has to make their own personal choice.

Here's another conflict. If you do everything listed here, you most likely will not see any bears—or any deer or moose or eagles or any other wildlife. Again, you make the choice. If you want to be as safe as possible, follow these rules religiously. If you want to see wildlife, including bears, do all of this in reverse, but then, you are increasing your chances of an encounter instead of decreasing it.

## CAMPING IN BEAR COUNTRY

Staying overnight in bear country is not dangerous, but it adds a slight additional risk to your trip. The main difference is the presence of more food, cooking, and garbage. Plus, you are in bear country at night when bears are usually most active. Once again, however, following a few basic rules greatly minimizes this risk.

**Storing food and garbage:** If the campsite doesn't have a bear pole, be sure to set one up or at least locate one before it gets dark. It's not only difficult to store food after darkness falls, but it's easier to forget some juicy morsel on the ground. Also, be sure to store food in airtight, waterproof bags to prevent food odors from circulating throughout the forest. For double protection, put food and garbage in zip-locked bags and then seal tightly in a larger plastic bag.

The following illustrations depict three popular methods. In any case, try to get food and garbage at least 10 feet off the ground.

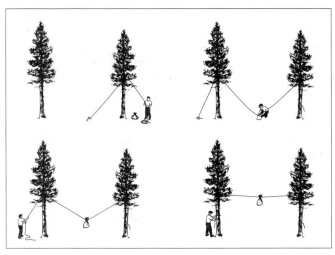

*Hanging food and garbage between two trees.*

*Hanging food and garbage over a tree branch.*

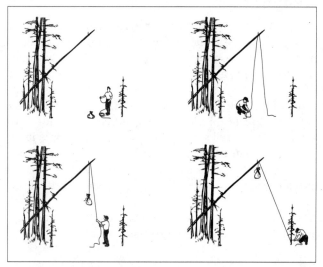

*Hanging food and garbage over a leaning tree.*

**Special equipment:** It's not really that special, but one piece of equipment you definitely need is a good supply of zip-locked bags. This handy invention is perfect for keeping food smell to a minimum and helps keep food from spilling on your pack, clothing, or other gear.

Take a special bag for storing food. The bag must be sturdy and waterproof. You can get dry bags at most outdoor specialty stores, but you can get by with a trash compactor bag. Regular garbage bags can break and leave your food spread on the ground.

You also need 100 feet of nylon cord. You don't need a heavy climbing rope to store food. Go light instead. Parachute cord will usually suffice unless you plan to hang large quantities of food and gear (which might be the case on a long backpacking excursion with a large group).

You can also buy a small pulley system to make hoisting a heavy load easier. Again, you can usually get by without this extra weight in your pack unless you have a massive load to hang.

**Getting the food up there:** People get hurt hanging their food at night, so be careful.

The classic method is tying a rock or piece of wood to the end of your rope and tossing it over the branch and then attaching it to the bag and hoisting it up 10 feet or more. If the load gets too heavy, wrap it around a small tree or branch for leverage.

If you can't tie the rope to the rock, put the rock in a small bag and then toss it over the bear pole. Use gloves so you don't get rope burns. And of course, don't let the rock or wood come down on your head (it happens!). Also, don't let anybody stand under the bag until you're sure its securely in place.

As a footnote, be careful not to leave your rope behind the next morning. Once you've untied your food, slowly pull your rope over the branch. Don't jerk it. If the rope gets stuck and you can't climb the tree, you have to leave it behind.

**What to hang:** To be as safe as possible, store everything that has any food smell. This includes cooking gear, eating utensils, bags used to keep food in your pack, all garbage, and even clothes with food smells on them. If you spilled something on your clothes, change into other clothes for sleeping and hang clothes with food smells with the food and garbage. If you take them into the tent, you aren't separating your sleeping area from food smells. Try to keep food odors off your pack, but if you failed, put the food bag inside and hang the pack.

**What to keep in your tent:** You can't be too careful in keeping food smells out of the tent. Just in case a bear has become accustomed to coming into that campsite looking for food, it's vital to keep all food smells out of the tent. This often includes your pack, which is hard to keep odor-free. Usually only take valuables (like cameras and binoculars), clothing, and sleeping gear into the tent.

If you brought a bear repellent, such as pepper spray, sleep with it. Also, keep a flashlight in the tent. If an animal comes into camp and wakes you up, you need the flashlight to identify it.

**The campfire:** Regulations prohibit campfires in some parts of Yellowstone, but if you're in an area where fires are allowed, treat yourself. Besides adding the nightly entertainment, the fire might make your camp safer from bears.

The campfire provides the best possible way to get rid of food smells. Build a small but hot fire and thoroughly burn everything that smells of food—garbage, leftovers, fish entrails, everything. If you brought food in cans or other incombustible containers, burn them, too. You can even dump extra water from cooking or dish water on the edge of the fire to erase the smell.

Be very sure you have the fire hot enough to completely burn everything. If you leave partially burned food scraps in the fire, you are setting up a dangerous situation for the next camper to use this site.

Before leaving camp the next morning, dig out the fire pit and pack out anything that has not completely burned, even if you believe it no longer carries food smells. For example, many foods like dried soup or hot chocolate come in foil packages that might seem like they burn, but they really don't. Pack out the scorched foil and cans (now with very minor food smells). Also, pack out foil and cans left by other campers.

**Types of food:** Don't get paranoid about the types of food you bring. All food has some smell, and you can make your trip much less enjoyable by fretting too much over food.

Perhaps the safest option is freeze-dried food. It carries very little smell, and it comes in convenient envelopes that allow you to "cook it" by merely adding boiling water. This means you don't have cooking pans to wash or store. However, freeze-dried food is very expensive, and many backpackers don't use it—and still safely enjoy bear country.

Dry, pre-packed meals (often pasta- or rice-based) offer an affordable compromise to freeze-dried foods. Also, take your favorite high-energy snack and don't worry about it. Avoid fresh fruit and canned meats and fish.

The key point is this. What food you have along is much less critical than how you handle it, cook it, and store it. A can of tuna fish might put out a smell, but if you eat all of it in one meal, don't spill it on the ground or on your clothes, and burn the can later, it can be quite safe.

Hanging food at night is not the only storage issue. Also, make sure you place food correctly in your pack. Use airtight packages as much as possible. Store food in the containers it came in or, when opened, in zip-locked bags. This keeps food smells out of your pack and off your other camping gear and clothes.

**How to cook:** The overriding philosophy of cooking in bear country is to create as little odor as possible. Keep it simple. Use as few pans and dishes as possible.

Unless it's a weather emergency, don't cook in the tent. If you like winter backpacking, you probably cook in the tent, but you should have a different tent for summer backpacking.

If you can have a campfire and decide to cook fish, try cooking in aluminum foil envelopes instead of frying them. Then, after removing the cooked fish, quickly and completely burn the fish scraps off the foil. Using foil also means you don't have to wash the pan you used to cook the fish.

Be careful not to spill on yourself while cooking. If you do, change clothes and hang the clothes with food odor with the food and garbage. Wash your hands thoroughly before retiring to the tent.

Don't cook too much food, so you don't have to deal with leftovers. If you do end up with extra food, however, you only have two choices. Carry it out or burn it. Don't bury it or throw it in a lake or leave it anywhere in bear country. A bear will most likely find and dig up any food or garbage buried in the backcountry.

**Taking out the garbage:** In bear country, you have only two choices—burn garbage or carry it out. Prepare for garbage problems before you leave home. Bring along airtight zip-locked bags to store garbage. Be sure to hang your garbage at night along with your food. Also, carry in as little garbage as possible by discarding excess packaging while packing.

**Washing dishes:** This is a sticky problem, but there is one easy solution. If you don't dirty dishes, you don't have to wash them. So try to minimize food smell by using as few dishes and pans as possible. If you use the principles of no trace camping, you are probably doing as much as you can to reduce food smell from dishes.

If you brought paper towels, use one to carefully remove food scraps from pans and dishes before washing them. Then, when you wash dishes, you have much less food smell. Burn the dirty towels or store them in zip-locked bags with other garbage. Put pans and dishes in zip-locked bags before putting them back in your pack.

If you end up with lots of food scraps in the dish water, drain out the scraps and store them in zip-locked bags with other garbage or burn them. You can bring a lightweight screen to filter out food scraps from dish water, but be sure to store the screen with the food and garbage. If you have a campfire, pour the dish water around the edge of the fire. If you don't have a fire, take the dish water at least 100 yards downwind and downhill from camp and pour it on the ground or in a small hole. Don't put dish water or food scraps in a lake or stream.

Although possibly counter to accepted rules of cleanliness for many people, you can skip washing dishes altogether on the last night of your trip. Instead, simply use the paper towels to clean the dirty dishes as much as possible. You can wash them when you get home. Pack dirty dishes in zip-locked bags before putting them back in your pack.

Finally, don't put it off. Do dishes immediately after eating, so a minimum of food smell lingers in the area.

**Choosing a tent site:** In Yellowstone, the cooking area and the food hanging area is desingated, but not the tent sites. Unfortunately, some campsites in Yellowstone have the well-used (not designated) tent sites too close to the bear pole or cooking area. Refrain from setting up your tent on these sites even if it is the ideal tent site by all other definitions. Store food at least 100 yards from the tent. You can store it near the cooking area to further concentrate food smells.

**Not under the stars:** Some people prefer to sleep out under the stars instead of using a tent. This might be okay in areas not frequented by bears, but it's not a good idea in bear country. The thin fabric of a tent certainly isn't any real physical protection from a bear, but it does present a psychological barrier to a bear who wants to come even closer.

**Do somebody a big favor:** Report all bear sightings to the ranger after your trip. This might not help you, but it could save another camper's life. If rangers get enough reports to spot a pattern, they manage the area to prevent potentially hazardous situations.

# The Bear Essentials of Hiking and Camping

- Knowledge is the best defense.
- There is no substitute for alertness.
- Hike with a large group and stay together.
- Don't hike alone in bear country.
- Stay on the trail.
- Hike in the middle of the day.
- Make lots of noise while hiking.
- Never approach a bear.
- Females with cubs are very dangerous.
- Stay away from carcasses.
- Defensive hiking works. Try it.
- Choose a safe campsite.
- Camp below treeline.
- Separate sleeping and cooking areas.
- Sleep in a tent.
- Cook just the right amount of food and eat it all.
- Store food and garbage out of reach of bears.
- Never feed bears.
- Keep food odors out of the tent.
- Leave the campsite cleaner than you found it.
- Leave no food rewards for bears.

## How to get Really Bear Aware

Most of the information in this section comes from BEAR AWARE, a handy, inexpensive guidebook recently published by Falcon Press Publishing. This small, "packable" book contains the essential tips you need to reduce the risk of being injured by a bear to the slimmest possible margin, and it's written for beginners and experts. This book is for:

- Day Hikers
- Tent Campers
- Hunters
- Anglers
- Outfitters
- Backpackers
- Backcountry Horsemen
- Mountain Bikers
- Trail Runners
- Photographers

In addition to covering the all-important subject of how to prevent an encounter, this book includes advice on what to do if you are involved in an encounter.

You can get this book at local bookseller, in Yellowstone visitor centers, or by calling FALCON at 1-800-582-2665.

# NORTHWEST SECTION

## *SHORT HIKES*

## 1   *BOILING RIVER*

| | |
|---|---|
| **Type of hike:** | Out-and-back. |
| **Type of trip:** | Day hike. |
| **Total distance:** | 1 mile or 1.6 kilometers (round-trip). |
| **Difficulty:** | Easy. |
| **Elevation gain:** | Minimal. |
| **Maps:** | Trails Illustrated (Mammoth Hot Springs); Gardiner USGS quad. |
| **Starting point:** | Boiling River Trailhead. |

**Finding the trailhead:** Drive south of Gardiner on the North Entrance Road through the entrance station for about 2 miles and turn either right or left into one of the Boiling River parking lots. There is so much traffic on this trail that the NPS has expanded the parking lot to the west side of the road. The trailhead is in the northeast corner of the parking lot on the east side of the road.

**The hike:** Until the mid-1980s, the Boiling River served mostly as a social hot tub for locals and park employees. Since then, the NPS has made it an official trail and swimming hole.

*On a hot summer day, you definitely won't have the Boiling River all to yourself.*

# BOILING RIVER • THE HOODOOS • OSPREY FALLS • BUNSEN PEAK • TERRACE MOUNTAIN • BEAVER PONDS • SEPULCHER MOUNTAIN

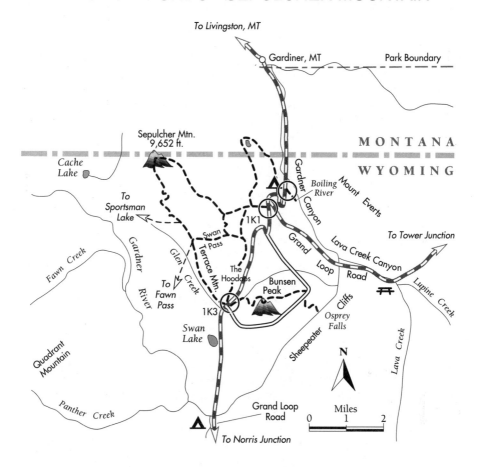

The Boiling River is created by a massive hot spring discharge 2 feet deep and 6 feet wide (probably from Mammoth Hot Springs) flowing into the Gardner River. The river has never been known to "boil," but it does get comfortably warm, and people have been soaking in this hot water for decades. Early park promoters touted it as the only place you could catch a trout and boil it on the hook.

Now, the NPS has constructed a nice trail along the banks of the Gardner River to the hot spring, and it has become a very popular, short day hike. On a hot summer afternoon, expect to see dozens of people at the hot spring. The trail is easy and flat all the way.

Because of the extreme popularity of this hike (over 200 hikers per day), the NPS has established special regulations. The trail has restricted hours

(5 a.m. to 9 p.m. in summer, 6 a.m. to 6 p.m. in winter), and pets, bicycles, soap, food, beverages, and nudity are prohibited. You can swim only in the Gardner River, not in the hot spring where it emerges from under a travertine ledge.

Another unusual tidbit of information is that this trail starts exactly at the 45th Parallel, precisely halfway between the North Pole and the Equator.

**Options:** You can also hike down to the Boiling River from the Mammoth Campground, but this is a much tougher hike on a less developed trail with a 300-foot climb to get back to the campground.

## 2   WRAITH FALLS

| | |
|---|---|
| **Type of hike:** | Out-and-back. |
| **Type of trip:** | Day hike. |
| **Total distance:** | 1 mile or 1.6 kilometers (round-trip). |
| **Difficulty:** | Easy. |
| **Elevation gain:** | 160 feet. |
| **Maps:** | Trails Illustrated (Mammoth Hot Springs); Blacktail Deer Creek USGS quad. |
| **Starting point:** | Wraith Falls parking area. |

See Map on Page 77

**Finding the trailhead:** Drive east 4.6 miles from Mammoth or 13.4 miles west of Tower and park at the Wraith Falls pullout on the south side of the road.

**The hike:** This trail takes you to a charming small waterfall on Lupine Creek where the stream cascades down a steep slope for about 100 feet.

The trail to the falls is in great shape and well used, and it has a small climb near the end with three switchbacks after you cross the creek on a footbridge. The trail ends at a viewpoint about 100 yards from the falls. In recent years, trees have fallen to partially block the view, but it's still nice.

## 3   GRIZZLY LAKE

| | |
|---|---|
| **Type of hike:** | Out-and-back. |
| **Type of trip:** | Day hike or overnighter. |
| **Total distance:** | 3.6 miles or 5.8 kilometers (round-trip). |
| **Difficulty:** | Moderate. |
| **Elevation gain:** | 400 feet. |
| **Maps:** | Trails Illustrated (Mammoth Hot Springs); Obsidian Cliff and Mount Holmes USGS quads. |
| **Starting point:** | Grizzly Lake Trailhead (1K8). |

See Map on Page 120

*Grizzly Lake.*

**Finding the trailhead:** Drive south 14.4 miles from Mammoth or 6.6 miles north of Norris and park at a pullout on the west side of the road.

**The hike:** The trail starts out nice and flat as it crosses Obsidian Creek on a footbridge and goes through a large meadow just south of Beaver Lake. At the west side of the meadow, the trail starts switchbacking up the side of the ridge. At this point, you may see a sign for the Howard Eaton Trail going to Mammoth, but that trail has been abandoned.

The Grizzly Lake Trail stays on top of the ridge for a quarter mile or more before switchbacking down the other side to the north end of the 136-acre lake. When you reach the lake, the trail follows the shoreline for about 100 yards before reaching the outlet. If you're staying overnight, carefully cross the outlet on a logjam to reach the campsites along Straight Creek below the lake.

The trail is in great shape all the way. It winds through a burned forest the entire distance except the large meadow at the trailhead and a few small meadows on top of the ridge. Grizzly Lake is a beautiful mountain lake tucked between two forested ridges, but it has been in the path of several forest fires, most recently the fires of 1988.

**Options:** You can make this a shuttle hike by leaving a vehicle at the Mount Holmes Trailhead (1K6). You can also hike out and back to Grizzly Lake from the Mount Holmes Trailhead.

**Side trips:** If you stay overnight at the lake and want a long day hike the next day, you can climb Mount Holmes. If you aren't this ambitious, you can hike along Winter Creek to the meadows below the mountain and return to camp. For both side trips first follow the trail along Straight Creek north from Grizzly Lake to the junction with the Mount Holmes Trail and turn left (west).

# 4    ARTISTS PAINTPOTS

| | |
|---|---|
| **Type of hike:** | Out-and-back. |
| **Type of trip:** | Day hike. |
| **Total distance:** | 1.2 miles or 1.9 kilometers (round-trip). |
| **Difficulty:** | Easy. |
| **Elevation gain:** | Minimal. |
| **Maps:** | Trails Illustrated (Mammoth Hot Springs); Norris Junction USGS quad. |
| **Starting point:** | Artists Paintpots Trailhead. |

See Map on Page 61

*Artists Paintpots.*

**Finding the trailhead:** Drive south from the Norris Junction for 3.9 miles or 8.9 miles north of the Madison Junction and park at the Artists Paintpot pull-out on the east side of the road at the south end of Gibbon Meadows.

**The hike:** This short hike skirts the south edge of massive Gibbon Meadows, staying in the unburned lodgepole all the way. The trail is partly boardwalk, and the rest is double wide, flat, and easy. Since elk commonly use Gibbon Meadows, you might see some on the way to the paintpots. However, you probably won't see many people. Even though this trail goes to several interesting thermal features, it doesn't get much use—at least when compared to the trails in geyser basins around Old Faithful.

At the end of the hike on the slopes of Paintpot Hill, the trail makes a convenient little loop that provides good views of the major thermal features, primarily colorful paintpot formations (which early explorers thought resembled an artist's palette) as well as hot pools and steam vents. To protect both yourself and these fragile natural features, stay on the designated trail.

# 5  HARLEQUIN LAKE

| | |
|---|---|
| **Type of hike:** | Out-and-back |
| **Type of trip:** | Day hike. |
| **Total distance:** | 1 mile or 1.6 kilometers (round-trip). |
| **Difficulty:** | Easy. |
| **Elevation gain:** | Minimal. |
| **Maps:** | Trails Illustrated (Mammoth Hot Springs); Mount Jackson USGS quad. |
| **Starting point:** | Harlequin Lake Trailhead. |

**Finding the trailhead:** Drive 1.5 miles west of Madison Junction or 12.5 miles east of West Yellowstone and park in the Madison Plateau parking area on the south side of the highway. The trail starts on the north side of the road.

HARLEQUIN LAKE

**The hike:** This is a short hike to a shallow, marshy lake. The trail goes through about a quarter mile of burnt timber before climbing a small hill on the top of which you can see the 10-acre lake. The trail goes around the south side of the lake, but gets increasingly faint. You can see a variety of waterfowl at the lake, but probably not the rare Harlequin duck for which it was named—but if you go early in the summer, you can see a million mosquitoes.

This trail does not show on some maps.

# 6   ICE LAKE

| | | |
|---|---|---|
| **Type of hike:** | Loop. | *See Map on Page 116* |
| **Type of trip:** | Day hike or overnighter. | |
| **Total distance:** | 4.5 miles or 7.2 kilometers. | |
| **Difficulty:** | Easy. | |
| **Elevation gain:** | Minimal. | |
| **Maps:** | Trails Illustrated (Mammoth Hot Springs); Norris Junction and Crystal Falls USGS quads. | |
| **Starting point:** | Ice Lake Trailhead (4K2). | |

**Finding the trailhead:** Drive 3.5 miles east from Norris Junction or 8.5 miles east from Canyon and park at the Ice Lake Trailhead and parking area on the north side of the road.

**Key points:**
  0.3 (0.5)   Spur trail to 4D3 (5★).
  0.5 (0.8)   Ice Lake.
  0.6 (0.9)   Junction with Howard Eaton Trail.
  0.8 (1.3)   4D1 (4★).
  1.5 (2.4)   4D2 (5★).
  2.3 (3.7)   Junction with Little Gibbon Falls/Wolf Lake Trail.
  3.4 (5.5)   Little Gibbon Falls.
  3.7 (5.9)   Virginia Meadows.
  4.0 (6.4)   Norris-Canyon Road.
  4.5 (7.2)   Ice Lake Trailhead.

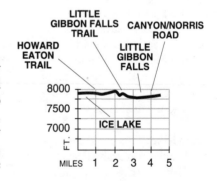

**The hike:** The trail to Ice Lake gets fairly heavy traffic, but most hikers go out and back to the lake. Few hikers turn this into one of the few easy loop trips in the park, as described here. Ice Lake is a fairly large, deep, forest-lined mountain lake, a pleasant destination for a short day hike or easy overnighter.

The trail to Ice Lake is good enough for wheelchairs up to the spur trail to 4D3 (the only wheelchair accessible backcountry campsite in the park). Wheelchairs can't go beyond this point, but the trail stays good. It traverses the west end of the lake and joins the Howard Eaton Trail just after rounding the end of the lake.

Turn right (east) at this junction and follow the north shore of the lake, going by 4D1 shortly after the junction. You pass the spur trail to 4D2 at the east end of the lake and ford the Gibbon River shortly thereafter. In summer, this river could be described as a creek, and you'll have no problem fording it. After the ford, the trail continues east for another 0.7 mile to the junction with the Little Gibbon Falls Trail (called Wolf Lake Trail on some maps).

Turn right (south) at this junction and go another mile or so to 25-foot Little Gibbon Falls, which actually resembles the larger Gibbon Falls downstream along the Norris-Madison section of the Grand Loop Road. From the falls, the trail drops into a spacious Virginia Meadows along the Gibbon River until you reach the highway.

The trail is in good shape and stays in a mostly burned lodgepole forest most of the way, including all around the lake. The trail gets a little rougher on the last leg of the trip by Little Gibbon Falls, but it's still distinct with the exception of one spot near the highway where it disappears for about 100 yards in the lush meadow along the river. An orange marker on the other side of the meadow marks the route.

When you reach the highway, walk about a half mile along the paved road back to your vehicle.

**Options:** Hikers can hike out and back to Ice Lake or Little Gibbon Falls or do this loop in reverse with no extra difficulty.

---

# 7    LITTLE GIBBON FALLS

| | |
|---|---|
| **Type of hike:** | Out-and-back. |
| **Type of trip:** | Day hike. |
| **Total distance:** | 1.2 miles or 1.9 kilometers (round-trip). |
| **Difficulty:** | Easy. |
| **Elevation gain:** | Minimal. |
| **Maps:** | Trails Illustrated (Mammoth Hot Springs); Crystal Falls USGS quad. |
| **Starting point:** | Little Gibbon Falls Trailhead. |

See Elevation Profile on Page 48
See Map on Page 116

**Finding the trailhead:** This trailhead is difficult to find. Drive 3.5 miles east from Norris Junction or 8.5 miles east from Canyon to the Ice Lake Trailhead. Using this trailhead as a reference point, go 0.4 mile east of this trailhead and park in a pullout on the right (south) side of the road. From here, walk about 100 feet down the road (east) and watch for an orange marker on the north side of the road. When we did this hike, there was no sign at the trailhead.

*Little Gibbon Falls.*

**The hike:** This is one of the little hidden jewels of Yellowstone that, for some strange reason, not many people see. The 25-foot waterfall is not even on the USGS topo maps for this area.

The first part of the trail goes through the north edge of large Virginia Meadows before climbing a small hill through burned lodgepole forest to the falls. You get a great view of the falls from a flat bench on the north side of the trail.

This used to be called Upper Falls of the Gibbon, but it was changed to Little Gibbon Falls because it resembles the larger Gibbon Falls along the Norris-Madison Road.

**Options:** You can also see Little Gibbon Falls as part of the Ice Lake Loop hike.

# 8  *BACON RIND CREEK*

|                     |                                            |
|--------------------:|:-------------------------------------------|
| **Type of hike:**   | Out-and-back.                              |
| **Type of trip:**   | Day hike.                                  |
| **Total distance:** | 4 miles or 6.4 kilometers (round-trip).    |
| **Difficulty:**     | Easy.                                      |
| **Elevation gain:** | Minimal.                                   |
| **Maps:**           | Trails Illustrated (Mammoth Hot Springs);  |
|                     | Divide Lake USGS quad.                     |
| **Starting point:** | Bacon Rind Trailhead (WK4).                |

*See Map on Page 53*

**Finding the trailhead:** Drive south from Belgrade, Montana, or north from West Yellowstone, Montana, on U.S. Highway 191 and turn west on the Bacon Rind Road between mileposts 22 and 23 and follow the gravel road about a half mile to the trailhead.

**The hike:** This trail has the distinction of being the only trail heading west from the Gallatin Valley in the park. After the park boundary (at the 2-mile mark), the trail keeps going up into the Lee Metcalf Wilderness in the Gallatin National Forest. However, the trail gets faint and marshy as you near the park boundary. The map may show the trail crossing Bacon Rind 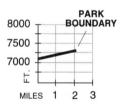 Creek before the park boundary, but it stays on the north side of the stream.

This is a flat, easy trail along the bottomlands of Bacon Rind Creek. The stream contains a healthy rainbow population, and willow thickets along the creek provide hiding places for moose and grizzly bears. If you plan to fish (catch-and-release only), be sure to get a park fishing permit.

The trail goes along the north side of the meandering stream as it winds its way through a beautiful mountain meadow with a strange (it looks almost manmade) square-shaped hill in the middle of it. The trail crosses marshy Migration Creek just before reaching the park boundary, so this might be a good place to take a break before returning to the trailhead.

# 9    FAN CREEK

**Type of hike:** Out-and-back.
**Type of trip:** Day hike or overnighter.
**Total distance:** 5-10 miles (round-trip).
**Difficulty:** Moderate.
**Elevation gain:** 430 feet.
**Maps:** Trails Illustrated (Mammoth Hot Springs);
Divide Lake and Quadrant Mountain USGS quads.
**Starting point:** Fawn Pass Trailhead (WK5).

**Finding the trailhead:** Drive south from Belgrade, Montana, or north from West Yellowstone, Montana, on U.S. 191 to just south of milepost 22 and park in the Fawn Pass Trailhead on the east side of the road.

**Key points:**

1.4 (2.2)   Fawn Pass Trail junction.
2.7 (4.3)   WC2 (5★).
3.0 (4.8)   Fan Creek ford.
5.5 (8.8)   Confluence of East and North forks of Fan Creek.

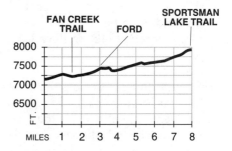

**The hike:** After hiking this trail, you could be easily convinced that Fan Creek is a shortened version of the original name, "Fantastic Creek." Although Fan Creek gets moderate to heavy use from trail riders taking long loop trips over to Gardners Hole and back over Fawn Pass, the area is lightly used by hikers, but not because it isn't worthy. On the contrary, it's one of the most beautiful mountain valleys in the park.

The terrain doesn't completely open up until after the Fawn Pass Trail Junction where you turn left (northeast). You can go as far as 5.5 miles where the East Fork and the North Fork merge, or you can go any lesser distance. At the 3-mile mark, you ford Fan Creek, but the crossing is less than knee-deep and easy after mid-July.

If you're looking for an easy day hike, possibly combined with some stream fishing, Fan Creek would be an excellent choice. There are no big hills, and the trail is in terrific shape the entire way. You might want to go early or stay late to watch elk and moose, which are quite abundant in the area.

The area east of upper Fan Creek (after WC3) is a part of the Gallatin Bear Management Area and closed to off-trail travel.

# FAN CREEK • BACON RIND CREEK

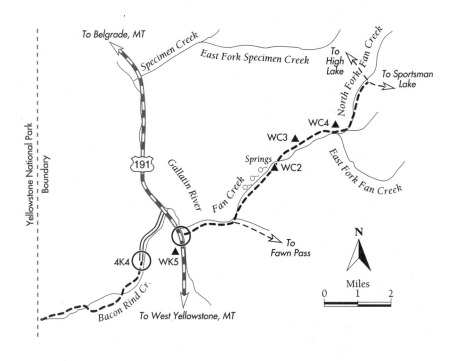

*Lower Fan Creek.*

**Options:** If you want an easy overnighter, you can stay at WC2, a delightful campsite. It's a short backpacking trip (only 2.7 miles one way on a nearly level trail), but for beginning backpackers, this could be just right.

# 10  UPPER GALLATIN RIVER

| | |
|---:|:---|
| **Type of hike:** | Out-and-back. |
| **Type of trip:** | Day hike or overnighter. |
| **Total distance:** | 9-13 miles (round-trip). |
| **Difficulty:** | Moderate. |
| **Elevation gain:** | 400 feet. |
| **Maps:** | Trails Illustrated (Mammoth Hot Springs); |
| | Divide Lake and Joseph Peak USGS quads. |
| **Starting point:** | Bighorn Pass Trailhead (WK6). |

**Finding the trailhead:** Drive south from Belgrade, Montana, or north from West Yellowstone, Montana, on U.S. 191 and park at the Bighorn Pass Trailhead about halfway between mileposts 20 and 21 on the east side of the road.

**Key points:**

4.5  (7.2)  Fawn Pass
              Cutoff Trail.
4.7  (7.4)  WB1 (5★).
5.8  (9.3)  Landslide.
6.6  (10.6)  WB6 (4★).

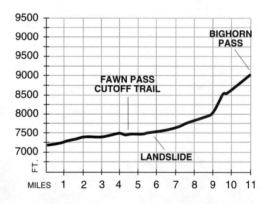

**The hike:** The Upper Gallatin Valley, like Fan Creek, gives you the option of going as far as you choose instead of having a specific destination. You can go to WB6 and the start of the Gallatin Range Bear Management Area, or you can turn back at any earlier point.

About a quarter mile after leaving the trailhead, you ford the Gallatin River. Sorry, no footbridge. After mid-July, however, it isn't a dangerous crossing. An ice jam took out this bridge in January 1995, but the NPS plans to replace it as soon as possible.

After the ford, the trail stays consistently flat and easy as you hike along the north edge of the treeless Gallatin Valley. You can fish the river (don't forget to get a permit), watch elk, or simply have a relaxing hike. This trip is well-suited for hikers who don't want to climb big hills or get too serious about anything, but wouldn't mind seeing some great scenery and wildlife.

As you walk up the valley, you can see Bighorn Pass in the distance looming over the unusually beautiful Gallatin Valley. Many mountain valleys are

# UPPER GALLATIN RIVER • BIGHORN PASS

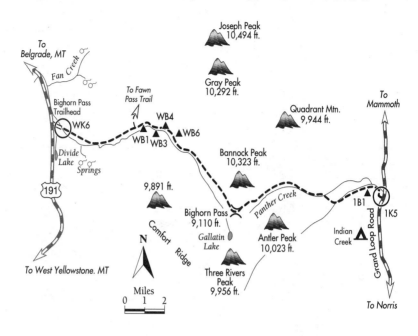

*Upper Gallatin Valley.*

narrow, V-shaped and forested, but the Gallatin Valley has directly opposite characteristics. One phenomenon added in 1995 to this already interesting landscape is a large landslide that buried about 200 yards of trail between the stock-parties-only WB3 and WB4 campsites and about 5 miles (one way) from the trailhead. When you look up at the hillside where the slide originated, it's hard to believe this happened on such a gentle slope.

**Options:** You can make this an easy overnighter by staying at WB1 or a longer overnighter by staying at WB6.

## 11   GNEISS CREEK

| | |
|---:|:---|
| **Type of hike:** | Out-and-back. |
| **Type of trip:** | Day hike or overnighter. |
| **Total distance:** | 6 miles (9.6 kilometers) to WA1; |
| | 8.6 miles (13.8 kilometers) to Gneiss Creek. |
| **Difficulty:** | Moderate. |
| **Elevation change:** | 212 feet. |
| **Maps:** | Trails Illustrated (Mammoth Hot Springs); |
| | Richards Creek USGS quad. |
| **Starting point:** | Gneiss Creek Trailhead (WK7). |

**Finding the trailhead:** Drive south from Belgrade, Montana, or north from West Yellowstone, Montana, on U.S. 191 to the trailhead near milepost 9 near the Fir Ridge Cemetery.

**Key points:**

0.3 (0.5)   Park boundary.
1.5 (1.8)   Campanula Creek.
3.0 (4.8)   WA1 (3★).
4.3 (6.9)   Gneiss Creek.

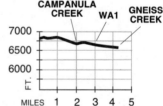

**The hike:** Gneiss Creek is a nice hike. It's an easy walk with no hills, and you actually lose elevation hiking in and gain coming back, but be sure to bring the insect repellent.

The trail passes through open terrain rich in wildlife, so you might want to go early in the morning to watch the elk, moose, bald eagles, and, perhaps, the mighty grizzly bear—all common in this area. This hike is popular with anglers, and Gneiss Creek offers some great fishing.

From the trailhead, you hike on an old road for less than a half mile until you reach the park boundary. Before and after the boundary sign, the trail stays on a small ridge among aspen groves and above Duck Creek to the south (also popular with fly-casters). The entire Duck Creek/Gneiss Creek valley is flat and marshy with slow-moving, braided streams and side channels.

*Watching a moose in a beaver pond on Campanula Creek on the Gneiss Creek Trail.*

At the 1.5-mile mark, you cross Campanula Creek, which flows into Gneiss Creek at approximately the point where the combined stream becomes Duck Creek. You can see a series of beaver dams in this area, an increasingly rare sight in the park because of the decline of beaver populations in recent years.

After Campanula Creek, you drop down into the bottomlands along Gneiss Creek and stay there until you reach WA1. After you get down in the lowlands, the trail gets faint in several places, so be careful not to get off the trail or miss WA1. After WA1, the trail is difficult to follow all the way to Gneiss Creek

## GNEISS CREEK

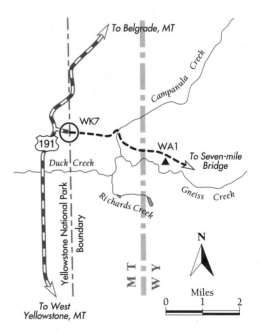

**Options:** You can make this an easy overnighter by staying at WA1. You could also try to hike through to Seven-mile Bridge on the west entrance road east of West Yellowstone (13.9 miles one way), but one 2-3 mile section of this trail goes through a heavily burned area that is plagued with heavy downfall.

---

# 12   PURPLE MOUNTAIN

|  |  |
|---|---|
| **Type of hike:** | Out-and-back. |
| **Type of trip:** | Day hike. |
| **Total distance:** | 6 miles or 9.8 kilometers (round-trip). |
| **Difficulty:** | Moderate. |
| **Elevation gain:** | 1,583 feet. |
| **Maps:** | Trails Illustrated (Mammoth Hot Springs); Madison Junction USGS quad. |
| **Starting point:** | Madison Junction (MK1). |

**Finding the trailhead:** From the Norris Junction drive east for about 0.25 mile to the trailhead on the west side of the road.

**The hike:** When looking at the map, this doesn't look like 3 miles to the top, but when you get on the trail it seems like it. It's a tough 1,500-foot, Category 2 climb to the summit of this 8,433-foot peak named because of its purplish color. This is a good choice for campers staying at Madison Junction and looking for some exercise without having to drive anywhere.

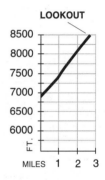

The trail passes through mostly burnt timber and ends with series of gradual switchbacks. About half-way up, you move into an open slope and get good views of the Gibbon River Valley—actually a better view than from the forested summit.

## PURPLE MOUNTAIN

# 13  GREBE LAKE

|  |  |
|---|---|
| **Type of hike:** | Out-and-back. |
| **Type of trip:** | Day hike or overnighter. |
| **Total distance:** | 6 miles or 9.6 kilometers (round-trip). |
| **Difficulty:** | Moderate. |
| **Elevation gain:** | Minimal. |
| **Maps:** | Trails Illustrated (Mammoth Hot Springs); Crystal Falls and Cook Peak USGS quads. |
| **Starting point:** | Grebe Lake Trailhead (4K3). |

See Map on Page 116

**Finding the trailhead:** Drive 8 miles east of Norris Junction or 4 miles west of Canyon and park in the Grebe Lake parking area on the north side of the road.

**The hike:** This is the easiest way to get to Grebe Lake, but it isn't as scenic as the routes via Wolf or Cascade lakes.

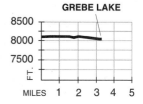

The trail starts out through meadows but shortly thereafter goes into heavily burned lodgepole for the rest of the way to the lake. The trail is flat and well-defined the entire way as if follows the route of an abandoned fire road.

*Grebe Lake.*

Some maps might show a trail going off to the right just before the lake, but that trail has been abandoned. Now, the trail comes out right at the lake where you can go left to 4G2 or right around the east shoreline of the lake to hook up with the Howard Eaton Trail.

The lake is surrounded by marshy meadows that produce a great crop of wildflowers and, unfortunately, an even better crop of mosquitoes. Be sure to bring mosquito netting and insect repellent.

**Options:** You can make this an overnighter by staying at any of the four excellent campsites at Grebe Lake. You can also make this a shuttle hike by coming back to the Norris-Canyon Road at Cascade Creek, Wolf Lake, or Ice Lake trailheads.

## 14  MONUMENT GEYSER BASIN

| | |
|---|---|
| **Type of hike:** | Out-and-back. |
| **Type of trip:** | Day hike. |
| **Total distance:** | 3 miles or 4.8 kilometers (round-trip). |
| **Difficulty:** | Moderate. |
| **Elevation gain:** | 600 feet. |
| **Maps:** | Trails Illustrated (Mammoth Hot Springs); Obsidian Cliff USGS quad. |
| **Starting point:** | Monument Geyser Trailhead. |

*Monument Geyser Basin.*

# MONUMENT GEYSER BASIN • ARTISTS PAINTPOTS

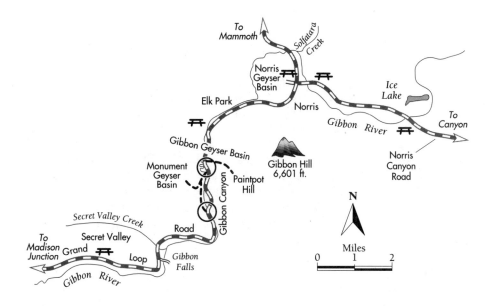

**Finding the trailhead:** Drive 8.2 miles north of Madison Junction or 4.6 miles south from the Norris Junction and park in the trailhead parking area just south of the bridge over the Gibbon River on the west side of the road.

**The hike:** Some maps show this trail starting at the river and starting to climb immediately. However, the trail follows the river on a level trail for at least a half mile before taking a sharp left to climb through heavily burned forest to the geyser basin. When it does start climbing, though, it's a serious Category 3 hill all the way to the geyser basin. The sign at the trailhead says 0.9 miles to the geyser basin, but it's at least 1.5 miles.

The destination is worth the climb, however. The Monument Geyser Basin has several interesting steam vents and chimneys. Be careful when exploring the area so you don't destroy any of the basin's fragile features or burn yourself by stepping through a thin crust.

# 15  SOLFATARA CREEK

| | |
|---|---|
| **Type of hike:** | Shuttle. |
| **Type of trip:** | Day hike. |
| **Total distance:** | 6.3 miles or 10.1 kilometers. |
| **Difficulty:** | Difficult. |
| **Elevation gain:** | 160 feet. |
| **Maps:** | Trails Illustrated (Mammoth Hot Springs); Obsidian Cliff and Norris Junction USGS quads. |
| **Starting point:** | Solfatara Creek Trailhead (4K1). |

**Finding the trailhead:** Drive 14 miles south of Mammoth or 7 miles north of Norris Junction. The trailhead is about a half mile south of Beaver Lake Picnic Area. If you start at the south end of the shuttle hike, the trailhead is at the far end of Norris Campground, less than 1 mile north of Norris Junction. This campground was closed in 1996. If it's still closed, park your vehicle at the entrance to the campground.

## Key points:

0.9  (1.5)  Lake of the Woods.
2.8  (4.5)  Whiterock Spring.
5.8  (9.3)  Junction with Howard Eaton
            Trail to Ice Lake.
6.3 (10.1)  Norris Campground.

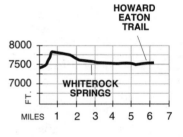

**The hike:** The Solfatara Creek Trail, named after a type of thermal vent, receives little use, especially south of Whiterock Spring. It's also low on the priority list for trail maintenance, so it can be difficult to follow, and you might be slowed by significant downfall.

From the trailhead, the trail starts out along Lemonade Creek, named for its greenish color caused by an infusion of sulphur from nearby thermal areas. After about a half mile, the trail leaves the stream bottom and climbs steadily for a half mile (about 400 feet up) through downed lodgepole and next to red, white, gray, and gold thermal slopes.

As the trail nears the top of this first short climb, it follows the telephone lines through unburned lodgepole. As you walk under the lines, look to your left (east). Through the trees, you can see Lake of the Woods, about 200 yards off the trail and almost hidden by the dense forest. After Lake of the Woods, the trail leaves the utility corridor and continues on to a large meadow. Here, the trail nearly disappears, so go to the other end of the meadow and to the right slightly to where the trail continues.

# SOLFATARA CREEK

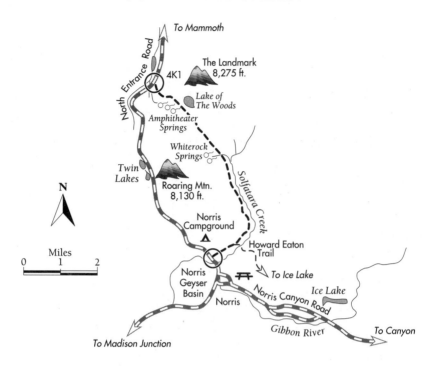

At 2.8 miles, you can see Whiterock Spring on your right (west), which is a stream with a thermal mud area. Along this section of the trail, you can also see lots of obsidian, used by the Sheepeater Indians and other tribes for arrowheads. In June, you can also find the gorgeous glacier lily along this trial.

After Whiterock Spring, the trail stays in lodgepole with large meadows to the left (east). Some sections of trail pass through burned areas with blowdowns. Watch for wildlife in the meadows.

At 5.8 miles, the trail intersects the route to Ice Lake. Go right (west) at this junction. From this point on, the trail is more heavily used and distinct. One last hill puts you in the Norris Campground.

**Options:** This hike can be done from either end with no noticeable difference in difficulty.

# 16  THE HOODOOS

| | | |
|---|---|---|
| **Type of hike:** | Shuttle. | |
| **Type of trip:** | Day hike. | |
| **Total distance:** | 3.8 miles or 6.1 kilometers. | |
| **Difficulty:** | Easy. | |
| **Elevation loss:** | 866 feet. | |
| **Maps:** | Trails Illustrated (Mammoth Hot Springs); Mammoth USGS quad. | |
| **Starting point:** | Glen Creek Trailhead (1K3). | |

See Map on Page 43

**Finding the trailhead:** Drive 4.7 miles south of Mammoth to just past the Golden Gate Bridge and park on the left (east) in the Glen Creek Trailhead parking lot. The trail starts on the west side of the road.

**Key points:**

0.2 (0.3)  Howard Eaton Trail junction.
1.3 (2.1)  The Hoodoos.
2.6 (4.2)  Snow Pass Trail junction.
3.1 (5.0)  Mammoth Terrace.
3.6 (5.8)  Beaver Ponds Trail junction.
3.8 (6.1)  Sepulcher Trailhead.

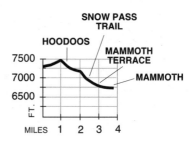

**The hike:** This enchanting short hike passes through some of the truly scenic parts of Yellowstone without getting far from the paved road. But it's far enough from the road to seem like backcountry.

It's a shuttle hike, but if you happen to be driving north toward Mammoth and need some exercise, and others in the car don't feel the need, have your friends or relatives drop you off at the Glen Creek Trailhead and meet you two hours later at Mammoth. They can drive down, and you can take the scenic route. If this doesn't work out for you, try to arrange a ride from Mammoth to the trailhead and hike back to your vehicle.

From the Glen Creek Trailhead, hike west for 0.2 mile to the junction with the Howard Eaton Trail. Take a right (north) on the Howard Eaton Trail, which goes through the Hoodoos to Mammoth. From this junction, the trail climbs through mostly forested terrain above the Mammoth-Norris section of Yellowstone's Grand Loop Road for about 400 feet over the next half mile or so and then drops down into the Hoodoos. These ghostly rock formations, actually huge chunks of travertine limestone, crashed down from Terrace Mountain (west of the trail) long ago.

After the Hoodoos, the trail veers off to the west out of sight of the highway and gradually drops down, through mostly open terrain, toward the Mammoth Terrace. At the 2.6-mile mark, you cross the Snow Pass Trail junction where you go straight instead of left or right (unless you're taking the Terrace Mountain loop option, in which case turn left).

In another half mile or so, you start through the Mammoth Terrace area, and the trail parallels the Mammoth Terrace Drive for a few hundred yards before hitting the junction with the Beaver Ponds Trail. You go right (east) and finish at the Clematis Trailhead (also called Beaver Ponds Trailhead) on the south edge of Mammoth. The trail is well-defined and marked the entire way.

**Options:** This hike can start at Mammoth, of course, but this would result in a steady uphill most of the way. This trail can also be part of the Terrace Mountain Loop. Refer to Terrace Mountain for details.

# 17   OSPREY FALLS

| | | |
|---:|:---|:---|
| **Type of hike:** | Out-and-back with loop option. | See Map on Page 43 |
| **Type of trip:** | Day hike. | |
| **Total distance:** | 9.2 miles or 14.8 kilometers (round-trip). | |
| **Difficulty:** | Moderate. | |
| **Elevation gain:** | 800 feet. | |
| **Maps:** | Trails Illustrated (Mammoth Hot Springs); Mammoth USGS quad. | |
| **Starting point:** | Glen Creek Trailhead (1K3). | |

**Finding the trailhead:** Drive 4.7 miles south of Mammoth to just past the Golden Gate Bridge and park on the left (east) in the Glen Creek Trailhead parking lot.

**Key points:**
   3.2 (5.1)   Osprey Falls spur trail and loop trail to Bunsen Peak.
   3.7 (5.9)   Rim of Sheepeater Canyon.
   4.6 (7.4)   Osprey Falls.

**The hike:** The first 4 miles of this hike are on an abandoned road closed to motorized vehicles but still open to mountain bikers. In fact, mountain bikers often ride into the Osprey Falls spur trail, hike down to the falls, and then ride back to the Glen Creek Trailhead.

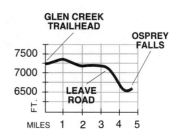

This is a great early morning hike. The trail is flat and easy (i.e. former road). It goes through mostly open terrain where you're likely to see many species of wildlife. If you go early, you can get down to the falls, enjoy a long rest there, and climb back up before the late afternoon heat makes the big climb out of Sheepeater Canyon seem harder.

*Taking a break at Osprey Falls.*

After 4 miles of easy hiking, the spur trail to Osprey Falls turns off to the right (south). Watch carefully for this junction. The road continues on, and if you're gawking around, you could walk right past it and have to back-track.

The trail down into Sheepeater Canyon is well-defined, but steep as it switchbacks down about 800 feet in 0.6 mile right to the foot of the falls. The NPS has posted warning signs at the top of the climb, but with average amount of caution, the trail is quite safe.

You end your hike at a great viewpoint close to the splash basin for the falls, close enough that you can feel the mist in the air. You definitely want to relax here for awhile and watch the Gardner River plunge 150 feet down into Sheepeater Canyon. It's so pleasant here that you'll have a hard time leaving—especially as you think of the short Category H climb you face to get back up to the road. It's worth the effort, though, as this is definitely one of the hidden jewels of Yellowstone.

Incidentally, Sheepeater Canyon is named after the only Indian tribe—the Sheepeaters, of course—hardy enough to spend the entire winter in what is now Yellowstone Park. And yes, they depended heavily on local herds of bighorn sheep for sustenence.

On your rest breaks on the way up, you can lunch on the omnipresent wild raspberries that grow all along this section of trail. Also, be sure to bring water. The only water source is the Gardner River below the falls.

**Options:** You can make a loop hike out of this trip by climbing over the top of Bunsen Peak. See the Bunsen Peak Trail for details.

# 18 BUNSEN PEAK

| | |
|---|---|
| **Type of hike:** | Out-and-back with loop option. |
| **Type of trip:** | Day hike. |
| **Total distance:** | 4.2 miles or 6.7 kilometers (round-trip). |
| **Difficulty:** | Moderate. |
| **Elevation gain:** | 1,300 feet. |
| **Maps:** | Trails Illustrated (Mammoth Hot Springs); Mammoth USGS quad. |
| **Starting point:** | Bunsen Peak Creek Trailhead (1K4). |

See Map on Page 43

**Finding the trailhead:** Drive 4.7 miles south of Mammoth to just past the Golden Gate Bridge and park on the left (east) in the Glen Creek Trailhead parking lot.

**The hike:** This trail offers the easiest way to get a spectacular mountaintop view of the northwestern corner of the park. However, some people wouldn't call this an easy hike. You go up 1,300 feet in 2.1 miles (a Category 2 climb). Fortunately, the trail is superbly switchbacked to minimize the impact of the elevation gain. In addition, the scenery along the way tends to absorb you so you

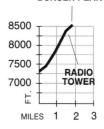

BUNSEN PEAK

*Gardners Hole and Swan Lake from Bunsen Peak.*

don't focus on the effort it takes to reach the summit of Bunsen Peak, named after the same fellow who invented the Bunsen burner, Robert Bunsen. If you want to be able to say you climbed a mountain in Yellowstone Park, this hike (or Mount Washburn) would be your least strenuous way to meet that goal.

Be sure to bring water, though. You won't find any on the mountain unless you hike in June or early July when you can find snowbanks.

From the top, you can see the large meadow below to the west known as Gardners Hole and of course, a river runs through it (the Gardner River). You can also see the town of Gardiner over the top of Terrace Mountain along with Mammoth Terrace in the foreground—and awesome 10,992-foot Electric Peak to the west, 10,336-foot Mount Holmes to the south, the mighty Absarokas to the north, and just about everything else. The telecommunications equipment on the summit is somewhat distracting, but the view is undeniably overwhelming.

You might want to hike this early in the morning before the afternoon heat makes the climb harder. If you go early, bring along some binoculars so you can watch wildlife from the summit.

**Options:** You can make a loop out of this hike by continuing east from the summit instead of retracing your steps to the trailhead. The trail winds through mostly burned lodgepole, over two secondary summits, and down to the abandoned road above the rim of Sheepeater Canyon. Turn right (west) on the trail and follow it back to the Glen Creek Trailhead. The loop option makes this about a 9-mile hike, not counting the trip down to see Osprey Falls.

**Side trips:** If you take the loop option and have extra time and energy, you can also take the side trip to Osprey Falls.

# 19   TERRACE MOUNTAIN

<table>
<tr><td align="right">Type of hike:</td><td>Loop.</td></tr>
<tr><td align="right">Type of trip:</td><td>Day hike.</td></tr>
<tr><td align="right">Total distance:</td><td>6.2 miles or 10 kilometers.</td></tr>
<tr><td align="right">Difficulty:</td><td>Moderate.</td></tr>
<tr><td align="right">Elevation gain:</td><td>760 feet.</td></tr>
<tr><td align="right">Maps:</td><td>Trails Illustrated (Mammoth Hot Springs); Mammoth USGS quad.</td></tr>
<tr><td align="right">Starting point:</td><td>Glen Creek Trailhead (K3).</td></tr>
</table>

See Map on Page 43

**Finding the trailhead:** Drive 4.7 miles south of Mammoth to just past the Golden Gate Bridge and park on the left (east) in the Glen Creek Trailhead parking lot.

**Key points:**

| | | |
|---|---|---|
| 0.2 | (0.3) | Junction with Howard Eaton Trail to Mammoth. |
| 2.1 | (3.4) | Fawn Pass Trail junction. |
| 2.6 | (4.1) | Snow Pass. |
| 3.3 | (5.3) | Junction with Clagett Butte Trail. |
| 3.7 | (5.9) | Junction with Howard Eaton Trail. |
| 5.3 | (8.5) | The Hoodoos. |
| 6.0 | (9.6) | Junction with Glen Creek Trail. |
| 6.2 | (10.0) | Glen Creek Trailhead. |

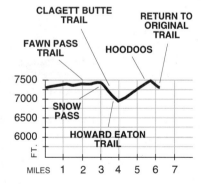

**The hike:** This nice little loop circles Terrace Mountain and goes through scenic Snow Pass and through the series of strangely shaped rock formations called the Hoodoos. This trail is also popular with cross-country skiers.

The hike starts out on a flat, double-wide Glen Creek Trail, which gradually angles to the north around the edge of Terrace Mountain. At the junction with the Sportsman Lake (straight) Fawn Pass (left) trails, go right (north) toward Snow Pass. After the junction, the trail climbs over the pass between

Terrace Mountain and Clagett Butte, named for Montana congressman William Horace Clagett, who in 1871 introduced legislation to designate Yellowstone as America's first national park. Apparently, Snow Pass gets its name from the snowbanks that often cling to the area until late summer.

After going through the pass, the trail descends to the junction with the Clagett Butte Trail. Go right (east) and right again (south) at next junction about a half mile up the trail. From here, follow the Howard Eaton Trail along the highway south of Mammoth through the Hoodoos back to the Glen Creek Trailhead. The trail stays out of sight of the highway most of the last 2.5 miles, with the exception of a short section in the last mile after the Hoodoos. The trail is in good shape and easy to follow all the way.

**Options:** This loop can be done counterclockwise just as easily. You can also start the loop at the Clematis Creek (Beaver Ponds) or Snow Pass trailheads, adding some elevation gain and distance to the trip.

## 20  CACHE LAKE

| | |
|---|---|
| **Type of hike:** | Out-and-back. |
| **Type of trip:** | Day hike. |
| **Total distance:** | 9.8 miles or 15.8 kilometers (round-trip). |
| **Difficulty:** | Moderate. |
| **Elevation gain:** | 720 feet. |
| **Maps:** | Trails Illustrated (Mammoth Hot Springs); Mammoth USGS quad. |
| **Starting point:** | Glen Creek Trailhead (1K3). |

See Map on Page 94

**Finding the trailhead:** Drive 5 miles south of Mammoth to just past Golden Gate and park at the Glen Creek Trailhead on the east side of the road.

**Key points:**

0.2 (0.3) Junction with Howard Eaton Trail to Mammoth.

2.1 (3.4) Fawn Pass Trail junction.

2.9 (4.7) Sepulcher Mountain Trail junction.

3.7 (5.9) Cache Lake Spur Trail junction.

4.9 (7.9) Cache Lake.

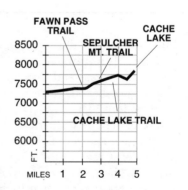

**The hike:** Cache Lake is a great destination for a moderate day hike. It's a charming little (18 acres) lake surrounded by open meadow and marsh. Massive Electric Peak provides a sensational backdrop behind the shallow mountain lake.

*Cache Lake with Electric Peak as backdrop.*

The first 2.1 miles of trail to the Fawn Pass Trail junction is flat, well-used and double-wide in some places. It goes through a sagebrush flat just south of Terrace Mountain. At the junction, go straight (west) into a narrow valley along Glen Creek. The trail continues to follow the creek, gently climbing through an open, unburnt forest past the Sepulcher Mountain Trail junction (where you stay left and continue going west) until you see the Cache Lake Spur Trail going off to the right (north).

The trail sign at this junction says it's 1.2 miles to Cache Lake from this point, but it's about half that distance. The grade increases on the spur trail, but it's not a serious hill.

**Options:** You could make this a moderate overnighter by staying at 1G3 or 1G4, adding 4 miles to the total distance.

# 21  *BEAVER PONDS*

| | |
|---|---|
| **Type of hike:** | Loop. |
| **Type of trip:** | Day hike. |
| **Total distance:** | 5.1 miles or 8.2 kilometers. |
| **Difficulty:** | Moderate. |
| **Elevation gain:** | 226 feet. |
| **Maps:** | Trails Illustrated (Mammoth Hot Springs); Mammoth USGS quad. |
| **Starting point:** | Sepulcher Mountain Trailhead (1K1) (also called Beaver Ponds and Clematis) in Mammoth. |

See Map on Page 43

**Finding the trailhead:** Drive south from Gardiner to Mammoth Hot Springs. The trailhead is on the right (west) just below the main hot springs by Liberty Cap.

## Key points:

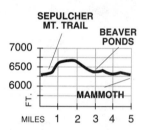

|  |  |
|---|---|
| 0.2 (0.3) | Junction with Howard Eaton Trail. |
| 0.7 (1.6) | Junction with Sepulcher Mountain Trail. |
| 3.0 (4.8) | Beaver Ponds. |
| 5.0 (8.0) | Intersection with old road. |
| 5.1 (8.1) | Mammoth. |

**The hike:** If you stay at Mammoth and have some extra time to get away from the traffic-choked roads, this gentle 5-mile loop trail is a good option. There is an excellent chance of seeing elk (if you haven't already seen enough right in Mammoth), moose, and black bear.

The trail begins just to the right (north) of Clematis Creek before Liberty Cap. Ordinarily, you could park and start at the same trailhead as the boardwalk trail around the hot springs, but the footbridge didn't survive the high water of the spring of 1996, so when we did this hike, it was necessary to start from the bus parking area on the east side of the creek.

The trail starts with a gradual uphill with brilliant colors of Mammoth Hot Springs on the left (south). Then, the trail crosses Clematis Creek on a bridge that did survive the high water.

At 0.2 mile is the junction with the Golden Gate/Howard Eaton Trail, which takes you behind the hot springs and to Terrace Mountain. Stay right (west) and continue toward Beaver Ponds. The trail crosses another bridge and climbs more steeply, passing one unmarked junction with a game trail. Stay right and keep switchbacking uphill.

At 0.7 mile is the marked junction with the Sepulcher Ridge Trail. The junction has a unique marker. An old carved stump signals, "Mountain Trail/ Ranger Nature Trail." That old nature trail is now called the Beaver Ponds Trail so turn right (north).

*Beaver ponds along Beaver Ponds Trail.*

After this junction the trail levels out and crosses meadows of dandelions and aspen with bark chewed off by winter-starved elk. In the spring you might see some larkspur and shooting stars along the way. The section of trail offers sweeping views of Gardner River valley and across to the Absaroka Range to the north.

After a short descent, the trail passes the first of several ponds. The Beaver Ponds consist of several marshy lakes graced by cattails and lilypads.

The return trip is relatively flat across a sagebrush plateau with good scenery all around, especially at Mount Everts (which would be better described as a ridge) across Gardner Canyon. When you see the town of Mammoth, the trail intersects an old road. Again, stay right. This last 0.1-mile descent to Mammoth terminates behind the main lodge, where you can make your way back to the trailhead.

| | |
|---|---|
| **Type of hike:** | Shuttle with loop option. |
| **Type of trip:** | Moderate day hike or overnighter. |
| **Total distance:** | 4.5 miles or 7.2 kilometers. |
| **Difficulty:** | Moderate. |
| **Elevation loss:** | 800 feet. |
| **Maps:** | Trails Illustrated (Mammoth Hot Springs); Mammoth and Blacktail Deer Creek USGS quads. |
| **Starting point:** | Lava Creek Picnic Area. |

See Map on Page 77

**Finding the trailhead:** From Mammoth, drive 4.4 miles east and park at the Lava Creek Picnic Area. Leave a vehicle at the Lava Creek Trailhead, a marked pullout just south of the campground at Mammoth.

**Key points:**
0.2 (0.3)  Junction with Lava Creek Trail and cutoff trail to Blacktail Ponds.
0.3 (0.5)  Undine Falls.
1.8 (2.9)  1A3 (3★).
3.7 (4.9)  Gardner River Bridge.
4.5 (7.2)  Lava Creek Trailhead (1N3).

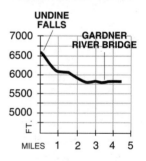

**The hike:** This trail receives much higher use than Rescue Creek and much of that use is horse-riding trips along Lava Creek. Undine Falls is more easily seen from the road to Tower Junction, but from this trail, you get a less-crowded and different perspective of the 60-foot waterfall.

Shortly after leaving the picnic area, you reach the Lava Creek Canyon Trail where you go left (west). The right turn leads to the Blacktail Ponds.

In less than a quarter mile, you get a great view of Undine Falls, which gets its name from mythological water spirits who were extraordinarily wise, usually female, and thought to live around waterfalls. In folklore, an undine could acquire the soul of a mortal man, marry him, and bear his children. Imagine this as you view the misty landscape around the waterfall.

From the falls, the trail drops steadily through mostly open terrain with little shade and no water. At the bottom of the descent, you see a backcountry campsite off to your left. If you're not alert, you can miss it.

After the campsite, you continue through shadeless terrain with good views of the Lava Creek and Gardner River drainages. Less than 1 mile from the trailhead, you cross the Gardner River on a rustic, wooden (but sturdy) bridge and then take a short, steep ascent past a horse corral to Mammoth Campground.

*Undine Falls in June.*          *Undine Falls in August.*

**Options:** You can also start this hike at the Blacktail Creek Trailhead (1N5), but this adds 2.5 miles to the trip. You can also do this shuttle in reverse, but that means an 800-foot elevation gain instead of a downhill trip. To make a loop trip out of this hike, combine it with the Rescue Creek hike, which requires walking on the north entrance road for about 3 miles. You could also combine it with the west section of the trail through the Black Canyon of the Yellowstone for a long overnight hike. Refer to the Rescue Creek and Black Canyon of the Yellowstone hike descriptions.

## 23  RESCUE CREEK

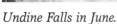

| | |
|---|---|
| **Type of hike:** | Shuttle with loop option. |
| **Type of trip:** | Day hike or overnighter. |
| **Total distance:** | 8 miles or 12.8 kilometers. |
| **Difficulty:** | Moderate. |
| **Elevation loss:** | 1,018 feet. |
| **Maps:** | Trails Illustrated (Mammoth Hot Springs); Gardiner, Mammoth, and Blacktail Deer Creek USGS quads. |
| **Starting point:** | Blacktail Creek Trailhead (1N5). |

**Finding the trailhead:** From Mammoth, drive 6.8 miles east and turn into the Blacktail Creek Trailhead on the north side of the road. Leave a vehicle or arrange to be picked up at the Rescue Creek Trailhead (1N2), which is 0.5 mile south of the entrance station on the east side of the highway.

**Key points:**

| | | |
|---|---|---|
| 0.3 | (4.8) | Junction with trail to Blacktail Ponds and Lava Creek. |
| 0.6 | (9.6) | Junction with Crevice Lake Trail. |
| 3.0 | (4.8) | 1A2 (4★). |
| 7.8 | (12.5) | Gardner River footbridge. |
| 8.0 | (12.8) | Rescue Creek Trailhead. |

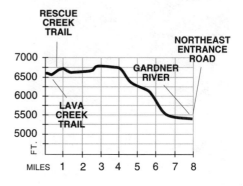

**The hike:** This trail is prime but often passed up by people eager to get deep in the backcountry of Yellowstone. Although it's close to Mammoth, it appears to get little use. Like many trails in Yellowstone, elk, deer, and bison probably use it more than hikers.

At the 0.3-mile mark, stay right (south) at the junction with the trail to Blacktail Ponds and Lava Creek. (If you chose the loop option, this is where you would rejoin the trail.)

About a quarter mile farther down the trail, take a left (northwest) at the junction with the trail that drops down to Crevice Lake and the Yellowstone River. From this junction, the trail stays on the east side of the Rescue Creek valley, going through scattered meadows and forest partially burned in 1988. You go past a few marshy areas and get good views of Everts Mountain. Watch for elk, abundant along this section of trail.

At the 3.0-mile mark, you see 1A2 on your left. After the campsite, the trail crosses a flat, sage prairie with views of the Gardner and Yellowstone valleys. Solitary poles with faded orange markers show the way. You get a nice look at the massive Absaroka Range to the north in the Gallatin National Forest.

The trail continues through meadows and intermittent stands of aspen and Douglas-fir and in the shadow of Rattlesnake Butte and Turkey Pen Peak. After passing several old stately junipers, the trail switchbacks down to the bridge over the Gardner River, and then a short climb takes you up to the trailhead.

**Options:** You could start at Rescue Creek Trailhead and do the trip in reverse, but you would face a 1,000-foot elevation gain that you can avoid by starting at the Blacktail Creek Trailhead. Also, for a large loop, you can combine the Rescue Creek hike with either the Lava Canyon hike or the

# RESCUE CREEK • LAVA CREEK CANYON • WRAITH FALLS

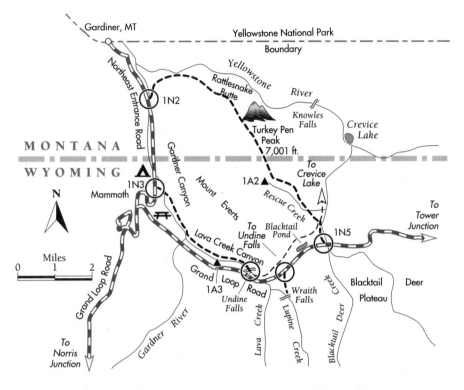

Black Canyon of the Yellowstone hike (east to Crevice Lake). But this section of trail is very hard to follow at times, and you might end up just walking cross country parallel to the road to Undine Falls. See the Lava Creek Canyon and Black Canyon of the Yellowstone hike descriptions.

## 24  CREVICE LAKE

| | | |
|---|---|---|
| **Type of hike:** | Out-and-back. | *See Map on Page 125* |
| **Type of trip:** | Day hike or overnighter. | |
| **Total distance:** | 8.4 miles or 13.5 kilometers (round-trip). | |
| **Difficulty:** | Moderate. | |
| **Elevation gain:** | 1,038 feet. | |
| **Maps:** | Trails Illustrated (Mammoth Hot Springs); Ash Mountain and Blacktail Deer Creek USGS quads. | |
| **Starting point:** | Blacktail Creek Trailhead (1N5). | |

**Finding the trailhead:** Drive east of Mammoth for 6.8 miles or west of Tower for 11.2 miles and turn into the pullout for the Blacktail Creek Trailhead on the north side of the road.

## Key points:
    0.4 (0.6)   Junction with trail to Lava Creek Trail.
    0.7 (1.1)   Junction with Rescue Creek Trail.
    1.5 (2.4)   1A1 (3★).
    3.8 (6.1)   Suspension Bridge and spur trail to 1Y6 (3★) and 1Y8 (4★).
    4.0 (6.4)   Junction with Yellowstone River Trail.
    4.2 (6.7)   Crevice Lake.

**The hike:** This trail is a popular starting point for longer trips along the Yellowstone River, but it also offers a taste of the river without an extended trip through the Black Canyon.

From the trailhead, hike past one of the Blacktail Ponds, which are sometimes closed to protect nesting sandhill cranes. Hopefully you can get a glimpse of one of the rare birds.

At 0.4 miles is the faint but marked junction with the trail to Lava Creek and Undine Falls. Turn right (south) and continue past several fenced off areas used for soil and wildlife studies. After a short climb, at the 0.7-mile mark, stay right (south) at the junction with the Rescue Creek Trail.

The trail is flat or downhill the rest of the way and mostly through open terrain. Watch for bison and elk. The rolling, prairie-like terrain continues until just before the spur trail to backcountry campsite 1A1 where the trial drops suddenly into the Blacktail Creek Valley.

After 1A1 the trail follows the left side of Blacktail Creek valley until just before the suspension bridge where you see the junction with the spur trail to 1Y6 and 1Y8. The spur trail leads past an old fire cabin used to cache firefighting supplies. When I did this hike, these two sites were closed, because the bridge over Blacktail Creek was washed out. In mid-summer, however, Blacktail Creek doesn't need a bridge, and you can safely rock hop or wade across the stream. Both campsites were easily accessible.

Back at the main trail, cross the metal suspension bridge high above the river. The trail climbs onto a flat area (with blooming bitterroot in June) until the Yellowstone River Trail junction. Turn left (northwest) for a visit to Crevice lake. The next section is flat to downhill through a dry juniper and Douglas-fir forest.

Crevice Lake is on the left (south) just below the trail. It's a small (18 acres) but deep (up to 98 feet) lake along the Yellowstone River. The lake has an abundance of damselflies, so if it had any fish (which it doesn't), they would be fat.

Take a nice long rest along the river or at the lake and prepare for your 1,000-foot climb back up to the highway.

**Options:** Although this makes a nice day hike, you can stay overnight at several campsites in the area.

**Side trips:** If you stay overnight, you can hike out and back (either east or west) along the Yellowstone on a delightful trail.

# 25   CYGNET LAKES

| | |
|---|---|
| **Type of hike:** | Out-and-back. |
| **Type of trip:** | Day hike. |
| **Total distance:** | 8 miles or 12.8 kilometers (round-trip). |
| **Difficulty:** | Moderate. |
| **Elevation gain:** | Minimal. |
| **Maps:** | Trails Illustrated (Old Faithful); Crystal Falls and Norris Junction USGS quads. |
| **Starting point:** | Cygnet Lakes Trailhead. |

## CYGNET LAKES

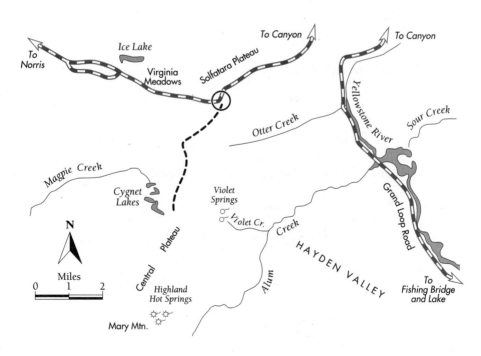

**Finding the trailhead:** Drive 4.7 miles west of Canyon Junction or 7.3 miles east of Norris Junction and park in a pullout on the south side of the road.

**The hike:** The trail to Cygnet Lakes is flat and fried, but in fair shape. With the exception of a few short sections, it's easy to follow. It goes through intermittently burned lodgepole all the way to the lakes.

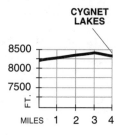

The lakes are marshy and covered with lilypads and surrounded by a large meadow where you're likely to see waterfowl and other wildlife. Like the Mary Lake area, this is good grizzly habitat, so be alert. Bear management prevents overnight camping in the Cygnet Lake area.

**Options:** Your map might show a trail extending south of Cygnet Lakes to Mary Lake, but this section of trail is unmaintained and difficult to follow.

## LONG HIKES

## 26  SKY RIM

|                    |                                                          |
| ------------------ | -------------------------------------------------------- |
| **Type of hike:**  | Loop (actually a "lollipop").                            |
| **Type of trip:**  | Long day hike.                                           |
| **Total distance:** | 21.1 miles or 34 kilometers, plus 0.6 mile (0.9 kilometer) for round-trip side trip to Big Horn Peak. |
| **Difficulty:**    | Difficult.                                               |
| **Elevation gain:** | 3,150 feet.                                              |
| **Maps:**          | Trails Illustrated (Mammoth Hot Springs); Big Horn Peak USGS quad. |
| **Starting point:** | Dailey Creek Trailhead (WK1).                            |

**Finding the trailhead:** Drive north from West Yellowstone or south from Bozeman to the Dailey Creek Trailhead between mileposts 30 and 31 on U.S. Highway 191. Black Butte Trailhead is between mileposts 28 and 29.

**Key points:**

| | | |
|---|---|---|
| 1.8 | (2.9) | Black Butte Cutoff Trail junction. |
| 2.6 | (4.2) | Teepee Creek Trail junction, WF2 (3★). |
| 4.9 | (7.8) | Dailey Pass. |
| 5.7 | (9.1) | Sky Rim Trail Junction. |

# SKY RIM

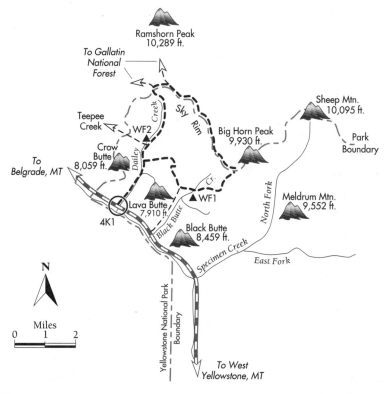

Ramshorn Peak
10,289 ft.

To Gallatin
National
Forest

Sky Rim

Creek

Teepee
Creek

WF2

Big Horn Peak
9,930 ft.

Sheep Mtn.
10,095 ft.

Crow
Butte
8,059 ft.

Dailey

Park
Boundary

To
Belgrade, MT

Cr.

Meldrum Mtn.
9,552 ft.

Lava Butte
7,910 ft.

WF1

North Fork

4K1

Black Butte

Black Butte
8,459 ft.

Specimen Creek

East Fork

N

Yellowstone National Park Boundary

Miles
0    1    2

To West
Yellowstone, MT

*Hiking the Sky Rim Trail.*

## Key points (cont'd):

11.2 (17.8)  Black Butte Creek Trail junction.
15.7 (25.3)  Trail to WF1 (4★).
15.9 (25.6)  Black Butte Creek Trail junction.
18.0 (28.9)  Dailey Creek Trail junction.
21.1 (34.0)  Dailey Creek Trailhead.

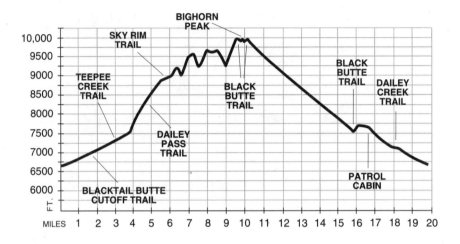

*The Sky Rim Trail follows the park boundary on the Gallatin Divide.*

**The hike:** For serious hikers who like to "get high" and have lots of panoramic mountain scenery, the Sky Rim loop trail is probably the best long hike in Yellowstone. It's also one of the most difficult, but it's ideal for the well-conditioned hiker who likes to get up early and spend the entire day walking with minimal time devoted to rest and relaxation.

Besides being one of the nicest parts of the park, the far northwest corner is also the newest. It was added to the park in 1927.

Be sure to take plenty of water on this hike. The stretch between Upper Dailey Creek all along Sky Rim, up Big Horn Peak, and down to Black Butte Creek is a very long haul without any reliable water sources. Take more water than you normally would on a long day hike.

Also, watch the weather closely. We had a perfect day when we hiked this route, but it was easy to see that you really don't want to be on Sky Rim in bad weather. At best, it wouldn't be much fun because you couldn't see the scenery, but more likely, it would be dangerous because of slippery footing and the specter of hypothermia. If you get caught in a thunderstorm on Sky Rim, you could become a lightning rod.

August is the best time to take this hike. You stand a good chance of good weather, and you avoid hiking the ridgeline with hunters who tend to take over the place in early September when the early big game seasons open in Montana.

The first 1.8 miles up Dailey Creek (incorrectly shortened to Daly Creek on some maps) starts out in the shadow of mighty Crown Butte just outside the park to the north. The well-defined trail winds through expansive open meadows broken here and there by scattered stands of trees. The scenery stays like this until about a mile past backcountry campsite WF2 when the trail slips into the trees for the climb up to Dailey Pass. The trail is heavily rutted in spots, which makes walking difficult.

When you get to Dailey Pass, you're actually at a four-way junction. The faint trail to the left (not shown on some maps) follows the ridgeline and park boundary, and the trail going straight heads out of the park into the Gallatin National Forest. You go right (east) and continue to climb along the ridgeline.

After the Category 1 climb up to the pass with only a few short switchbacks near the end, it seems like it should be about as high up as you can get, but you aren't even close to the top. The trail follows the ridge for 0.8 mile to the Sky Rim Trail junction. Parts of this trail go along a sharply angled ridgeline, so be careful not to fall off either side. We almost missed this junction because it's natural to keep heading up the ridge and the trail sign is behind you. At this junction, another trail heads north out of the park into the Buffalo Horn region of the Gallatin National Forest.

From the Sky Rim Trail, the view is fantastic. Off to the west looms the Taylor-Hilgards of the Madison Range with 11,316-foot Hilgard Peak and in the foreground, expansive Dailey Creek where you just hiked. Off to the

*Looking west into the Madison Range from the Sky Rim Trail.*

east is the sprawling Tom Minor Basin in the shadow of Canary Bird, Ramshorn, and Twin peaks with a majestic backdrop of the Absaroka Range and its highest point, Mount Cowen (11,205 feet).

From here, the already strenuous route gets more strenuous. The next leg of your trip, 5.5 miles along Sky Rim, goes over two more big climbs and is followed by the last pitch up to the Black Butte Creek Trail Junction, one of the few Category H climbs in the park. In fact, this is the most precipitous section of designated trail in the park, but it's not dangerous.

The scenery stays sensational all the way to Big Horn Peak. The trail gets faint in spots and about 1 mile from the next junction, more or less disappears on grassy flanks of Big Horn Peak. You won't get off the designated route as long as you don't drop off the ridgeline.

At the junction, take the short, out-and-back side trip to the very top of Big Horn Peak. It's hard to believe the scenery can get any better, but it actually does. This short but nerve-wracking (use caution!) side trip is definitely worth the little extra effort. From the true summit of Big Horn Peak you get a good view of the Gallatin Skyline Trail continuing over to Sheep Mountain to the south.

In addition to the mountain vistas that surround the Sky Rim, you also have a good chance of seeing elk, deer, and moose on the open slopes and along Dailey Creek. Also, watch for bighorn sheep, commonly seen on Big Horn Peak. In the fall, grizzlies frequent the Gallatin Skyline area to feed on whitebark pine nuts, abundant along this high-elevation trail.

From here, it's all downhill as you switchback down Big Horn Peak into Black Butte Creek. The trail is in better shape than the trail up Dailey Creek and along Sky Rim, so if you are behind schedule, you can make up some lost time. After about a half mile, you leave the open slopes of Big Horn Peak behind and hike into a lush, unburned forest and through the Gallatin Petrified Forest.

The trail stays in the forest the rest of the way. The trail to WF1 goes off to the left (south) just before the junction with the Black Butte Cutoff Trail. If you left a vehicle at the Black Butte Trailhead, you can skip the cutoff trail. If not, turn right (north), go through a large meadow and climb over a forested ridge past a patrol cabin, and back into spacious Dailey Creek. At the junction with the Dailey Creek Trail, turn left (west) and retrace your steps back to the Dailey Creek Trailhead.

**Options:** You could start at Black Butte Trailhead or take the route counter-clockwise with the same degree of difficulty. The climbs on the counter-clockwise route tend to be longer but more gradual as opposed to the short, steep climbs of the clockwise route. If you have 2 vehicles, you can skip the cutoff trail and shorten your trip by about two miles by leaving one vehicle at the Black Butte Trailhead. Because of the location of the campsites, you can't really turn this into an overnighter without making it more difficult. However, you could base camp at WF1 or WF2 and make the long day hike about 2 miles shorter.

**Side trips:** You would really miss something if you didn't take the short side trip (0.3 mile one way) to the top of Big Horn Peak. You can continue along the Gallatin Skyline Trail to Shelf Lake (3 miles one way), but make sure you have enough daylight. You could also camp at Shelf Lake and come out Specimen Creek, but this would be a Herculean day with an overnight pack to get to Shelf Lake along Sky Rim.

---

# 27  CRESCENT LAKE

|  |  |  |
|---|---|---|
| **Type of hike:** | Loop (actually a "lollipop"). | See Map on Page 89 |
| **Type of trip:** | Backpacking trip. | |
| **Total distance:** | 22 miles or 35.4 kilometers. | |
| **Difficulty:** | Difficult. | |
| **Elevation gain:** | 2,745 feet. | |
| **Maps:** | Trails Illustrated (Mammoth Hot Springs); Sportsman Lake and Big Horn Peak USGS quads. | |
| **Starting point:** | Specimen Creek Trailhead (WK3). | |

**Finding the trailhead:** Drive north from West Yellowstone, Montana, or south from Belgrade, Montana, on U.S. 191 to trailhead between mileposts 26 and 27.

**Key points:**
    2.0   (3.2)   Specimen Creek Trail junction.
    2.2   (3.5)   WE1 (4★).
    5.3   (8.6)   WE4 (3★).
    6.0   (9.7)   Shelf Lake Trail junction.

**Key points (cont'd):**
- 7.4 (12.0)  Crescent Lake, WE6 (4★).
- 11.7 (18.8)  High Lake, WD5 (2★).
- 11.9 (19.2)  WD4 (5★).
- 12.4 (20.1)  Park Boundary and Mill Creek Trail junction.
- 15.3 (24.7)  Sportsman Lake Trail junction.
- 16.2 (26.1)  WD1(2★).
- 20.0 (32.3)  Specimen Creek Trail junction.
- 22.0 (35.4)  Specimen Creek Trailhead.

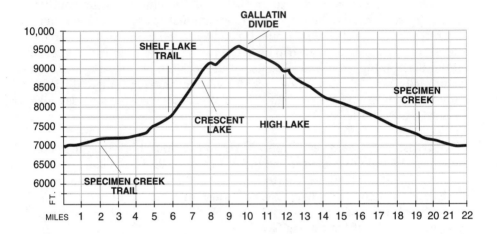

**Recommended itinerary:** I recommend a four-day trip with the first two nights at Crescent Lake and the third at High Lake. Spend the second day hiking without an overnight pack on day hikes to Shelf Lake, Sheep Mountain, or Big Horn Peak. On the third day, hike from Crescent Lake to High Lake and then out to the trailhead on the fourth day.

**The hike:** The hike starts out spectacularly and then gets better. The first 2 miles of trail meander along Specimen Creek and through a mature, unburned forest. This section is flat, easy, and the trail is in great shape, and you can almost always see moose in the meadows along the stream.

If you chose the clockwise route, turn left (northeast) at the first junction. Less than a quarter mile down the trail, you break out into a big meadow where the North Fork and East Fork of Specimen Creek merge. Backcountry campsite WE1 is on your left.

From here, head into an open forest broken up by a few large meadows and gradually climb up to the Shelf Lake Trail junction. Turn right (east) here and climb on a switchbacked trail to the outlet of Crescent Lake and backcountry campsite WE6, where you probably want to spend the night. Sorry, no fish in Crescent Lake—even though it's big enough (18 acres) and deep enough (48 feet).

*Crescent Lake.*

(If you're thinking about hanging your pack at the junction and taking a short side trip up to Shelf Lake or camping there instead of Crescent Lake, be aware of the very steep, 2.1-mile, Category 1 climb to Shelf Lake. It's straight up with no switchbacks.)

From Crescent Lake, the trail climbs about 1,000 feet over 2.3 miles (Category 2) to 9,660 feet on the Gallatin Skyline. This is rugged hiking, but the terrain is fairly open except for the sections around Crescent and Sedge lakes. When you reach ridgeline, the trail turns right (south) toward High Lake. Some old maps might show a trail along the ridge over to Sheep Mountain, but there is no trail. On the way up to the ridgeline, keep your map and compass out. Many hikers have gotten momentarily lost in this stretch of trail, so follow the trail carefully from Crescent Lake. Also, make sure you're on the right trail. Some game trails are better than the official trail. If you hike this route in July, you might run into some snow in this section, which makes staying on the official trail even more difficult. Go slowly and carefully to stay on the correct route.

Watch for elk which are very abundant along this section of trail, and soak in some spectacular scenery. To the left (east), look down into the Cinnabar Basin in the Gallatin National Forest with the mighty Absaroka Range as a backdrop. To the right (west), you can see the general route you'll be taking down the East Fork of Specimen Creek and back to the Gallatin River and U.S. 191. Don't get too wrapped up in the scenery, however, and get off the trail.

You stay on the divide surrounded by scenic vistas for about 2 miles before quickly dropping down about 400 feet to High Lake, where you probably will want to spend the night (if you have a permit, of course). This isn't one of those mountain lakes nestled in the backend of a cirque surrounded by craggy peaks. Instead, High Lake is more like a gentle jewel in the heart of a lush, high-elevation swale. The small (7 acres) lake hosts a hardy, self-sustaining cutthroat population. To fish (catch-and-release only), you need a park fishing license purchased before you hit the trail.

From High Lake it's all downhill. You can take two days to hike the last 10 miles by staying at backcountry campsite WD1, but most well-conditioned backpackers won't have trouble covering this downhill stretch in one long day.

About a half mile after leaving the lake, you see a junction marking the park boundary and Mill Creek Trail heading off to the left (east) into the Gallatin National Forest. Turn right (west) here and head down through a series of gorgeous, high-altitude meadows to the Sportsman Lake Trail junction, where you stay right (west).

From this junction, the trail stays in a mature, mostly unburned forest all the way to the trailhead. You pass through one huge meadow about 1 mile after the junction in the upper reaches of the East Fork of Specimen Creek and cross the East Fork twice and the main Specimen Creek once on bridges.

**Options:** You can take the loop in either direction, of course. However, it's close to a toss up. I give a slight edge to the clockwise route because it avoids making the tough choice between hiking 10.1 uphill miles to High Lake on the first day with my pack at its heaviest or taking two days to cover this leg and staying at WD1, which is a marginal campsite. On the clockwise route, I hiked 7.4 miles the first day to a great campsite at Crescent Lake, and then on my last day, I rolled out early and did the 10.1 miles downhill from High Lake with a lighter pack.

You can do this loop with only two nights out by either skipping the side trip to Shelf Lake or getting up early on the second day and do it before backpacking over to High Lake. You can also make this a longer trip by staying at Shelf Lake and taking two days to get to High Lake.

This area is also a setup for a base camp hike. If you like this option, I suggest setting up the base camp at Crescent Lake, and from here, take day trips to High Lake, Shelf Lake/Sheep Mountain, Big Horn Peak, or up to the divide west of High Lake.

**Side trips:** From Crescent Lake, you can day hike out and back to Shelf Lake, Sheep Mountain, or Big Horn Peak, but keep in mind that it's a 2.1-mile (one way), 1,400-foot, Category 1 climb to get up to Shelf Lake. There isn't an official trail from Shelf Lake up to Sheep Mountain, but it's an easy scramble. There is an official trail over to Big Horn Peak. From Crescent Lake, you can also take short off-trail hikes to an unnamed lake just southwest of your campsite and to Crag Lake to the southeast.

| | |
|---|---|
| **Type of hike:** | Out-and-back. |
| **Type of trip:** | Long day hike. |
| **Total distance:** | 14 miles or 22.6 kilometers (round-trip). |
| **Difficulty:** | Difficult. |
| **Elevation gain:** | 3,119 feet. |
| **Maps:** | Trails Illustrated (Mammoth Hot Springs); Big Horn Peak USGS quad. |
| **Starting point:** | Black Butte Trailhead (WK2). |

**Finding the trailhead:** Drive south from Belgrade, Montana, or north from West Yellowstone, Montana, on U.S. Highway 191 to just south of milepost 29.

**Key points:**

| | | |
|---|---|---|
| 2.0 | (3.2) | Dailey Creek Cutoff Trail junction. |
| 2.2 | (3.6) | Trail to WF1 (4★). |
| 6.7 | (10.8) | Sky Rim Trail junction. |
| 7.0 | (11.3) | Big Horn Peak. |

## BIG HORN PEAK • CRESCENT LAKE

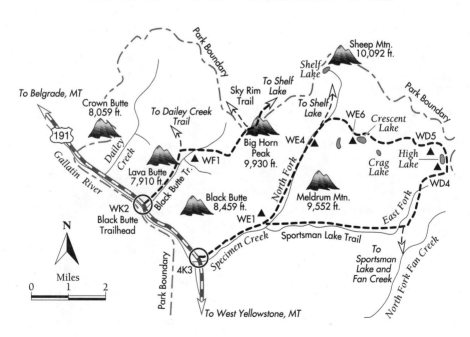

**The hike:** This is the shortest route to one of the park's most sensational views.

The trail remains in an unburnt forest along Black Butte Creek for about 3 miles before angling off to the southeast and switchbacking up to the summit of Big Horn Peak. This is a Category 1 climb, but it doesn't get super steep until you get near the top, and the well-designed and switchbacked trail makes it easier. You hike through the Gallatin Petrified Forest and can see exposed petrified trees along the way, but please leave the petrified wood where you find it.

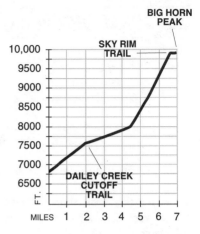

The trail is in excellent shape the entire way until you get near the summit where you break out into the open grassy slopes. Here, the trail gets faint in a few spots. Near the top, you'll see a junction with the trail going left (north) along the Sky Rim. Turn right (south) for another 0.3 mile to the summit of Big Horn Peak.

Make sure you have a clear day for this hike (life can be ugly up here in bad weather!), and be sure to take a map and leave yourself enough time on top to identify all the nearby mountains.

Don't forget your water bottles. The last reliable source is about halfway up.

*The last pitch to the top of Big Horn Peak.*

*View of Sheep Mountain and the Gallatin Skyline trail from Big Horn Peak.*

**Options:** You can turn this into an overnighter by staying at WF1, an easy 2.5-mile backpack from the Black Butte Trailhead and then day hike up to Big Horn Peak the next day.

## 29   *SPORTSMAN LAKE*

|   |   |
|---|---|
| **Type of hike:** | Shuttle. |
| **Type of trip:** | Long backpacking trip. |
| **Total distance:** | 23.2 miles  or 37.3 kilometers. |
| **Difficulty:** | Difficult. |
| **Elevation gain:** | 2,980 feet, not counting side trips to Cache Lake or up Electric Peak. |
| **Maps:** | Trails Illustrated (Mammoth Hot Springs); Mammoth, Quadrant Mountain, Joseph Peak, Electric Peak, Sportsman Lake, and Richards Creek USGS quads. |
| **Starting point:** | Glen Creek Trailhead (1K3). |

**Finding the trailhead:** Drive 4.7 miles south of Mammoth to just past the Golden Gate and park at the Glen Creek Trailhead parking lot on the east side of the road.

## Key points:

| | | |
|---|---|---|
| 0.2 | (0.3) | Junction with Howard Eaton Trail to Mammoth. |
| 2.1 | (3.4) | Fawn Pass Trail junction. |
| 2.9 | (4.7) | Sepulcher Mountain Trail junction. |
| 3.7 | (5.9) | Cache Lake Trail junction. |
| 5.7 | (9.1) | Electric Peak Spur Trail junction. |
| 5.8 | (9.2) | 1G3 (3★). |
| 5.9 | (9.3) | 1G4 (4★). |
| 9.9 | (15.9) | Electric Pass. |
| 12.7 | (20.4) | Sportsman Lake, 4D3 (5★), and 4D2 (3★). |
| 15.7 | (25.3) | High Lake Cutoff Trail. |
| 20.6 | (33.2) | 4C2 (5★). |
| 21.9 | (35.3) | Fawn Pass Trail junction. |
| 23.2 | (37.3) | U.S. Highway 191. |

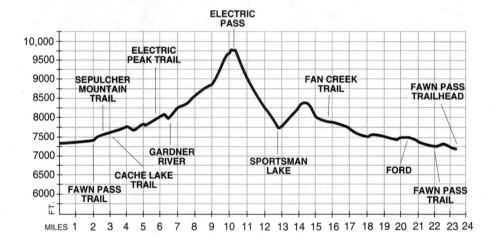

**Recommended itinerary:** I recommend a four-day trip that leaves a day for climbing Electric Peak. Hang your pack and take the side trip to Cache Lake on first day while hiking to 1G3 or 1G4 and spend two nights at one of these campsites. Weather permitting, climb Electric Peak on the second day. Stay at Sportsman Lake (WD3, if possible) the third night and hike out the fourth day. If the 10.5 miles on the last day scares you, you can stay in one of the three campsites in Fan Creek and have a very easy day on the fifth day of the hike. The information you get from the backcountry office might say that only WC2 is open to hikers, but the NPS will sometimes allow hikers to camp at WC3 and WC4 if they aren't already reserved by stock parties.

**The hike:** If you like to take a break in the middle of a long backpacking trip for a mountain climb, the Sportsman Lake trip is perfect for you. It offers easy access to Electric Peak. If you don't like to climb mountains, Sportsman Lake is almost perfect.

*Studying the map on Electric Pass.*

The only drawback of this hike (like several others in the Gallatin Range) is the long vehicle shuttle. Leave a vehicle at the other end or team up with another party and meet at Sportsman Lake and trade vehicle keys.

This trail goes through the no-off-trail-travel zone designated by the NPS for the Gallatin Range to minimize the impact of hiking on this key grizzly habitat. This restriction doesn't apply to the hike up Electric Peak, which is a NPS-designated route.

The first section of trail up to the Fawn Pass Trail junction goes through sagebrush-carpeted flats on a double-wide trail on the south side of Terrace Mountain. At the Fawn Pass Trail junction, go straight (west) and head into a small valley, through a short section of burned forest along Glen Creek and past the Sepulcher Mountain Trail going off to the right (north). You go left (west) at this junction.

At the 3.7-mile mark, you can hang your pack for a short side trip up to Cache Creek. The sign says 1.2 miles, but it only took us about 10 minutes to get to the lake. This spur trail is in great shape, and you get a great view of Electric Peak with the lake in the foreground.

After the Cache Lake Trail junction, the trail continues gradually climbing through an open, unburned forest. Just after the junction with the Electric Peak Spur Trail, the trail drops down into the Upper Gardner River valley for a quarter mile or so to 1G3 or 1G4 (just after fording the stream) where you probably want to spend your first night. These campsites serve as a base camp for a climb up Electric Peak.

Even though the trail up to Electric Pass barely qualifies as a Category 2 climb, it doesn't seem that difficult. About halfway up, you break out of the

# SPORTSMAN LAKE • CACHE LAKE
# • ELECTRIC PEAK

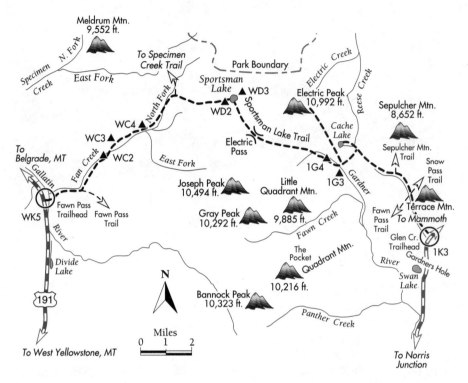

unburned timber and stay in the open the rest of the way to the pass. Electric Pass is less severe than Bighorn Pass, but more rigorous than Fawn Pass.

Even though you might see some signs of past campsites on the pass (mainly used by locals climbing Electric Peak), it's illegal to camp here, and the NPS keeps a close watch on the place. Plus, this is a high-use area for grizzlies, and there are no trees high enough to hang food out of a bear's reach.

After resting awhile on the pass, head down to Sportsman Lake. When you see how steep the climb is on the west side of the pass, you'll be glad you started at Golden Gate. After about 1 mile of open terrain, where the trail gets faint and you have to use cairns to find you way, the trail heads into deep timber and stays there all the way to Sportsman Lake. Be sure to make noise while in this dense timber so you don't surprise one of the bears inhabiting this area.

Sportsman Lake is difficult to see from a distance or even when you're standing in the huge meadow at the foot of the lake. When you reach the trail sign in the meadow below the lake, take a moment to make sure you take the correct trail. At this crossroads junction, go straight. The trail to the right goes to WD3 and used to go up Mol Heron Creek into the Gallatin

*Sportsman Lake.*

National Forest (an essentially abandoned and non-existent route). The lefthand trail goes to the patrol cabin you can see on the edge of the meadow. You probably want to camp at Sportsman Lake because it's another 8 miles to the next designated campsite (WC2) and 10.5 miles to the trailhead on U.S. 191. Sportsman Lake is only 4 acres but it has a healthy cutthroat population, so if you plan to fish (catch-and-release only), don't forget your park fishing license.

When you leave Sportsman Lake, you climb for almost 1 mile through a heavily burned forest. When you reach the top of the ridge, you drop into unburned timber and stay there past the cutoff trail to Specimen Creek, and another mile or so, until you break out into the splendor of Fan Creek. This trail gets light use by hikers, which may mystify you when you see how truly splendid it is. The area does get heavy use from stock parties, however.

From here, it's a scenic hike (flat, stream grade downhill on an excellent trail) through open country all the way to the trailhead. Watch for moose and bears. You have to ford Fan Creek once at about 3 miles from the trailhead. This ford can be difficult early in the year, but is usually easy by late July.

**Options:** This shuttle can be done just as easily in reverse. The elevation gain and spacing of campsites are similar from both trailheads. I give a slight edge to starting on the east end because the climb up Electric Pass seems more difficult from the west. If you don't feel up to climbing Electric

*Upper Fan Creek.*

Peak, cut a day off the trip, and you can trim it to three days by hiking all the way out from Sportsman Lake on the last day. A well-conditioned hiker could do this entire route in one day without the burden of an overnight pack and without taking any side trips.

**Side trips:** Refer to the Electric Peak and Cache Lake trail descriptions.

## 30  *ELECTRIC PEAK*

|  |  |
|---|---|
| **Type of hike:** | Out-and-back. |
| **Type of trip:** | For well-conditioned, experienced hikers only. A side trip on a multi-day backpacking trip, a moderate overnighter, or a strenuous day hike. |
| **Total distance:** | 8.4 miles or 13.5 kilometers (round-trip from beginning of spur trail). |
| **Difficulty:** | Very difficult. |
| **Elevation gain:** | 2,812 feet from beginning of spur trail; 3,700 feet from Glen Creek Trailhead. |
| **Maps:** | Trails Illustrated (Mammoth Hot Springs); Mammoth, Quadrant Mountain, and Electric Peak USGS quads. |
| **Starting point:** | Junction with Electric Peak spur trail accessed from Glen Creek Trailhead (1K3). |

See Map on Page 94

**Finding the trailhead:** Drive 4.7 miles south of Mammoth to just past the Golden Gate and park at the Glen Creek Trailhead parking lot on the east side of the road.

**Key points:**

| | | |
|---|---|---|
| 0.2 | (0.3) | Junction with Howard Eaton Trail to Mammoth. |
| 2.1 | (3.4) | Fawn Pass Trail junction. |
| 2.9 | (4.7) | Sepulcher Mountain Trail junction. |
| 3.7 | (5.9) | Cache Lake Trail junction. |
| 5.7 | (9.1) | Electric Peak Spur Trail junction. |
| 5.8 | (9.2) | 1G3 (3★). |
| 5.9 | (9.3) | 1G4 (4★). |
| 9.9 | (15.9) | Summit of Electric Peak. |

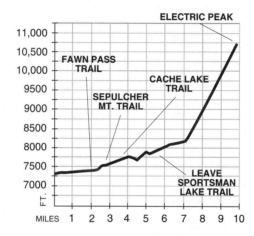

*Heading for Electric Peak.*

**Recommended itinerary:** If you aren't climbing Electric Peak as part of a longer backpacking trip, I suggest making it a three-day trip with two nights at 1G3 or 1G4. Hike in and set up camp on the first day; include a side trip to Cache Lake on the way in. Get up early and climb the mountain the second day, and hike out the third day.

**The hike:** Electric Peak, at 10,992 feet, is commonly believed to be the highest point in Yellowstone National Park, but in reality, it's the sixth highest. However, it might be the most sensational hike in the park. It's certainly the high point of the northwestern corner of Yellowstone.

This trail description stretches the definition of the word "hike." Actually, this is a moderately difficult mountain climb with a well-defined approach trail.

If you plan to stay overnight, reserve 1G3 or 1G4 and spend your first day of the three-day hike enjoying a leisurely 5.8-mile hike into the headwaters of the Gardner River. The first part of the hike to the Fawn Pass Trail junction goes through sagebrush flats on a double-wide trail on the south side of Terrace Mountain. At the Fawn Pass Trail junction, go straight (west) and head into a small valley, through a short section of burned forest along Glen Creek and past the junction with the Sepulcher Mountain Trail, which goes off to the right (north). You go left (west) at this junction.

At the 3.7-mile mark, you can hang your pack for a short side trip up to Cache Creek. The sign says 1.2 miles, but it's probably about half that distance. This spur trail is in great shape, and you get a great view of Electric Peak from the lake.

After the Cache Lake Trail junction, the trail continues gradually climbing through an open, unburned forest. Just after the Electric Peak Spur Trail, the trail drops down into the Upper Gardner River Valley for a quarter mile or so to 1G3 or 1G4, just after your ford the stream. These campsites serve as your base camp for a climb up Electric Peak.

The first 2 miles of the official route up the southeastern flank of Electric Peak are a well-defined trail without too much climbing, but be alert not to accidentally get on game trails, which might look better than the official route. Then, about halfway up, the trail gets less defined and starts climbing very steeply (Category H climb) until you get within about a half mile of the summit where the trail disappears in the rocks. From this point on, it's a cross between scrambling and climbing until you get to the summit. For most of the way, you can see the route commonly taken by hikers who have gone before you. Be very careful on this last stretch, which can be hazardous, especially if you aren't an experienced rock climber.

Because of heavy snowpack, don't try Electric Peak until mid-July, and even then, check with the backcountry office at Mammoth for current conditions. Also, be sure to take plenty of water since you won't see any on this route, with the possible exception of a few snowbanks surviving the summer sun. And finally, watch the weather closely. If you wake up to a rainy day, you might want to abandon your plans. If you get lucky on the weather, start at dawn and get up to the summit by mid-morning to minimize the chance of getting caught in an afternoon thunderstorm, common in Yellowstone. You definitely do not want to be caught near the summit in a thunderstorm. Early explorers named this mountain for how "electric" it became during lightning storms.

It goes without saying that the view from the summit is overwhelming. You can look down at Sepulcher and Terrace mountains and Bunsen Peak and everything else in the northwestern corner of the park. You can follow the Gardner River from its humble beginnings to where it merges with the Yellowstone just before the town of Gardiner. On a clear day, you'll want to allow an hour or so for absorbing the view before heading down.

It's hard on your lungs going up and hard on your knees going down, but you won't be sorry you climbed Electric Peak.

**Options:** In some cases, the summit of Electric Peak is a destination of a long day hike from Glen Creek Trailhead but only by very well-conditioned, experienced hikers. This would probably rank as the hardest but most spectacular day hike in the park, rivaled only by the Sky Rim, Mount Holmes, and Mount Sheridan (from Heart Lake Trailhead) hikes. In many cases, it's a long side trip on the Sportsman Lake or Gallatin Skyline backpacking trips.

**Side trips:** You'll be missing something if you don't take the short side trip to Cache Lake on your way in or out.

# 31  THE GALLATIN SKYLINE

|  |  |
|---|---|
| **Type of hike:** | Shuttle. |
| **Type of trip:** | A long, strenuous backpacking adventure. |
| **Total distance:** | 40.3 miles or 64.9 kilometers. |
| **Difficulty:** | Difficult. |
| **Elevation gain:** | 2,680 feet, not including climbs up Electric Peak or Sheep Mountain. |
| **Maps:** | Trails Illustrated (Mammoth Hot Springs); Mammoth, Quadrant Mountain, Joseph Peak, Sportsman Lake, Electric Peak, and Big Horn Peak USGS quads. |
| **Starting point:** | Glen Creek Trailhead (1K3). |

**Finding the trailhead:** Drive 5 miles south of Mammoth to just past the Golden Gate and park at the Glen Creek Trailhead parking lot on the east side of the road.

**Key points:**

| | | |
|---|---|---|
| 0.2 | (0.3) | Junction with Howard Eaton Trail to Mammoth. |
| 2.1 | (3.4) | Fawn Pass Trail junction. |
| 2.9 | (4.7) | Sepulcher Mountain Trail junction. |
| 3.7 | (5.9) | Cache Lake Trail junction. |
| 5.7 | (9.1) | Electric Peak Spur Trail junction. |
| 5.8 | (9.2) | 1G3 (3★). |
| 5.9 | (9.3) | 1G4 (4★). |
| 9.9 | (15.9) | Electric Pass. |
| 12.7 | (20.4) | Sportsman Lake, 4D3 (5★), and 4D2 (3★). |
| 15.7 | (25.3) | Sportsman Lake Creek Cutoff Trail. |
| 16.8 | (27.0) | High Lake Trail. |
| 19.7 | (31.7) | Mill Creek Trail junction. |
| 20.2 | (32.5) | High Lake, WD4 (5★) and WD5 (2★). |
| 24.7 | (39.7) | Crescent Lake, WE6 (4★). |
| 25.3 | (40.7) | Junction with Specimen Creek and Shelf Lake trails. |
| 27.1 | (43.6) | Shelf Lake, WE5 (5★) and WE7 (5★). |
| 27.3 | (43.9) | Gallatin Divide. |
| 30.1 | (48.4) | Big Horn Peak. |
| 30.3 | (48.7) | Junction with Black Butte Trail. |
| 35.8 | (57.6) | Junction with trail to Buffalo Horn Pass. |
| 36.6 | (58.9) | Dailey Pass. |
| 38.9 | (62.6) | Teepee Creek Trail junction, WF2 (3★). |
| 39.6 | (63.7) | Black Butte Cutoff Trail junction. |
| 41.4 | (66.6) | Dailey Creek Trailhead. |

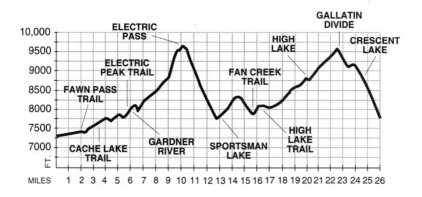

**Recommended itinerary:** This trip requires a minimum of six days, but I recommend taking seven, adding an extra day to climb Electric Peak.

| | | |
|---|---|---|
| First night | — | Preferred—1G4, alternate—1G3. |
| Second night | — | Same campsite. |
| Third night | — | Preferred—WD3, alternate—WD2. |
| Fourth night | — | Preferred—WD4, alternate—WD5. |
| Fifth night | — | Preferred—WE5, alternate—WE7. |
| Sixth night | — | Outside park on Sky Rim. |

*The trail on the west side of Electric Pass.*

**The hike:** Regardless of how experienced or well-conditioned you are (and you must be both), this hike is a true adventure. This is not a hike you decide to do a few days in advance. Instead, it's a hike you plan months ahead, going over every detail to keep your pack as light as possible but still be prepared for all types of weather. If you're looking for a "get high" backpacking trip to really experience the essence of the Yellowstone high country, this is how you'll want to spend your summer vacation.

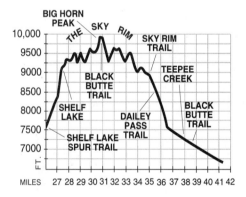

You hike above treeline much of the way, backpacking right over the top of one mountain (Big Horn Peak), and you'll probably want to take side trips to the top of two more (Electric Peak and Sheep Mountain). You visit five gorgeous high-altitude mountain lakes, camping at three of them. You'll probably see lots of wildlife, and you'll definitely see some of the most outstanding mountain scenery in the northern Rockies. When you finish, you'll definitely have that "hard body" feeling, and your jeans won't be so tight. And finally, for those who like an extra dose of wildness, you'll live with Yellowstone's most famous resident, the grizzly bear, for a week or more since this route goes through some of the park's best bear habitat. (This means no off-trail trail hiking on some sections of the route to minimize the impact of our behavior on bear behavior.)

# GALLATIN SKYLINE

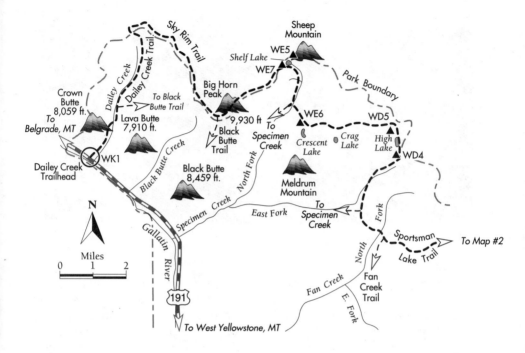

Planning is the key to making this trip a success. Since it's a shuttle (and a long one at that), you'll have to leave a vehicle or arrange for a pick up at the Dailey Creek Trailhead.

Waiting until August maximizes your chances of getting a week of good weather. Bad weather can really take the fun out of this trip (and make it dangerous) because you're often exposed at high altitude. (Fortunately, you can safely "bail out" if you get in trouble by hiking back to the Glen Creek Trailhead on the first two days or out to U.S. 191 down Fan, Specimen, or Black Butte creeks after you cross Electric Pass.)

It might be tempting to wait for the wonderful weather that often hits this area in September, but this is also the time the early big game seasons opens in Montana. You'll run into hordes of hunters on the divide, which is mostly devoid of people the rest of the year.

The first 2.1 miles of trail to the Fawn Pass Trail junction goes through sagebrush-carpeted flats on a double-wide trail along the south edge of Terrace Mountain. At the Fawn Pass Trail junction, go straight (west) and head into a small valley, through a short section of burned forest along Glen Creek and past the Sepulcher Mountain Trail junction, where you go left (west). At the 3.7-mile mark, you can hang your pack and take a short side trip up to Cache Creek.

# GALLATIN SKYLINE

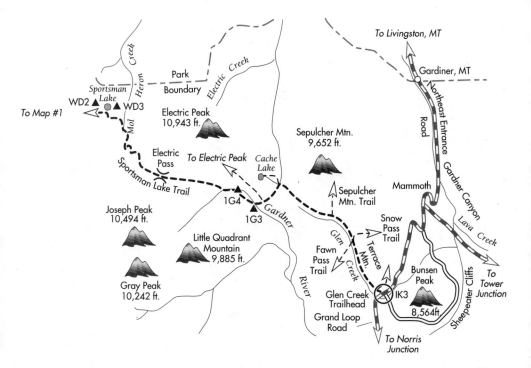

After the Cache Lake Trail junction, the trail gradually climbs through open, unburned timber. Just after the Electric Peak Spur Trail, the trail drops into the Upper Gardner River valley for a quarter mile or so to 1G3 or 1G4 (just after an easy ford of the stream). These campsites serve as base camps for a day trip up Electric Peak.

Even though the trail up to Electric Pass barely qualifies as a Category 2 climb, it doesn't seem that difficult. About halfway up, you break out of the unburned timber and stay in open terrain the rest of the way to the pass.

After resting awhile on the pass, head down to Sportsman Lake. After about 1 mile of treeless landscape (where the trail gets faint and cairns mark the route), the trail heads into deep timber and stays there until Sportsman Lake.

Sportsman Lake could be called "Hidden Lake" because even though you're standing in the open meadow at the foot of the lake you can't see it, nor can you see it coming down from the pass. A trail sign in the huge meadow below the lake marks a four-way crossroads. Eventually, you'll go straight, but if you're staying at WD3, take a right. The spur trail used to go up Mol Heron Creek into the Gallatin National Forest (now essentially abandoned), but now, it only goes to WD3.

*Viewing Shelf Lake and Sheep Mountain from the Gallatin Skyline Trail.*

*Gallatin Skyline Trail between Sheep Mountain and Big Horn Peak.*

When you leave Sportsman Lake, you climb for almost 1 mile through a heavily burned forest. When you reach the top of the ridge, you drop into unburned timber and stay there until you reach the cutoff trail to Specimen Creek and the High Lake Trail.

Turn right (north) here, and follow the cutoff trail through open timber and one large meadow before joining the trail to High Lake. Turn right (east), and tackle the Category 2 climb to High Lake, which sits in a open, high-elevation bowl. It also hosts a hardy, self-sustaining cutthroat population. If you plan on fishing (catch-and-release), don't forget your park fishing license.

When leaving High Lake, you face a 400-foot hill to get up to the Gallatin Divide. Once on the divide, plan on soaking in the serious scenery, and watch for elk along this section of trail. To the right (east) is the Cinnabar Basin in the Gallatin National Forest with the mighty Absaroka Range in the background. To the left (west), look into the expansive Gallatin Valley and its main artery, the Gallatin River. Don't get too wrapped up in the scenery, however, and get off the trail. It gets faint in places, especially after you veer left and head down to Crescent Lake. You can easily get diverted onto one of the many game trails in the area, which are often more distinct than the official trail. This trail gets especially difficult to follow in the fall.

After Crescent Lake, the trail switchbacks down to the junction with the Specimen Creek Trail. Turn right (north) here, and start the 2.1-mile, Category 1 climb up to Shelf Lake. This is a very tough hill, and you'll probably be worn out after three days of backpacking—and you'll probably be hiking this section in the hot mid-day sun. It goes straight up, and whoever built it forgot the switchbacks.

When you get to Shelf Lake, however, your effort will be well-rewarded. This is an enchanting, if not ominous, place just below the Gallatin Divide and Sheep Mountain. Both campsites at this lake are among the best in the park. If you spend two nights here, use part of the rest day to scramble up to the top of 10,095-foot Sheep Mountain, the highest peak in this section of the park. It has a big, metal reflector screen for telecommunications on the summit.

From Shelf Lake, stay on the Gallatin Divide for the next 8.5 miles. Start early because this is your toughest day, and before leaving the lake, load up on all the water you can carry. With the exception of late-season snowbanks (which you usually can find as late as early August), you won't find any water on the ridgeline.

This section makes this trip one of the most unusual and scenic backpacks found anywhere. From Shelf Lake to Big Horn Peak and the Black Butte Trail junction, the going is fairly easy. After the junction, however, you face the toughest part of the trip. The trail more or less disappears for about a half mile after the junction, but the official route stays on the ridgeline, and the walking is fairly easy but essentially off-trail. At this point, you can rejoice that you aren't lugging your pack up this pitch, a Category H hill from the north.

The trail goes up and down over two smaller summits on the ridge. Between each summit is a flat saddle where you can spend your last night out. The park boundary goes right on the ridgeline and is marked in many places.

*Dailey Creek.*

Be sure that you're camped outside of the park. These are all marginal camp-sites with no water sources, but the night on this high divide is a special treat. (The NPS may put an official campsite along this stretch, so check on this before you leave on this trip.)

From this last camp, it's downhill to Dailey Pass. You pass two junctions with trails going off to the right (northeast) into the Gallatin National Forest. You stay left at both junctions.

The trip down from the pass may be difficult on your knees, but once you break out into the openness of Dailey Creek, it's easy walking the last 4 miles to the trailhead.

**Options:** You can trim one day off this trip by skipping the climb to Electric Peak. You could lengthen the trip by staying an extra night at Shelf Lake or staying at Crescent Lake instead of going all the way from High Lake to Shelf Lake in one day. You could also tack one more day on the trip by staying at WF2 in Dailey Creek. You could start at the Dailey Creek Trailhead, but this might mean a more difficult trip.

**Side trips:** The Cache Lake and Electric Peak side trips have their own trail descriptions. The side trip up Sheep Mountain is an easy scramble.

# 32  FAWN PASS

|  |  |
|---|---|
| **Type of hike:** | Shuttle. |
| **Type of trip:** | Long day hike. |
| **Total distance:** | 20.8 miles or 33.5 kilometers. |
| **Difficulty:** | Difficult. |
| **Elevation gain:** | 2,030 feet. |
| **Maps:** | Trails Illustrated (Mammoth Hot Springs); Divide Lake, Joseph Peak, Quadrant Mountain, and Mammoth USGS quads. |
| **Starting point:** | Fawn Pass Trailhead (WK5). |

**Finding the trailhead:** Drive south from Belgrade, Monana, or north from West Yellowstone, Montana, on U.S. 191 to the Fawn Pass Trailhead just south of milepost 22 on the east side of the road.

**Key points:**

| | | |
|---|---|---|
| 1.3 | (2.1) | Junction with Fan Creek Trail. |
| 4.0 | (8.0) | Bighorn Pass Cutoff Trail. |
| 9.0 | (14.5) | Fawn Pass. |
| 15.7 | (25.3) | 1F2 (4★). |
| 16.3 | (26.2) | Fawn Creek footbridge. |
| 16.8 | (27.0) | Gardner River footbridge, 1G2 (5★). |
| 18.7 | (30.1) | Sportsman Lake Trail junction. |
| 20.8 | (33.5) | Glen Creek Trailhead. |

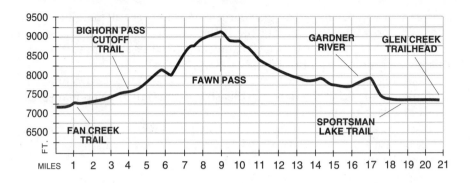

The hike: Because of the prohibition of camping in the bear management area in the Gallatin Range, this hike is a poor choice for backpacking, but a great choice for a delightful, albeit long, day hike—as long as you can start early, and you're fit enough to enjoyably hike 20 miles in a single day. For safety reasons, the NPS recommends groups of four or more hikers for this bear-rich area.

Since you really need to get up early to finish the hike in daylight, you'll undoubtedly be treated with some great wildlife watching. It seems like everywhere you look, you see elk bounding away, but also keep your eyes pealed for the mighty grizzly commonly seen on this hike.

*Fawn Pass.*

# FAWN PASS

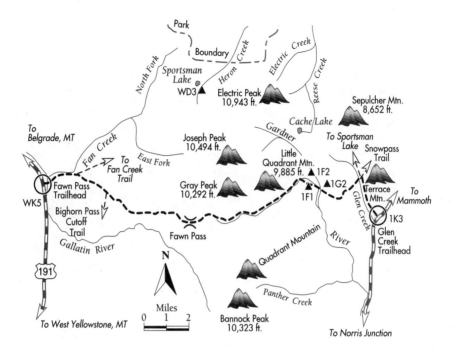

Even though you gain more than 2,000 feet elevation, this Category 2 climb doesn't seem that bad because its evenly spread over 9 miles. A strong hiker can make it up to the pass in 5-6 hours without extra effort.

The trail is in excellent shape all the way to the pass. The bear management area starts at the Bighorn Pass Cutoff Trail, which means no off-trail travel beyond this point. The trail gradually climbs through intermittently burned forest with lots of open meadows. You might be surprised when you get to the pass. It isn't a severe divide like many passes. Instead, it's gentle and lush. This is great bear habitat, and if you're careful and patient, you might be able to see a grizzly on Fawn Pass.

On the way down, you follow beautiful Fawn Creek as it flows through open terrain lined by unburned forest and wildflower-carpeted meadows until you cross it just before you reach the Gardner River. Both Fawn Creek and the Gardner River have footbridges. Just before you reach the river, a major social trail veers off to the right, but you go left. The righthand trail is an unofficial trail that goes over to the stock-only 1G5 campsite.

Just before you reach the river, the trail levels out and goes through open terrain for about 1 mile. Then, after you cross the Gardner River footbridge, you climb over a small but steep hill and drop down to the Electric Pass Trail junction. Turn right (east) here, and hike the last flat, easy 2.1 miles to the Glen Creek Trailhead. The hill out of the Gardner River can be annoying coming near the end of the trip after you've already hiked over a major pass,

*Fawn Creek with Electric Peak dominating the horizon.*

but you might be glad you hiked from the west since the hill looks even steeper from the east.

**Options:** You can do this hike from either end, of course, but if you start on the west end, you can avoid a big hill between the Electric Peak Trail junction and the Gardner River. You can also make this an overnighter by staying at 1G2 or 1F2, but these campsites are poorly located, and you end up hiking 15.7 miles in one day with an overnight pack. This makes a 20.8-mile hike with a daypack more appealing. Actually, the best way to do this hike is team up with another party, start an opposite ends, meet for lunch on Fawn Pass, and trade vehicle keys.

**Side trips:** The hike goes through the Gallatin Range bear management area, so no off-trail travel is allowed over most of the Fawn Pass area.

# 33  BIGHORN PASS

See Map on Page 55

| | |
|---|---|
| **Type of hike:** | Shuttle. |
| **Type of trip:** | Long day hike. |
| **Total distance:** | 19.4 miles or 31.2 kilometers. |
| **Difficulty:** | Difficult. |
| **Elevation gain:** | 1,790 feet. |
| **Maps:** | Trails Illustrated (Mammoth Hot Springs); Mammoth, Quadrant Mountain, Joseph Peak, Three Rivers Peak, and Divide Lake USGS quads. |
| **Starting point:** | Bighorn Pass Trailhead (1K5) at Indian Creek Campground. |

**Finding the trailhead:** Drive 8.7 miles south of Mammoth or 12.8 miles north of Norris Junction and park in the small parking area at the entrance to Indian Creek Campground on the west side of the highway.

## Key points:

| | | |
|---|---|---|
| 0.4 | (0.6) | Leave Indian Creek Campground. |
| 0.8 | (1.3) | 1B1 (1★). |
| 2.2 | (3.5) | Indian Creek footbridge. |
| 3.0 | (4.8) | Panther Creek footbridge. |
| 8.4 | (13.5) | Bighorn Pass. |
| 12.8 | (20.6) | WB6 (4★). |
| 13.0 | (20.9) | Landslide. |
| 14.9 | (24.0) | WB1 (5★). |
| 15.1 | (24.2) | Fawn Pass Cutoff Trail junction. |
| 19.4 | (31.2) | U.S. Highway 191. |

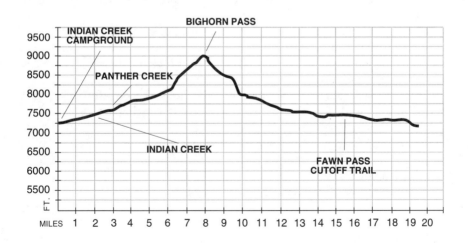

*The trail to Bighorn Pass through the meadows along Panther Creek.*

**The hike:** Like the Fawn Pass Trail, the route over Bighorn Pass goes through the Gallatin Range bear management area, a vital cub-rearing area where the NPS manages recreation to minimize the impact on bear behavior patterns. You can't camp inside the boundaries of the area, and that restriction more or less turns this into a long day hike instead of an overnighter. This is, however, little problem for a well-conditioned hiker. The NPS also prohibits off-trail travel in the bear management area and recommends groups of four or more hikers.

Also like Fawn Pass, this is a bothersome shuttle. It's best to team up with another party, start at opposite ends of the trail, meet on the pass for lunch, and trade vehicle keys. If this isn't possible, you'll have to leave a vehicle at one end of the trail or arrange to be picked up.

The hike starts out with a 0.4-mile walk along the edge of the Indian Creek Campground. This is a popular cross-country skiing area, so after the campground, you'll see several ski loops veering off in both directions for the next few miles. Since you have to get up early to make this entire trip in one day, you'll probably see elk and other wildlife in the large meadows along Indian and Panther creeks.

The trail stays on a bench on the eastern edge of the meadow until shortly after 1B1, where it drops down into the meadow and stays there for another half mile or so until you cross Indian Creek on a footbridge. The trail continues in open terrain as you climb over an almost unnoticeable divide over to Panther Creek.

After crossing Panther Creek (also on a footbridge), the trail follows the creek to within 1 mile or so of the pass. This is a beautiful, wildlife-rich area through mostly open terrain broken by a few stands of unburned timber. If you go in late-July, you'll be treated by carpets of wildflowers. When I hiked this route, the trail was faint in spots and not marked very well between Indian and Panther creeks, nor was it marked well on the west side of Panther Creek. It was, however, well-marked the rest of the way. Watch for moose, common along this section of trail.

Although this is rated a Category 2 climb, it really doesn't seem very steep, possibly because the scenery is so great that you forget the steady uphill grade. The pass is more austere than the gentle Fawn Pass. I hiked over the pass in mid-July, and there was a huge cornice on top that was difficult and dangerous to climb over, so I wouldn't recommend hiking Bighorn Pass any earlier. All three major passes in the section of Gallatin Range in the park (Bighorn, Fawn, and Electric) are all fairly tame, but even though this is not really a rugged hike, Bighorn Pass may be the most difficult of the three.

As you start down the west side of the pass, you can easily see the burn patterns of the 1988 fires. The west side burned more heavily than the east side, but still sporadically. You can also see the grand sweep of the Gallatin River valley below you, including the trail you'll be hiking on the way out.

You stay on the timbered slopes of the pass for about 4 miles. This is serious bear country so be alert and make noise. Visibility is not as good on the west side as it was coming up Panther Creek on the east side. When you

*An unusual landslide wiped out a section of trail along the Upper Gallatin River.*

break out into the meadows along the Gallatin River just before WB6, you have great visibility the rest of the way.

About 2 miles later, between stock-only campsites WB4 and WB3, you can witness a very recent natural phenomenon. In the spring of 1996, there was a giant landslide that buried the trail for about 200 yards. The trail has been temporarily routed around the slide, but after the slide area stabilizes, the NPS plans to re-route the trail over the top. When you look up at the ridge to the north, you'll be amazed and puzzled by how this slide could happen. It's not a steep-sloped valley, and you really would never expect such a landslide to occur here.

The rest of the trail wanders pleasantly along the north edge of the open valley. This part of the trail gets heavy use from stock parties, so the trail is very distinct. If you get all warmed up while walking in the late afternoon sun at the end of your long day hike, you can look forward to getting cooled off while fording the Gallatin River at the end of the hike about a quarter mile from the trailhead. It isn't a difficult ford in late July, but earlier in the season, it can be. The feeder streams coming into the Gallatin from the north all have footbridges, but there's no bridge over the main river. An ice jam obliterated this bridge in January 1995, but the NPS plans to replace it as soon as possible.

(Incidentally, when you get to U.S. 191, you might notice that the distance listed there is 18.5 miles instead of 19.4, but the longer distance is probably closer to the truth.)

**Options:** Although the trail up to the pass seems slightly more precipitous on the west side, hiking from the west would not be much more difficult.

---

# 34  CHAIN OF LAKES

|  |  |
|---|---|
| **Type of hike:** | Shuttle. |
| **Type of trip:** | Short backpacking trip that could be a long day hike. |
| **Total distance:** | 10.3 miles or 16.6 kilometers. |
| **Difficulty:** | Easy overnighter, moderate day hike. |
| **Elevation gain:** | 160 feet. |
| **Maps:** | Trails Illustrated (Mammoth Hot Springs); Norris Junction, Crystal Falls, and Cook Peak USGS quads. |
| **Starting point:** | Cascade Creek Trailhead (4K4). |

**Finding the trailhead:** Drive about a half mile west of Canyon Junction and park in the parking area on the north side of the road.

**Key points:**

| | | |
|---|---|---|
| 2.1 | (3.4) | Junction with Cascade Lake Trail. |
| 2.3 | (3.7) | Spur trail to 4E4 (1★). |
| 2.4 | (3.8) | Junction with trail to Observation Peak and to 4E3 (3★). |
| 2.5 | (4.0) | Cascade Lake. |
| 2.7 | (4.3) | 4E2 (1★). |
| 4.9 | (7.9) | 4G3 (4★), junction with trail to Grebe Lake Trail and 4G2 (5★). |
| 5.0 | (8.0) | Grebe Lake. |
| 5.2 | (8.4) | 4G4 (5★). |
| 5.4 | (8.7) | 4G5 (5★). |
| 6.4 | (10.3) | 4G6 (5★). |
| 6.5 | (10.4) | Wolf Lake. |
| 6.6 | (10.6) | 4G7 (3★). |
| 7.5 | (12.0) | Ford of Gibbon River. |
| 8.6 | (13.8) | Junction with Little Gibbon Falls/Wolf Lake Trail. |
| 9.3 | (14.9) | Second ford of Gibbon River. |
| 9.5 | (15.3) | 4D2 (5★). |
| 9.6 | (15.4) | Ice Lake. |
| 9.7 | (15.7) | 4D1 (4★). |
| 9.8 | (15.8) | Junction with trail to Norris. |
| 10.1 | (16.2) | Spur trail to 4D3 (5★). |
| 10.3 | (16.6) | Ice Lake Trailhead. |

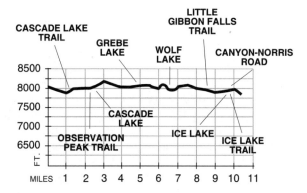

**Recommended itinerary:** This route is best suited for a weekend backpacking trip, staying overnight at any of the four excellent campsites at Grebe Lake. If you want to spend more time fishing (and not too much time carrying your pack each day), extend this to three days by staying at Cascade and Wolf lakes—although, in general, the campsites aren't as nice at these two lakes as they are at Grebe Lake.

**The hike:** This is the only hike in Yellowstone where you can see four mountain lakes in 10 miles. In fact, there is no other hike where you can see more than two. It's also an ideal trip for beginning backpackers, especially those who like to have extra time for fishing.

# CHAIN OF LAKES • GREBE LAKE • ICE LAKE • LITTLE GIBBON FALLS • CASCADE LAKE • OBSERVATION PEAK

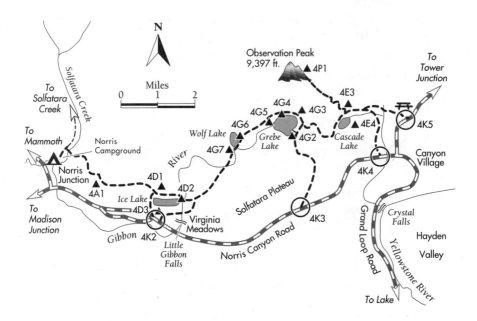

Since this is a shuttle hike, leave a vehicle or arrange to be picked up at the Ice Lake Trailhead. Also, be sure to bring lots of insect repellent and netting. This area, particularly Grebe Lake, produces hordes of mosquitoes. When we did this hike in early July, we were convinced that Grebe Lake served as the factory for all the mosquitoes in all of Yellowstone. If you want to avoid bugs, delay your trip until mid-August.

The first 2.5 miles goes through intermittently burned lodgepole and scenic Cascade Meadows. The trail is in terrific shape the entire way with bridges over all marshy spots. This stretch of trail gets heavy stock use.

Just before the lake, the Cascade Lake Trail joins from the east. Take a left (west) and head for Cascade Lake, which you can see about a half mile ahead. Just before the lake, the trail to Observation Peak and 4E3 turns off to the right (north). Cascade Lake (36 acres and deep) is in a big open park (just right for fly casting), and the trail goes on the north side of it.

The trail to Grebe Lake is flat with some marshy spots and not quite as nice as the trail to Cascade Lake. Grebe Lake is a huge lake (136 acres), also in an open park nicely suited for fly casting. Some older maps may still show a trail heading off to the left (south) just before reaching Grebe Lake to the Grebe Lake Trailhead. This trail has been abandoned. Now, the trail

*Hiking along Grebe Lake.*

to the Grebe Lake Trailhead follows the east edge of Grebe Lake, turning off just before reaching 4D3.

Grebe Lake is full of fish (rainbow and grayling) that have a super-abundant food source—the clouds of bugs produced in the marshy areas around the lake. Consequently, this lake attracts fish-eating birds—mergansers, pelicans, ospreys, and, of course, grebes.

Walking around Grebe Lake can be a real challenge because the west end features a nearly impassable marsh. However, you can easily walk the shoreline on the other three sides of the lake.

The trail between Grebe Lake and Wolf Lake (also in excellent shape) passes through burned forest before opening up into a gorgeous meadow at the inlet of the lake. You have to ford the inlet stream and a long but shallow backwater (actually the Gibbon River as it leaves the lake) to get to 4G7 and to continue on the trail. Wolf Lake is also large (51 acres), fairly deep, with a fairly open shoreline (although not as open as Cascade and Grebe lakes) and good fishing.

After leaving Wolf Lake, you head into the unburned timber and climb a fairly serious hill and then drop back into the Gibbon River valley. You have to ford the river, but it's only a small stream at this point after mid-July. After the ford, the trail follows the stream for about a half mile before going into a heavily burned forest. Just before Ice Lake (after you've taken a right (west) at the Little Gibbon Falls/Wolf Lake Trail Junction), you ford the Gibbon River once more, but it's still an easy, safe crossing after mid-July.

*Fording the shallow outlet of Wolf Lake, the start of the Gibbon River.*

Ice Lake contrasts with the other three lakes on this trip. It's completely surrounded by trees—most victims of the 1988 fires. Fortunately, it contains no trout because it would be a flycaster's nightmare.

At the west end of Ice Lake, take a left (south) at the junction with the trail going straight (east) to Norris. From here, it's an easy half mile hike back to the trailhead and the Norris-Canyon Road.

**Options:** This shuttle hike can be done from either direction with no added difficulty. You can also start at the Cascade Lake Trailhead (4K5). If you want a shorter hike, you can hike out to the Grebe Lake or Wolf Lake trailheads.

If you want a longer hike, you can hike out to Norris, but this trail goes through burnt forest with no views for the first half of the 4.5-mile trip from Ice Lake to Norris. After 4F1, the trail goes through the huge Norris Meadow, and just before reaching the junction with the Solfatara Creek Trail, you ford the Gibbon River one more time. Here, however, the river has grown to the point where the ford can be difficult and dangerous early in the year.

**Side trips:** Observation Peak makes a nice side trip for hikers staying at Cascade Lake. Refer to the Observation Point hike.

# 35  MOUNT HOLMES

| | |
|---|---|
| **Type of hike:** | Out-and-back. |
| **Type of trip:** | Long day hike or overnighter. |
| **Total distance:** | 18.8 miles or 30.2 kilometers (round-trip). |
| **Difficulty:** | Difficult. |
| **Elevation gain:** | 3,000 feet. |
| **Maps:** | Trails Illustrated (Mammoth Hot Springs); Mount Holmes and Obsidian Cliff USGS quads. |
| **Starting point:** | Mount Holmes Trailhead (1K6). |

**Finding the trailhead:** Drive 11.6 miles south of Mammoth or 9.4 miles north of Norris Junction and park in the parking area on the west side of the road.

**Key points:**

|  |  |  |
|---|---|---|
| 0.8 | (1.3) | Ford Winter Creek. |
| 1.8 | (2.9) | Junction with trail to Grizzly Lake. |
| 4.6 | (7.4) | 1C4 (3★). |
| 4.8 | (7.7) | Winter Creek patrol cabin and trail to Trilobite Lake. |
| 4.9 | (7.8) | Spur trail to 1C5 (1★). |
| 9.4 | (15.0) | Summit of Mount Holmes. |

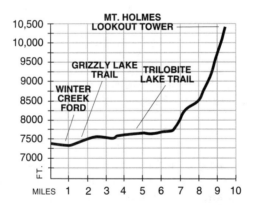

**The hike:** The northwest section of Yellowstone has an abundance of outstanding trails to mountaintops. This is one of the best, and like the Electric Peak, Big Horn Peak, and Sepulcher Mountain climbs, it's for well-conditioned hikers without heart or lung problems. Bunsen Peak and Purple Mountain are more suited to the non-mountain-goat hiker.

To make it to 10,336-foot Mount Holmes and back in the same day, start at dawn or as early as you can. You don't want to hike out at night, and you want to spend some time on the summit soaking in the view and feeling good about your fitness level. And, as is true with all hikes in Yellowstone,

# MOUNT HOLMES • GRIZZLY LAKE

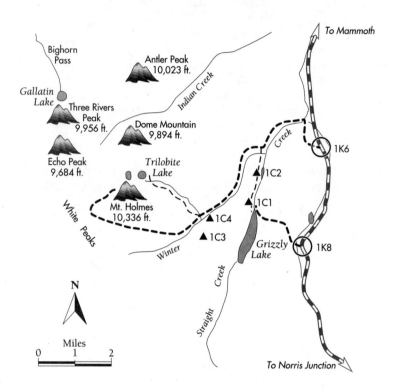

you can often expect "Yellowstone rollers"—early afternoon thundershowers that normally are sort of pleasant unless, of course, you're caught on an exposed mountain summit, like Mount Holmes, where you can become a lightning rod.

The trail starts out through Willow Creek Meadows and along a powerline corridor and then crosses Winter Creek (no bridge). Immediately after the ford of Winter Creek, the trail takes a sharp left and heads through burned timber up to the junction with the Grizzly Lake Trail. Go right (west) here and around a big bald knob where you get your first good view of mighty Mount Holmes with Trilobite Point in the foreground. Then, the trail drops down to Winter Creek and follows it through lush meadows to the patrol cabin and campsites.

After the cabin, the trail goes up and up and up. Even though it's a Category 1 hill, the trail is expertly designed to minimize the impact on your lungs and calf muscles as it swings around the backside of the mountain into a saddle between Mount Holmes and White Peaks before the last three or four switchbacks to the summit. From the top, you can see it all—Electric Peak to the north, the Grand Teton to the south, and everything in-between.

The trail is in great shape all the way, and passes through burned forest until you reach the treeline on the upper reaches of Mount Holmes. However, you won't find the view unpleasant at any point along the way.

**Options:** If a 18.8-mile day hike is too much for you, camp at 1C4 or 1C5 and hike Mount Holmes the next morning, which makes it less than 10 miles (round-trip) from your campsite. You can also hike into the Winter Creek meadows, enjoy the view of the mountain instead of climbing it, and then hike out—either as a day hike or overnighter.

When we did this trip, we scrambled down the northeast slope of Mount Holmes to Trilobite Lake and then hiked out to the Winter Creek patrol cabin on the Trilobite Lake Trail, but this option is for very experienced hikers only. The way to Trilobite Lake requires off-trail route-finding and some rock climbing skills, and the trail from Trilobite Lake to Winter Creek is in bad shape and hard to find in places.

**Side trips:** You can take side rips to Trilobite Lake (5 miles round-trip on a poorly maintained trail) or Grizzly Lake (3 miles round-trip on a good trail).

# 36  *SEPULCHER MOUNTAIN*

| | |
|---|---|
| **Type of hike:** | Loop. |
| **Type of trip:** | Long day hike. |
| **Total distance:** | 12.1 miles or 19.4 kilometers. |
| **Difficulty:** | Difficult. |
| **Elevation gain:** | 3,312 feet. |
| **Maps:** | Trails Illustrated (Mammoth Hot Springs); Mammoth and Quadrant Mountain USGS quads. |
| **Starting point:** | Sepulcher Mountain Trailhead (1K1) in Mammoth. |

See Map on Page 43

**Finding the trailhead:** The trailhead is on the south edge of Mammoth by Liberty Cap.

**Key points:**

| | | |
|---|---|---|
| 0.2 | (0.3) | Junction with Howard Eaton Trail to Golden Gate. |
| 0.5 | (0.8) | Junction with Beaver Ponds Trail. |
| 1.2 | (1.9) | Junction with Clagett Butte Trail. |
| 5.2 | (8.3) | Summit of Sepulcher Mountain. |
| 8.2 | (13.2) | Junction with Sportsman Lake Trail. |
| 9.0 | (14.9) | Junction with Fawn Pass Trail. |
| 10.2 | (16.4) | Junction with Clagett Butte Trail. |
| 10.9 | (17.5) | Junction with Sepulcher Mountain Trail. |
| 11.6 | (18.6) | Junction with Beaver Ponds Trail. |
| 12.1 | (19.4) | Clematis Creek Trailhead. |

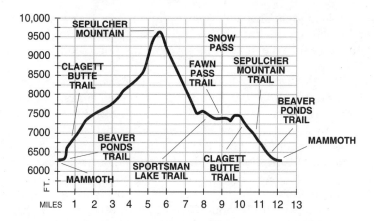

**The hike:** This loop hike isn't the easiest way to see Sepulcher Mountain, but it's the shortest and most convenient route—and you don't have to arrange a ride or get two vehicles to do the shuttle option. It's also a good choice for hikers who like to climb mountains on a good trail instead of with ropes and other equipment.

There are lots of junctions along this loop, so keep your map handy so you don't get on the wrong trail. Also, carry plenty of water. It can get dry on the mountain after the snow melts.

The trail begins just to the right of Clematis Creek before Liberty Cap. Ordinarily, you could park and start at the same trailhead as the boardwalk trail around the hot springs, but the footbridge didn't survive the high water during spring of 1996. Now, you start from the bus parking area on the east side of the creek.

The trail starts with a gradual uphill with brilliant colors of Mammoth Hot Springs on the left. Then, the trail crosses Clematis Creek on a bridge that did survive the high water.

At 0.2 mile is the junction with the Golden Gate/Howard Eaton Trail, which takes you behind the hot springs and to the Hoodoos. Turn right (west) and cross the bridge. The trail starts to climb more steeply, passing one unmarked junction with a game trail. Stay right and keep switchbacking uphill.

At 0.7 mile, go left (west) at the Sepulcher Ridge Junction. From here, the trail climbs steeply through a burn left behind by the 1988 fires, going past the Clagett Butte Trail where you go right (west). The trail turns into switchbacks near the top of the ridge and then traverses along the east side of the ridge and into a whitebark pine and subalpine fir forest. From here, the trail goes through several big meadows and along a steep, rocky ridge before reaching the summit. When you—finally—get to the summit, you can see the mountain's namesake—ghastly rock formations that reminded early explorers of sepulchers (grave markers).

The trail is in good shape until near the top where it gets a little faint, but still easy to follow. This is a difficult, Category 1 climb, so plan on a nice

*Electric Peak from the summit of Sepulcher Mountain.*

long break on top and soak in the sensational vistas of Paradise Valley and the Absaroka Range to the north, Electric Peak (a 1,000 feet higher) and Cache Lake to the west, Gardners Hole and Golden Gate to the south, and lots more.

The trail down the south slopes goes through more open terrain, commonly carpeted with wildflowers in July. It's a tough-on-your-knees, 2,300-foot descent to the junction with the Sportsman Lake Trail, some of it through long, tedious switchbacks. Go left (east) at this junction and hike along Glen Creek until the terrain opens up as you move into an enormous, high-altitude meadow called Gardners Hole at the junction with the trail going right to Fawn Pass and straight to Golden Gate. You go left (north) toward Snow Pass and Mammoth.

From this junction, the trail climbs slightly to go through Snow Pass and then drops to the junction with the seldom-used Snow Pass Trail. Go left (north) on the Clagett Butte Trail and hike less than 1 mile back to the Sepulcher Mountain Trail where you were earlier in the day. Turn right (east) and take the steep downgrade back to Mammoth.

**Options:** The loop can be done in either direction without more effort. You could also make a loop out of this trip by starting at the Glen Creek Trailhead. This allows you to start with 2 miles of easy, flat hiking and saves about 900 feet in elevation gain over the entire loop, but adds almost 2 miles to the trip. The easiest way to see the top of Sepulcher Mountain is to make it a shuttle from Glen Creek Trailhead to Mammoth.

| | | |
|---|---|---|
| **Type of hike:** | Shuttle. | |
| **Type of trip:** | A short backpacking trip that could be done as a long day hike. | |
| **Total distance:** | 18.5 miles or 29.6 kilometers. | |
| **Difficulty:** | Moderate. | |
| **Elevation loss:** | 1,060 feet. | |
| **Maps:** | Trails Illustrated (Mammoth Hot Springs); Tower/Canyon and Tower Junction, Blacktail Deer Creek, Ash Mountain, and Gardiner USGS quads. | |
| **Starting point:** | Hellroaring Trailhead (2K8). | |

**Finding the trailhead:** Drive 14.5 miles east from Mammoth or 3.5 miles west from Tower and pull into the Hellroaring Trailhead. The actual trailhead is about a half mile down a service road. To find the west trailhead in Gardiner, turn on the first road going east on the north side of the Yellowstone River and park by a sign for the Yellowstone River Trail between a private campground and a church.

## Key points:

| | | |
|---|---|---|
| 0.8 | (1.3) | Junction with trail to Tower. |
| 1.0 | (1.6) | Suspension bridge over Yellowstone. |
| 1.6 | (2.6) | Junction with trail to Coyote Creek and Buffalo Plateau. |
| 1.8 | (2.9) | Spur trail going north along the east side of Hellroaring Creek to 2H6 (4★) and 2H8 (4★) and to stock bridge. |
| 1.9 | (3.0) | Spur trail going south along the east side of Hellroaring Creek to 2H4 (4★) and 2H2 (5★). |
| 2.0 | (3.2) | Ford of Hellroaring Creek. |
| 2.1 | (3.4) | Spur trail going south along the west side of Hellroaring Creek to 2H3 (4★) and 2H1 (5★). |
| 2.2 | (3.5) | Spur trail going north along the west side of Hellroaring Creek to 2H5 (4★), to the stock bridge, and into Gallatin National Forest. |
| 4.5 | (7.2) | Little Cottonwood Creek, 1R3 (4★). |
| 5.9 | (9.5) | 1R2 (5★). |
| 6.0 | (9.6) | Cottonwood Creek, 1R1 (5★). |
| 8.3 | (13.1) | 1Y9 (5★). |
| 9.0 | (14.5) | 1Y7 (4★). |
| 9.8 | (15.7) | 1Y5 (4★). |
| 10.0 | (16.1) | Blacktail Creek Trail junction, trail to 1Y6 (3★) and 1Y8 (4★). |
| 10.1 | (16.2) | Crevice Lake. |
| 10.5 | (16.9) | 1Y4 (5★). |
| 11.6 | (18.6) | Crevice Creek. |
| 11.9 | (19.1) | Knowles Falls. |
| 12.3 | (19.8) | 1Y2 (4★). |
| 13.2 | (21.2) | 1Y1 (5★). |
| 18.5 | (29.6) | Gardiner. |

# BLACK CANYON OF THE YELLOWSTONE
## • CREVICE LAKE

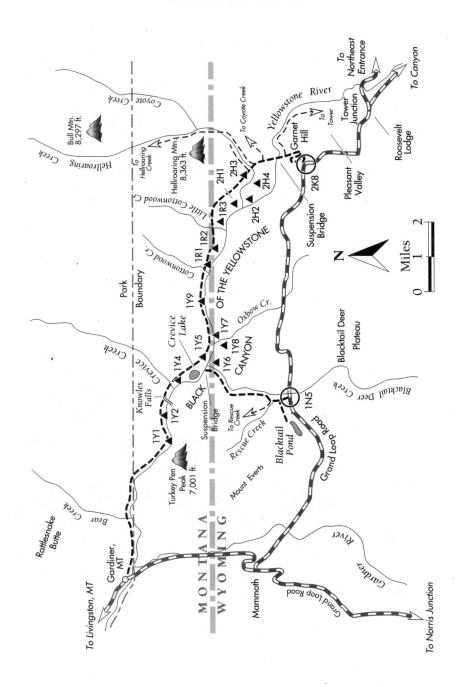

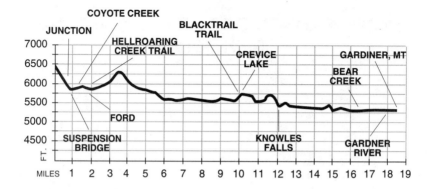

Recommended itinerary: There are many ways to enjoy the Black Canyon, but I recommend a three-day trip with the first night at 1R2 or 1R1, and the second at 1Y2 or 1Y1, and then out to Gardiner on the third day.

The hike: The Black Canyon of the Yellowstone is one of the classic backpacking trips of the northern Rockies. It seems to have everything. It's downhill all the way on an excellent trail with a wide choice of 4Y and 5Y campsites. Wildlife is abundant; the fishing is fantastic, and the scenery rivals almost any other hike since the trail closely follows the mighty Yellowstone River most of the way.

*Hiking the Black Canyon of the Yellowstone.*

Arranging the shuttle is the first order of business. It's better to start at the east end of the trail because you lose more than 1,000 feet in elevation along the way.

After leaving the Hellroaring Trailhead, you hike through meadows and a few stands of trees down a steep hill to the suspension bridge over the Yellowstone River, going left (north) at the junction with the trail to Tower just before reaching the bridge. Here's where you pat yourself on the back for your good plan to start at this end of the shuttle hike. If you did it in reverse, you would face this steep hill right at the end of your hike when you might not be in the mood for it.

The suspension bridge is one of the highlights of the trip, but don't conjure up images of "Indiana Jones" movies. This is a very sturdy metal bridge. From here to near Gardiner, you're in the Black Canyon of the Yellowstone.

Shortly after crossing the bridge, you break out into the open terrain around Hellroaring Creek. When you reach the junction with the trail up Coyote Creek, go left (west).

When you get to Hellroaring Creek, be alert or you'll get on the wrong trail. Well-defined trails go up both sides of the creek to campsites, and when we hiked this trip, many of the trail signs were missing. There used to be a footbridge across Hellroaring Creek (a large tributary to the Yellowstone), but high spring runoff claimed it a few years ago. Watch for trail markers on the west side of the creek so you know where to ford. This ford can be dangerous in June and early July, so if it looks too adventuresome for you, hike about 1 mile north along the creek and cross on a stock bridge and then back down the west side of the creek to the main trail.

After Hellroaring Creek, you gradually climb over a ridge and drop into Little Cottonwood Creek and then over another hill into Cottonwood Creek. The section of the trail between Hellroaring and Cottonwood creeks stays high above the river on mostly open hillsides. Then, just after Cottonwood Creek, it drops down to the river's edge.

Also, just before Cottonwood Creek, you pass from Wyoming to Montana. If you're an angler, though, this doesn't matter, as long as you have a park fishing license and know the regulations.

From Cottonwood Creek to the Blacktail Trail junction, the trail stays close to the river, offering up some spectacular scenery and plenty of pleasant resting places. You might notice frequent carcasses and scattered bones along this trail. That's because this is winter range for the park's large ungulates. Each year, winter kills some weaker members of the herd, and wolves, bears, and cougars take down a few more.

At the Blacktail Trail junction, continue straight (west) along the north side of the river, passing Crevice Lake just after the junction. Then, 1.6 miles later, cross Crevice Creek on a sturdy footbridge. Some older maps show a trail going up Crevice Creek to the park boundary, but this route has been abandoned. Shortly after Crevice Creek, drop your pack and take a short side trip down to see majestic Knowles Falls, a 15-foot drop on the Yellowstone.

From the falls to Gardiner, the trail continues close to the river, except one short section just after 1Y2, where the trail climbs over a rocky ridge. The river goes through a narrows here, getting white and frothy, so you might feel a bit safer being farther away. Just before Gardiner, you can see the confluence between the Gardner River and the Yellowstone. (Yes, Gardiner the town and Gardner the river have different spellings for no clearly definable reason. Interestingly, Jim Bridger originally called the river "Gardener Creek.")

The trail is in superb condition the entire way with the exception of one short section between Bear Creek and Gardiner. Here, the trail is etched out of a steep, clay hillside. If you draw a rainy day, this stretch can be slippery, so be careful.

**Options:** In addition to the three-day trip described here, this route makes an excellent four-day trip, staying the first night at one of the six excellent campsites along Hellroaring Creek, the second at 1R2 or 1R1, and the third at 1Y2 or 1Y1 before hiking out on the fourth day. This gives you plenty of time for fishing and relaxing. If you only have two days, stay overnight at 1Y9, 1Y7, or 1Y5. If you aren't interested in such a long hike, you can hike out and back to Hellroaring Creek, either as a day hike or as an easy overnighter, staying at one of the six campsites near the confluence of Hellroaring Creek and the Yellowstone. You can also trim about 4 miles off the trip by leaving the Black Canyon at the Blacktail Trail junction. If you like long day hikes, a well-conditioned hiker can make it to Gardiner in a day.

*Fishing the Black Canyon of the Yellowstone.*

*Luxury accommodations in the Black Canyon of the Yellowstone.*

**Side trips:** If you stay at Hellroaring Creek, you might enjoy a short day hike up the creek to the park boundary.

## BACKCOUNTRY CAMPSITES

These campsites serve backpacking trips in the northwest section of the park and are on the Mammoth Hot Springs Trails Illustrated map. Stock-party-only sites are not covered.

Please keep in mind that the rating serves as a general guide only. We only visited these campsites once, and it might have been an especially good or especially bad day. For example, campsites clouded with bugs in July may be bug-free in September, and campsites without a view on a rainy day might have a good view on a clear day.

All campsites in Yellowstone allow campfires unless otherwise indicated. Likewise, all campsites are supposed to have bear poles, but just in case, be prepared to improvise.

As this book goes to print, the NPS is in the process of moving campsites located right on the trail. Bears use the trails as travel cooridors, which increases the chance of an encounter.

**Gneiss Creek:** WA1 (3★) is a private (300 yards south of trail), mixed-site. Plenty of tent sites, an accessible water source, and a good view out over the meadows along Gneiss Creek. In July, expect to share this campsite with millions of mosquitoes. Closed until July.

**Bighorn Pass:** WB1 (5★) is a private, hiker-only campsite located on a bench above the Gallatin River on the south side of the huge meadow across from the Fawn Pass cutoff trail. A delightful site about a quarter-mile walk across a huge meadow from the trail. Great view, plenty of tent sites, and an easily accessible water source (the river). Firewood is sparse[1].

WB6 (4★) is a fairly private, hiker-only site with a good water source and a nice view across the big meadows lining the Upper Gallatin River. Good tent sites. No off-trail travel from this campsite.

**Fan Creek:** WC2 (5★) is the only hiker-only campsite in Fan Creek. It's almost private (about 75 yards off trail) and has a fantastic view from the food area, which is on a small bench overlooking the expansive meadows along Fan Creek—great for wildlife viewing. Excellent tent sites, but a short walk to water[2].

**East Fork of Specimen Creek:** WD1 (2★) is not in the big meadow along the trail as shown on some maps. In 1995, it was moved. Now it's on the north side of the trail and tucked back in the trees just west of the East Fork of Specimen Creek. Private (200 yards off the trail), hiker-only site, good water source (East Fork), but no view.

**Sportsman Lake:** WD2 (3★) is a poor cousin to WD3. It's a mixed site that gets heavy use from stock parties, and the view isn't nearly as nice as from WD3. Good water source and lots of tent sites. No off-trail travel from campsite.

WD3 (5★) is an excellent, but difficult to find, campsite. It's on the northeast side of the big meadow below Sportsman Lake. (Right after you cross the stream, you might see an old campsite—that's not 4D3.) From this private, hiker-only site you get a great view of the lake and the massive mountain meadow where you're likely to see moose. Good water sources and plenty of tent sites safely removed from the food area.

**High Lake:** WD4 (5★) is a hiker-only site near the outlet of High Lake[3]. It has limited tent sites and marginal privacy, but the view is so fabulous that

---

[1]WB3 and WB4—stock only sites, but the NPS will sometimes allow hikers to stay at these sites if the other two sites are taken. Ask about getting one of these campsites. Also, you might see WB5 on older maps, but the NPS eliminated that site in 1995.

[2]WC3 and WC4 are reserved for stock parties only, which is too bad because it would be much more convenient spacing to camp a mile or two earlier when hiking from Sportsman Lake. However, the NPS sometimes allows hikers to stay at WC3 or WC4. Hikers can request these campsites the morning they leave for the trailhead, but they can't reserve them in advance.

[3]If you can't get WD4 or WD5, you can camp outside the park in the Gallatin National Forest along a short section of trail just south of High Lake. You'd have to haul water from the lake, but you could have a campfire.

staying here is a rare delight. You can sit in the food area and watch the cutthroats nail flies on the surface of the lake. Good water source. No campfires.

WD5 (2★) is a difficult-to-find, mixed site on the west end of High Lake about 300 yards from the trail. There is no discernible trail to the site, so go to the west end of the lake and head across the marshy inlet area and up the steep slope on the other side of the lake. It's in a flat area on the other side of the hill. No view of the lake. A long walk to water. Private. Good tent sites. No campfires.

**North Fork of Specimen Creek:** WE1 (4★) is a mixed site right along the trail with no privacy, but it has everything else—a great view up the North Fork of Specimen Creek, good water source, and plenty of tent sites.

WE4 (3★) isn't in the location shown on some maps. It's about 0.75 mile west of the Shelf Lake Trail junction on the north side of the trail—and only 20 feet from the trail. No privacy. Good water source. Plenty of tent sites. A fair view of a small meadow along the North Fork of Specimen Creek with Meldrum Mountain as a backdrop.

**Crescent Lake:** WE6 (4★) is between Crescent Lake and the trail (and close to both) at the west end of the lake near the outlet. This hiker-only site has a great view of the lake (where you can easily get water). Limited tent sites, and one commonly used tent site is too close to the food area and bear pole. It's better to use one of the tent sites above the trail.

**Shelf Lake:** If you decide to camp at Shelf Lake, you'll be treated with two extraordinary hiker-only campsites. WE5 (5★) is on the northeast side of the lake on a little bench overlooking the lake about 300 yards of the trail in a little grove of subalpine fir and whitebark pine to protect your camp from the elements, which can be a big issue here since you're camping at 9,200 feet. Like all campsites above or near treeline, it's quite damaging to have a campfire, and the NPS rightfully disallowed them at Shelf Lake.

WE7 (5★) is on the northwest side of the lake and is similar to WE5 but less protected from weather. Both Shelf Lake campsites have limited tent sites and outstanding views, but be prepared for high altitude weather. The lake serves as an easy water source for both campsites.

**Black Butte Creek:** WF1 (4★) is a private, mixed site about a quarter mile off the trail. A decent view of a small meadow. Good water source (Black Butte Creek). You ford Black Butte Creek just before the campsite.

**Dailey Creek:** WF2 (3★) is a mixed site right along the trail with little privacy. Be alert because it's easy to walk right by this seldom-used campsite without noticing the sign on a tree away from the trail. Look for this site just east of the Teepee Creek junction, not west of it as shown on some maps. Good water source (Dailey Creek) and tent sites. A fair view of the meadows along Dailey Creek. Firewood is sparse.

**Crevice Lake:** 1A1 (3★) is a not-so-private, mixed site right next to Blacktail Creek and the trail among aspen and Engelmann spruce. The steep slopes of the valley limit the view. Good water source. Adequate tent sites.

**Rescue Creek:** 1A2 (5★) is one of the best campsite locations in the park. You can sit in camp as the sun goes down and look down the valley and up the ridge, without obstruction. The private, hikers-only campsite is about 300 yards across the valley and appears to receive low use. The food area is on the edge of meadow with the opportunity to watch wildlife from the comfort of a warm fire. Plenty of room for tents. Lots of firewood. Good water access (10 feet from food area).

**Lava Creek Canyon:** 1A3 (3★) is a hiker-only site limited to small parties, but still shows the signs of heavy use. Has shade, a good water source, and a decent view. Firewood is sparse.

**Indian Creek:** 1B1 (1★) is one of the least desirable campsites in the park. The hiker-only site is located right along the trail in an unprotected, heavily burned area less than a mile from the trailhead. Limited tent sites. A short walk to get water.

**Grizzly Lake:** 1C2 is slightly nicer than 1C1, but 1C1 is closer to the lake. Both of these hiker-only sites have readily accessible water sources (Straight Creek). Like Grizzly Lake itself, the forest around both campsites has been heavily burned.

1C1 (3★) is right along the trail less than a half mile north of Grizzly Lake. You can enjoy a view along Straight Creek, but the site is fairly exposed and lacks privacy.

1C2 (3★) is about 1 mile from the lake. It's farther from the trail and has a nicer view than 1C1 over a flatwater section of Straight Creek.

**Winter Creek:** 1C4 (3★) is a not-so-private, mixed site on the south side of the trail less than a quarter mile east of the Winter Creek patrol cabin. Plenty of tent sites, good water source, and a fair view out into the meadow.

1C5 (1★) is a private, mixed site more often used by stock parties than 1C4. It's a good half-mile hike through a marshy meadow to the difficult-to-find site. Look for a sign immediately after crossing Winter Creek, after the patrol cabin and head to the far south side of the meadow (no defined trail). Regrettably, this site was located back in the timber instead of on the edge of the meadow where you could watch wildlife, and a long haul from water. Marginal tent sites.

**Upper Gardner River:** 1G3 (3★) would have a great view if the food area was moved slightly to the west where you could sit in camp and look out over a beautiful meadow, split by the Upper Gardner River, and see Electric Peak in the background. But the present food area offers no view. This private (300 yards off the trail), hiker-only site has adequate tent sites and a fairly accessible water source (the Gardner River, about 100 yards from camp). One of the traditionally used tent sites is too close to the bear pole, so don't camp there.

1G4 (4★) is similar to 1G3 (private, hiker-only) but has a better view (although you still can't see Electric Peak). Good tent sites and water source (about 25 feet to the Gardner River).

**Fawn Pass:** 1F2 (4★) is a private, hiker-only site 150 yards north of the trail about a half mile west of the Fawn Creek footbridge, and on a bench above Fawn Creek. Excellent tent sites, but getting water is difficult. Regrettably, 1F2 wasn't located in several nearby locations where you could see Electric Peak with the Fawn Creek valley in the foreground, like you can from the trail.

1G2 (5★) is a private, hiker-only site just north of the trail on the east bank of the Gardner River. Good view, tent sites, and water source.

**Black Canyon of the Yellowstone:** 1R1 (5★) is a charming, mixed site right on the bank of the Yellowstone River and nicely private (about 200 yards off the trail) with plenty of tent sites. The bear pole is on a steep slope, making hanging food difficult. Good water source. No campfires.

1R2 (5★) is a hiker-only site very similar to 1R1. No campfires.

1R3 (4★) is a mixed site along Little Cottonwood Creek on a bench far above the Yellowstone with plenty of tent sites but close enough to the trail to make it only semi-private. Great view of the open country above the river

*Relaxing in a scenic campsite in the Black Canyon of the Yellowstone.*

from the food area, and you should be able to see elk from camp—and maybe some wolves chasing them. If you're an angler, you might not like this campsite because it's a steep climb down to the river. A good choice for a large party. No campfires.

1Y1 (5★) is the westernmost, near-perfect campsite on this trip. The trail is a little too close to the site for complete privacy. Great view. Easy water source (the river). Good tent sites. Even a little beach formed by the still water pool just below a big rapids. No campfires.

1Y2 (4★) has everything but privacy. The trail actually goes between the tent sites and bear pole. The hiker-only site has a sensational view of the rapids starting just below camp. The high water in 1996 deposited fresh sand on the tent sites, which makes it so soft you won't notice if you forgot your sleeping pad. Good water source. No campfires.

1Y4 (5★) is a private, hiker-only site along a slow section of the river just above Knowles Falls. Great view and excellent tent sites. Good water source. No campfires.

1Y5 (4★) is a private, hiker-only site right along the river. Limited tent sites and might be a marginal choice for a party with more than two tents. Good water source and view, but no campfires. 1Y5, 1Y7, and 1Y9 are similar sites.

1Y6 (3★) is the first hiker-only campsite on the spur trail, about 0.3 mile from the Blacktail Creek Trail on the south side of the river over the suspension bridge. Private site in sparse juniper and Douglas-fir with a good view of the river. Good water source. Adequate tent sites. No campfires.

1Y7 (4★) is similar to 1Y5, a private, mixed site along the river with a special tent site under a big Douglas-fir. Good view and water source.

1Y8 (4★) is the second hiker-only campsite on the spur trail, about 0.8 mile from the main trail on the south side of the river. It's more open and has a better view than 1Y6. Very private and appears to receive lighter use than 1Y6. Good water source and tent sites. No campfires.

1Y9 (5★) is another great campsite right along the river with privacy, lots of good tent sites, easy water source, and a great view. No campfires.

Also see Crevice Lake campsites on page 132.

**Ice Lake:** 4D1 (4★) is a hiker-only site on the south side of the trail at the west end of Ice Lake. It has a good view and easy water source, but limited tent sites and little privacy (right along the trail).

4D2 (5★) is a private, hiker-only site on a bench above the east end of Ice Lake with good tent sites and easy access to water. Good view of the lake.

4D3 (5★) is the only backcountry campsite in Yellowstone accessible by wheelchair. This private, hiker-only site has a good view of the lake, good tent sites, and believe it or not, a luxurious outdoor privy.

**Cascade Lake:** 4E2 (1★) is a private, hiker-only site on the north side of the trail just west of Cascade Lake. It's tucked away in the trees, with no view, on a steep hillside with only one good tent site, which is probably why it's limited to small groups of no more than four people. Parties with two tents will have a hard time finding another tent site. A 300-yard walk to water.

4E3 (3★) is a hiker-only site about 200 yards up the trail to Observation Peak. This private site has a good view of Cascade Lake, but you have to haul water up from the stream along the trail.

4E4 (1★) is a mixed site southeast of the lake. It's a private site (about 200 yards off the trail) with the food area and sleeping area separated by a marshy meadow, which means early in the year you might get your feet wet every time you go between the food area and tent site. Marginal view and water source.

**Grebe Lake:** All four Grebe Lake campsites are excellent. Located along the shore of the lake (the readily accessible water source) with good views.

4G2 (5★) is the only hiker-only site at Grebe Lake. It's a private site on the south side of the lake. Great view from the food area and you can almost fish from camp.

4G3 (4★) is a not-so-private, mixed site right along the trail on the north side of Grebe Lake. If you're an angler, you can almost fish from camp. Firewood is sparse.

4G4 (5★) is nestled in the trees on the north side of the lake. This private, mixed site doesn't appear to get much use from stock parties.

4G5 (5★) is very similar to 4G4.

**Wolf Lake:** 4G6 (5★) is about 50 yards north of the trail on the edge of the meadow that holds Wolf Lake. It's a semi-private, mixed site with a good view of the lake, an easy water source, and good tent sites.

4G7 (3★) is an exposed, hiker-only site on the south side of the trail on the west side of the outlet. Lacks privacy. Good view of the lake and easy water source.

**Norris Meadows:** 4F1(5★) is incorrectly marked as 4N1 on some older maps. This private, hiker-only site is on a small bench overlooking Norris Meadows—ideal for wildlife watching. Good water source and tent sites. This trail gets little use, so you probably won't see many people coming through the meadow.

**Observation Peak:** 4P1(3★) is an unusual campsite. It's a hiker-only site essentially on the summit of Observation Peak. You don't have a view from camp, but it's only about 50 yards to the summit where you get an incredible view of the Yellowstone River valley. Lots of tent sites, but no water source unless you get there early enough in the year to find snowbanks. Otherwise, be sure to carry enough water with you for your overnight stay.

## *SHORT HIKES*

## 38   *TROUT LAKE*

| | | |
|---|---|---|
| **Type of hike:** | Out-and-back. | See Map on Page 172 |
| **Type of trip:** | A popular and accessible | |

fishing destination and a great place to view spawning wild trout.

**Total distance:** 1.2 miles or 1.9 kilometers (round-trip).
**Difficulty:** Easy.
**Elevation gain:** 100 feet.
**Maps:** Trails Illustrated (Tower/Canyon); Mount Hornaday USGS quad.
**Starting point:** Trout Lake Trailhead.

**Finding the trailhead:** Drive 18.6 miles east of Tower Junction or 10.4 miles west of the Northeast Entrance and park in the turnout on the north side of the road, 1.8 miles west of Pebble Creek Campground.

*Fishing Trout Lake.*

**The hike:** This trail is popular with anglers, but it also provides a pleasant day hike for non-anglers. The rainbow-cutthroat hybrids in the lake are big and hard to catch, but rewarding for the successful angler.

From the trailhead, the trail heads steeply uphill. Although a fairly steep hill, the trip to Trout Lake is so short that it still ranks as an easy hike. The path climbs under Douglas-fir cover to the outlet of the lake, which rests in a big meadow filled with wildflowers. The excellent trail around the lake provides more hiking opportunity.

The 12-acre lake is catch-and-release fishing (don't forget to get a park fishing permit) but the inlet is closed to fishing during the spawning season to protect spawning trout, which put on quite a show. Be careful not to disturb them at this crucial time.

# 39 *YELLOWSTONE RIVER PICNIC AREA TRAIL*

|                  |                                                          |
|------------------|----------------------------------------------------------|
| **Type of hike:** | Out-and-back with loop option |
| **Type of trip:** | Day hike. |
| **Total distance:** | Up to 4 miles or 6.4 kilometers (round-trip). |
| **Difficulty:** | Moderate. |
| **Elevation gain:** | 200 feet. |
| **Maps:** | Trails Illustrated (Tower/Canyon); Tower Junction USGS quad. |
| **Starting point:** | Yellowstone River Picnic Area Trailhead (2K7). |

See Map on Page 154

**Finding the trailhead:** Drive 1.5 miles east of Tower Junction and pull into the Yellowstone River Picnic Area on the south side of the road.

**The hike:** This is a delightful day hike when you need some exercise and especially convenient if you stopped here for a picnic. You can go as far as 2 miles before the trail joins the Specimen Ridge Trail, or you can walk along the ridge overlooking the Yellowstone for whatever distance suits you before returning to the picnic area.

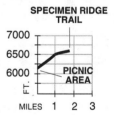

Several social trails leave the picnic area, and they join up with the official trail about a half mile later. The official trail starts by the trail sign on the east side of the picnic area just north of the vault toilet and appears to head east, but it quickly turns south and gradually climbs up to the ridge above the river.

After a short climb, the trail levels out and goes along the rim of the Yellowstone—great views of the narrows section of the river, but if you have children, watch them carefully. It would be a very serious fall down into the river bottom.

*The Narrows Section of the Yellowstone River from the Yellowstone River Picnic Area Trail.*

Hikers often see bighorn sheep along this trail. If you do, please don't try to approach or feed them.

**Options:** If you want to take a loop hike (also 4 miles total), continue on the trail until you reach the Specimen Ridge Trail. Turn left (north) here and walk downhill nearly to the highway where you'll see a trail heading along the road back to the picnic area.

# 40  LOST LAKE

See Map on Page 154

|  |  |
|---|---|
| **Type of hike:** | Out-and-back, loop or shuttle. |
| **Type of trip:** | Day hike. |
| **Total distance:** | 4 miles or 6.4 kilometers (loop option). |
| **Difficulty:** | Moderate. |
| **Elevation gain:** | 500 feet. |
| **Maps:** | Trails Illustrated (Tower/Canyon); Tower Junction USGS quad. |
| **Starting point:** | Roosevelt Lodge. |

**Finding the trailhead:** From Tower Junction, go south to the Roosevelt Lodge and park near the lodge. The trail starts at the south edge of the lodge.

**The hike:** Lost Lake is a charming little (only 6 acres) mountain lake lost in the forest behind Roosevelt Lodge.

From the lodge, the trail gradually climbs through unburned forest on gentle switchbacks up to the top of the ridge where you reach a junction. The left trail goes east past Lost Creek Falls and back to Roosevelt Lodge via the horse corral or to Tower Campground. Go right (west) for about another half mile to Lost Lake, which is preceded by a big meadow. The lake is shallow with yellow pond lilies along the shoreline. Sorry, no fish.

From the lake, keep going west until you come out in the parking lot for the Petrified Tree. You can drive here, but by walking down from the lake, you can avoid retracing your steps and make a small loop out of this hike.

The trail back to Roosevelt Lodge leaves the northeast end of the parking area (marked by an orange marker) and goes behind Tower Ranger Station, where you cross the creek and then proceed to Roosevelt Lodge.

**Options:** If you want to make this a shorter hike, walk out and back to the lake. If you want a shuttle (and a good view of Lost Creek Falls) take a left at the top of the ridge and hike another 3 miles to Tower Campground, taking a right (south) at the junction just past the falls. This trail comes out on the paved road up to the campground. You can walk down the road about a

*Lost Lake.*

quarter mile to the general store. This is a nice, flat trail through open forest and large meadows until it drops steeply down to the campground. As a third option, you can make a different loop out of this trail by taking a left (north) at the junction just past Lost Creek Falls (instead of the right heading to Tower Campground) and drop down to the corral just east of Roosevelt Lodge.

# 41  *TOWER FALL*

| | | |
|---|---|---|
| **Type of hike:** | Out-and-back. | |
| **Type of trip:** | Day hike. | |
| **Total distance:** | 1 mile or 1.6 kilometers (round-trip). | |
| **Difficulty:** | Easy. | |
| **Elevation gain:** | 200 feet. | |
| **Maps:** | Trails Illustrated (Tower/Canyon); | |
| | Tower Junction USGS quad. | |
| **Starting point:** | Tower Fall store. | |

See Map on Page 154

*Tower Fall.*

**Finding the trailhead:** Drive 2.5 miles south of Tower Junction or 15.5 miles north of Canyon Junction on the Tower-Canyon section of the Grand Loop Road and park in the large parking lot for the Tower Fall store.

**The hike:** The trip to Tower Fall is one of the shortest, but most-rewarding, hikes in the park. From the overlook (about 100 yards from the store), you get a great perspective of the 132-foot waterfall. Then, by walking down a double-wide, carefully switchbacked trail for another half mile, you get the rest of the story.

The trail takes you right down to where Tower Creek disappears into the Yellowstone. Then, with a short walk to your left, you end up right to the foot of the falls, a truly awesome sight.

Take along a sweater. Even on a warm August afternoon, the mist thrown up by the falls can cast a coolish atmosphere over the shaded canyon gouged out by the crashing water.

The 1870 Washburn party named the waterfall for the large tower-like rocks at the brink of the falls, one of which crashed to the depths of the canyon in 1986. No, luckily, there weren't any park visitors under the falls at the time!

# 42  RIBBON LAKE

| | |
|---|---|
| **Type of hike:** | Out-and-back. |
| **Type of trip:** | Day hike or overnighter. |
| **Total distance:** | 4 miles or 6.4 kilometers (round-trip). |
| **Difficulty:** | Easy. |
| **Elevation gain:** | Minimal. |
| **Maps:** | The Yellowstone Association's map/brochure for Canyon; Trails Illustrated (Tower/Canyon); Canyon Village USGS quad. |
| **Starting point:** | Artist Point Trailhead (4K8). |

See Map on Page 143

**Finding the trailhead:** Drive south 2.3 miles past Canyon Junction and turn left crossing the Chittenden Bridge. Go 1 mile until the road terminates at the heavily used Artist Point Viewpoint. The trail starts on the right as you walk down to the viewpoint.

## Key Points:

0.5 (0.8)  Point Sublime junction.
1.0 (1.6)  Junction with trail to Clear Lake.
2.0 (3.2)  Ribbon Lake Camp 4R1 (3★) and 4R2 (4★).

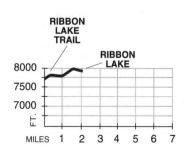

**The hike:** This trail from Artist Point is the perfect hike for someone just getting in to overnight camping and hiking. You aren't that far from the trailhead, and the hike in is easy walking. In addition, the 11-acre Ribbon Lake has a small population of rainbow trout (catch-and-release only with a park fishing permit). You can also have a campfire, and this trip has several possible side trips, one of which can give you a view that rivals that from Artist Point. The trail is in excellent shape the entire way.

At Artist Point, the trail leaves the paved area before the viewpoint and takes off to the right (northeast) toward Point Sublime. The trail climbs along the edge of the canyon with an already-sublime view. At 0.5 mile, turn right (south) and leave the trail to Point Sublime and head for Ribbon Lake— unless you first want to take a short side trip to Point Sublime before going to Ribbon Lake.

In less than a half mile is the junction with the trail to Clear Lake where you turn left (northeast). This junction may not show on some maps.

After the junction the trail stays in the trees until you reach Ribbon Lake, which is actually two lakes connected by a foot-deep, narrow channel. The smaller lake is surrounded by sedge meadows and may be completely covered with yellow pond lilies.

At Ribbon Lake a spur trail veers left to camps 4R1 and 4R2 and Silver Cord Cascade overlook, where you can see a small stream from Ribbon Lake plummet 1,200 feet to the canyon bottom, the longest drop in the park. Even if you aren't camping, take the short side trip on this trail for a view of the cascade and the Grand Canyon of the Yellowstone. It's eerie to suddenly emerge from the trees and look down at the river hundreds of feet below. The forest offers no clue that you're so close to the edge.

**Options:** Instead of re-tracing your steps you can complete the Clear Lake Loop, which requires a half mile walk on the paved South Rim Road, to get back to your vehicle. This lengthens your trip by about 1.5 miles.

**Side trips:** Two short, must-see side trips are Point Sublime and the Silver Cord Cascade overlook. You can also take a short trip over to Clear Lake.

## 43  CANYON RIM SOUTH

|  |  |
|---|---|
| **Type of hike:** | Out-and-back or shuttle. |
| **Type of trip:** | Day hike. |
| **Total distance:** | 3.2 miles or 5.2 kilometers (one way). |
| **Difficulty:** | Easy. |
| **Elevation gain:** | 150 feet. |
| **Maps:** | The Yellowstone Association's map/brochure for Canyon; Trails Illustrated (Tower/Canyon); Canyon Village USGS quad. |
| **Starting point:** | Wapiti Lake Trailhead (4K7). |

# CANYON RIM SOUTH/NORTH
# • RIBBON LAKE • CLEAR LAKE LOOP

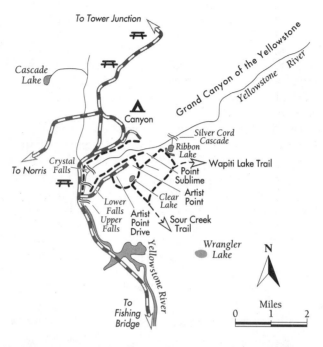

*Lower Falls from Artist Point on the Canyon Rim Trail.*

**Finding the trailhead:** Drive south 2.3 miles from the Canyon Junction, turn left (east) crossing the Chittenden Bridge and park in the large parking area on your right immediately after crossing the bridge.

**The hike:** To see the sights of the South Rim of the Grand Canyon of the Yellowstone, you can drive to Uncle Tom's Trail parking area to see Upper Falls, get back into your vehicle, drive to Artist Point parking area and view Lower Falls, and call it a day. Or you can take a wonderful hike along the canyon rim to see it all and get some exercise, too.

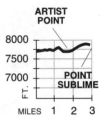

The trail from Chittenden Bridge to Point Sublime is 3.2 miles. You can hike all of it or whatever section suits you.

The scenery is world-renowned the entire way with many views of the mighty Yellowstone River and its Grand Canyon, Lower Falls and Upper Falls, all the way to Point Sublime, and a view of Silver Cord Cascades crescendoing down into the canyon from Ribbon Lake.

The trail gets heavy use, and parts of it are paved to accommodate this popularity. Even the unpaved sections are in superb condition. Unless you go down the Uncle Tom's Trail, there aren't any steep sections, although you face a few short upgrades to get through small valleys and a gradual upgrade to get from the river-level trailhead to Artist Point Overlook, about 150 feet above the river.

From the trailhead, the trail drops down to river-level right above Upper Falls where you get a good view of the footbridge on the other side of the river. Just before Uncle Tom's Trail parking area, you get the ideal view of Upper Falls from the Upper Falls Overlook. At Artist Point, you get the picturesque view of Lower Falls and the Grand Canyon. If you stop at Artist Point, you'll miss one of the great views in the park, Point Sublime. The grand expansiveness of the canyon is spread before you at Point Sublime.

If you can't arrange to leave a vehicle at Artist Point, retrace your steps to the Wapiti Lake Trailhead.

**Options:** You can hike sections of this trail out and back or you can leave a vehicle at Artist Point to keep from retracing your steps over part of the trip. You can also combine the South Rim and North Rim hikes by leaving a vehicle at Inspiration Point and starting at Artist Point or vice versa.

**Side trips:** Uncle Tom's Trail is a must-see side trip, but you can also take short hikes to Clear Lake or Ribbon Lake. You can also expand the hike to include the North Rim Trail. You can hike South Rim in the morning, eat at the picnic tables at the Wapiti Lake Trailhead, and hike North Rim in the afternoon.

| | |
|---:|:---|
| **Type of hike:** | Out-and-back. |
| **Type of trip:** | Day trip. |
| **Total distance:** | 1 mile or 1.6 kilometers (round-trip). |
| **Difficulty:** | Moderate. |
| **Elevation gain:** | 500 feet. |
| **Maps:** | The Yellowstone Association's map/brochure for Canyon; Trails Illustrated (Tower/Canyon); Canyon Village USGS quad. |
| **Starting point:** | Uncle Tom's Trail parking area. |

**Finding the trailhead:** Drive south 2.3 miles from the Canyon Junction, turn left (east) crossing the Chittenden Bridge, and go another 0.6 mile before parking on your left (west) in the Uncle Tom's Trail parking lot. The trail starts on your right (east) just as you enter the lot.

**The hike:** This may be the most unusual hike in the park. It's not really a trail. Instead, it's a series of stairs made of steel mesh, concrete, and asphalt, 328 steps from top to bottom. The "grand staircase" takes you to an incredible viewpoint near the base of the Lower Falls. The trail gets its

*Uncle Tom's Trail, actually a very long set of stairs.*

name from "Uncle" Tom Richardson who took park visitors into the canyon from 1898 to 1903 on this trail, which originally had 528 steps and rope ladders.

Although short, the trail can be quite strenuous coming up and is not recommended for people with heart or lung problems. However, the NPS has made it as easy as possible with handrails much of the way and benches to rest on while climbing out of the canyon.

# 45  CANYON RIM NORTH

|  |  |
|---|---|
| **Type of hike:** | Out-and-back or shuttle. |
| **Type of trip:** | Day hike. |
| **Total distance:** | 3 miles or 4.8 kilometers (one-way). |
| **Difficulty:** | Easy. |
| **Elevation gain:** | 150 feet. |
| **Maps:** | The Yellowstone Association's map/brochure for Canyon; Trails Illustrated (Tower/Canyon); Canyon Village USGS quad. |
| **Starting point:** | Wapiti Lake Trailhead (4K7). |

See Map on Page 143

**Finding the trailhead:** Drive south 2.3 miles from the Canyon Junction, turn left (east) crossing the Chittenden Bridge, and park in the large parking area on your right immediately after crossing the bridge.

**The hike:** Like the South Rim, the North Rim is loaded with world-famous scenery and short side trips. It's a nice half-day hike if you take in all the sights.

From the bridge, hike to the short (about a quarter mile) side trip to the Brink of the Upper Falls, a awe-inspiring (if not scary) view of the river plunging over the 109-foot Upper Falls.

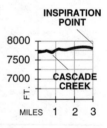

Next along the way is Crystal Falls on Cascade Creek, a nice contrast to the Upper and Lower falls. The trail goes over the top of the delicate waterfall. Then, you reach perhaps the most memorable spot on the trip—the side trip down to the Brink of the Lower Falls, where you can really feel the power of the mighty Yellowstone as in tumbles over the massive, 308-foot waterfall.

About a half mile down the trail is the side trip to Lookout Point and Red Rock Point. Both give additional views of Lower Falls. Lookout Point is a 50-foot walk, but Red Rock Point requires a steep quarter-mile drop.

Back on the Canyon Rim North Trail, your next stop is Grandview Point where you get one more version of the Lower Falls and Grand Canyon vista. The trail is mostly paved up to this point, but from here to Inspiration Point you hike on a normal, unpaved trail. Inspiration Point offers one more perspective of Lower Falls, but it includes the broad sweep of the Grand Canyon in the foreground. The Grand Canyon varies from 1,500 feet to 4,000 feet across and from 750 to 1,200 feet deep. Hot springs in the area weakened the rock and caused extreme erosion below Lower Falls to create the Grand Canyon.

**Options:** You can hike sections of this trail out and back, or you can leave a vehicle at Inspiration Point to keep from retracing your steps. You can also combine the North Rim and South Rim hikes by leaving a vehicle at Inspiration Point and starting at Artist Point or vice versa.

**Side trips:** Short side trips to Brink of the Upper Falls, Brink of the Lower Falls, Lookout Point and Red Rock Point add to this hike. Uncle Tom's Trail on the South Rim is the toughest climb down into the canyon. Red Rock Point is next toughest, followed by Brink of the Lower Falls.

## 46 BRINK OF THE LOWER FALLS

| | |
|---|---|
| **Type of hike:** | Out-and-back. |
| **Type of trip:** | Day hike. |
| **Total distance:** | 1.5 mile or 2.4 kilometers (round-trip). |
| **Difficulty:** | Moderate. |
| **Elevation gain:** | 600 feet. |
| **Maps:** | The Yellowstone Association's map/brochure for Canyon; Trails Illustrated (Tower/Canyon); Canyon Village USGS quad. |
| **Starting point:** | Brink of Lower Falls parking area near the end of the North Rim Drive. |

**Finding the trailhead:** Go through the Canyon Village and stay on the one-way North Rim Drive until just before it rejoins the Canyon to Lake Road, where you turn into the large parking area at Brink of the Lower Falls.

**The hike:** If you only take one short hike in the Canyon area, this probably would be your most memorable choice. At the end of the 0.75-mile trip (one way) to a concrete platform above the falls, you can't avoid the sensation of being overpowered by nature. The earth (and the platform) seems to quiver as the mighty river plunges over the 308-foot waterfall.

The trail is steep and includes several sections of stairs. It's not recommended for people with lung or heart problems—but highly recommended for anybody who doesn't. An interpretive display on the platform tells the story of how Lower Falls came to be.

## 47   THE THUNDERER

Type of hike:    Out-and-back.
Type of trip:    Day hike.
Total distance:  7.4 miles or 11.9 kilometers (round-trip) to
                 Chaw Pass.
Difficulty:      Difficult.
Elevation gain:  2,372 feet to Chaw Pass.
Maps:            Trails Illustrated (Tower/Canyon);
                 Abiathar Peak USGS quad.
Starting point:  Thunderer Trailhead (3K3).

See Map on Page 169

**Finding the trailhead:** Drive 11.6 miles east of the Tower Junction or 16.4 miles west of the Northeast Entrance and park in the Thunderer Trailhead parking area on the south side of the road.

**Key points:**

    0.2 (0.3)   Soda Butte Creek.
    3.7 (5.9)   Chaw Pass.
    5.3 (8.5)   Cache Creek Trail.

**The hike:** Less than a quarter mile after leaving the trailhead, you ford Soda Butte Creek, which can be slick and hazardous early in the year but safe after mid-July. From here, the trail climbs steadily for 3.5 miles to Chaw Pass, a Category 1 climb.

The trail is well-defined all of the way, passing through unburnt forest until Chaw Pass, which was burned by the 1988 fires. You get occasional glimpses through the trees of Amphitheater Valley to the north and The Thunderer to the south.

**Options:** This can be part of shuttle trips west to Lamar River Trailhead or east to Republic Pass and Cooke City.

# 48   WAHB SPRINGS

See Map on Page 169

|  |  |
|---|---|
| **Type of hike:** | Out-and-back. |
| **Type of trip:** | Day hike or overnighter. |
| **Total distance:** | 10 miles or 16.2 kilometers (round-trip). |
| **Difficulty:** | Moderate. |
| **Elevation gain:** | Maximum of 600 feet. |
| **Maps:** | Trails Illustrated (Tower/Canyon); |
|  | Opal Creek and Wahb Springs USGS quads. |
| **Starting point:** | Lamar River Trailhead (3K1). |

**Finding the trailhead:** Drive 14.4 miles east of Tower Junction or 14.6 miles west of the Northeast Entrance and park in the Lamar River Trailhead parking area on the south side of the road. The parking lot for horse trailers is about 100 yards west of the trailhead parking area.

**Key points:**

1.4 (2.2)   Junction with Specimen Ridge Trail.
3.1 (5.0)   Junction with Lamar River Trail.
5.0 (8.0)   Wahb Springs.

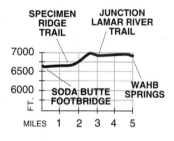

**The hike:** The Lamar River area was burnt heavily in 1988, but it's still excellent fishing and a popular hiking and horsepacking trail. The trail is as well-defined as trails get, mainly because of the heavy horse traffic and outfitter use in the area.

At the trailhead, you cross over Soda Butte Creek on a sturdy bridge. The first 1.4 miles of trail goes through the flat bottomland surrounding the confluence of the Lamar River and Soda Butte Creek. At the junction with the Specimen Ridge Trail, go left (south) and continue hiking through open sagebrush and grassland all the way to the junction with the Cache Creek Trail.

If you're staying overnight (and have a permit) go right (south) for one of the two campsites along Cache Creek or one of the campsites 1 or 2 miles farther down the Lamar River Trail. Then, spend the next day fishing and exploring the Lamar River Valley or going to Wahb Springs before retracing your steps to the trailhead.

You can reach Wahb Springs from the Cache Creek Trail by going left (southeast) at the junction and hiking 2 more miles. You can also bushwhack up Cache Creek, a preferred route for anglers, where they find that just below Wahb Springs, Cache Creek becomes strangely devoid of fish.

Wahb Springs is an impressive thermal area. Well-named Death Gulch comes into the springs from the south. The springs were named from the famous Meeteetse Wahb (Shoshone for "white bear"), an enormous grizzly bear described so eloquently by Ernest Thompson Seton in his classic book,

*Biography of a Grizzly*. After escaping cattlemen and government trappers for decades and taking a few bullets along the way, Wahb finally succumbed to the poison gases of Death Gulch.

It doesn't appear to be a problem today, but in the early days of Yellowstone, certain climatic conditions apparently created a hazardous inversion around the springs that allowed the gases to build up to lethal levels. That may sound strange when you read it, but when you get there, you'll understand.

# 49  GARNET HILL

| | |
|---|---|
| **Type of hike:** | Loop. |
| **Type of trip:** | Day hike. |
| **Total distance:** | 7.5 miles or 12.0 kilometers. |
| **Difficulty:** | Moderate. |
| **Elevation gain:** | 300 feet. |
| **Maps:** | Trails Illustrated (Tower/Canyon); Tower Junction USGS quad. |
| **Starting point:** | Tower Junction Trailhead (2K2). |

**Finding the trailhead:** Drive 0.3 mile east of Tower Junction and park in the large lot by the vault toilets east of the gas station. The trail starts about 100 yards down the Northeast Entrance Road.

**Key points:**

| | | |
|---|---|---|
| 1.5 | (2.4) | End of Stagecoach Road and cookout area. |
| 3.9 | (6.3) | Junction with Spur Trail to the Hellroaring Creek Trail. |
| 5.5 | (8.8) | Junction with angler's trail, stay right. |
| 6.9 | (11.1) | Unmarked junction, stay right. |
| 7.0 | (11.2) | Horse Concession Trail forks, stay left. |
| 7.5 | (12.0) | Northeast Entrance Road. |

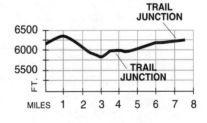

**The hike:** This is a good choice for an early season hike. Snow usually leaves the area in June, and if you hike around Garnet Hill early in the year, you can see an abundance of early season wildflowers, like the camas and bitterroot. Later, lupine lines the trail, and you might find a few unpicked wild raspberry patches.

This area is heavily used by the horse concession at Roosevelt Lodge. You might see a packtrain of dudes on docile mounts traveling the trails to a barbecue. The stagecoach rides from the lodge also use the first section of this loop to take the park visitors to the barbecue.

# GARNET HILL

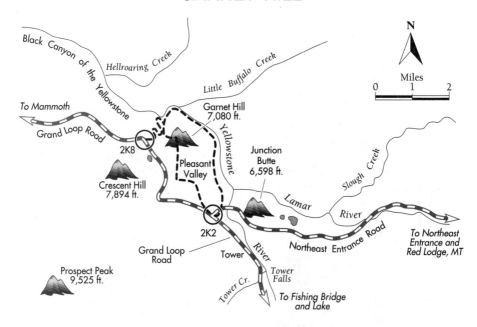

From the Northeast Entrance Road, take the stagecoach road for 1.5 miles through the sage-covered Pleasant Valley to a cookout area, where a regular trail starts. Follow this trail down Elk Creek for another 2.4 miles to a junction with a spur trail that connects with the Hellroaring Creek Trail. To stay on the Garnet Hill Loop, take a right (east).

From here, the trail continues around Garnet Hill (named for an abundance of small garnets, all valueless because of impurities) and back to Tower. Along the way, you get nice views of the Yellowstone, and you pass by two unofficial trail junctions, so be sure to stay on the main trail, marked with orange markers. You end up on the Northeast Entrance Road just east of your starting point. From here, walk along the road back to your vehicle at Tower Junction.

This area is mostly open terrain and can be quite hot and dry in July and August, so bring extra water. The 1988 fires burned much of the area, but a few Engelmann spruce and Douglas-fir survived.

**Options:** You can also start and finish this loop from the Hellroaring Trailhead, which comes out on the Mammoth-Tower Road about 1.5 miles west of Tower Junction. But starting the hike at Tower Junction is usually more convenient, and you can avoid a steep hill to get back up to Hellroaring Trailhead.

**Side trips:** You will be rewarded by a short side trip down to the suspension bridge over the Yellowstone.

|  |  |
|---|---|
| **Type of hike:** | Out-and-back. |
| **Type of trip:** | Day hike. |
| **Total distance:** | 4 miles or 6.4 kilometers (round-trip). |
| **Difficulty:** | Moderate. |
| **Elevation gain:** | 600 feet. |
| **Maps:** | Trails Illustrated (Tower/Canyon); Tower Junction USGS quad. |
| **Starting point:** | Hellroaring Trailhead (2K8). |

**Finding the trailhead:** Drive 14.5 miles east of Mammoth or 3.5 miles west of Tower and pull into a service road on the north side of the road. The trailhead is at the end of the dirt road, about a half mile from the Tower-Mammoth Road.

**Key points:**

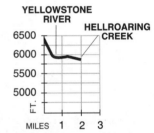

- 0.8 (1.3)  Junction with trail to Tower.
- 1.0 (1.6)  Suspension Bridge.
- 1.6 (2.6)  Junction with the trail to Coyote Creek and Buffalo Plateau.
- 2.0 (3.2)  Hellroaring Creek.

*Suspension bridge over the Black Canyon of the Yellowstone on the Hellroaring Trail.*

# HELLROARING CREEK • BULL MOUNTAIN LOOP

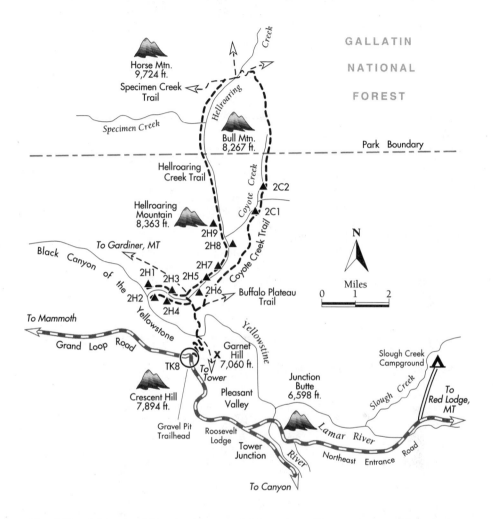

**The hike:** This day hike doubles as the first leg of longer hikes through the Black Canyon of the Yellowstone and around the Bull Mountain Loop. This trail is also a great choice for the beginning backpacker who can stay at one of six excellent campsites on Hellroaring Creek.

The trail switchbacks through open timber and sagebrush meadows for the first mile to the suspension bridge over the Yellowstone River. This isn't the suspension bridge you saw in the Indiana Jones movies. It's steel and sturdy. From the bridge, the trail goes into the open landscape on the Yellowstone and Hellroaring valleys.

The trail is in superb condition all the way. You pass by two trail junctions, the first to Tower (just before the suspension bridge) and the second up Coyote Creek (just after the suspension bridge). Go left (west) at both.

Once you get to Hellroaring Creek, take a break and explore the area for awhile before heading back to the trailhead. You can also follow the trail north for about 1.5 miles along the east side of the creek to a footbridge over this fairly large stream. If you decide to ford the creek, use caution. Even in low water, it's a difficult ford. In high water, it's dangerous, and you should strongly consider putting in the extra miles to use the footbridge.

## 51  TOWER CREEK

|  |  |
|---|---|
| **Type of hike:** | Out-and-back. |
| **Type of trip:** | Day hike. |
| **Total distance:** | 5.6 miles or 9.0 kilometers (round-trip). |
| **Difficulty:** | Moderate. |
| **Elevation gain:** | 200 feet. |
| **Maps:** | Trails Illustrated (Tower/Canyon); Tower Junction and Mount Washburn USGS quads. |
| **Starting point:** | Tower Campground. |

### TOWER CREEK • TOWER FALL • LOST LAKE • YELLOWSTONE RIVER PICNIC AREA TRAIL

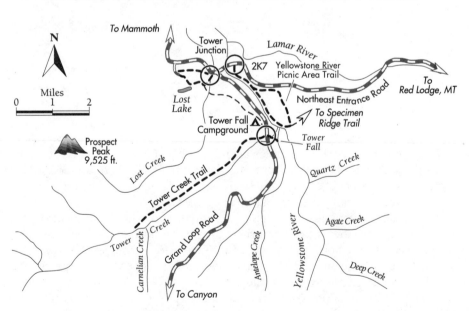

**Finding the trailhead:** Drive 2.5 miles south of Tower Junction or 15.5 miles north of Canyon to the Tower Fall general store and turn west into the campground. Park in the lot to the left of the entrance to the campground loop. The trail starts below campsite No. 1.

**The hike:** The trail starts in a Douglas-fir/Engelmann spruce forest along the south side of the creek for less than a quarter mile. Then it crosses Tower Creek on a bridge and goes into a heavily burned area and stays there for most of the trip. The trail stays on the north side of the creek, climbing at stream grade through open, blown down lodgepole. Plan on stepping over a few logs.

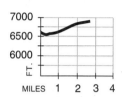

The trail passes several ponds with frogs, garter snakes, and dragonflies—and by a few patches of wild strawberries. After the trail drops into the floodplain, it ends right next to the river with a sign saying, "End of Maintained Trail."

---

## 52 MOUNT WASHBURN

|  |  |
|---|---|
| **Type of hike:** | Out-and-back. |
| **Type of trip:** | Day hike. |
| **Total distance:** | 5.2 miles or 8.3 kilometers (round-trip). |
| **Difficulty:** | Moderate. |
| **Elevation gain:** | 1,491 feet. |
| **Maps:** | Trails Illustrated (Tower/Canyon); Mount Washburn USGS quad. |
| **Starting point:** | Chittenden Road Trailhead (2K6). |

**Finding the trailhead:** Drive 9.7 miles north of Canyon or 8.7 miles south of Tower and turn into the well-signed Chittenden Road. Follow the gravel road for about a mile to a locked gate and a large parking lot off to the left.

**The hike:** The Chittenden Road continues up to the top of the mountain, but it's for official use only. You have to walk or ride a mountain bike to the summit.

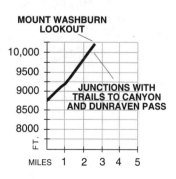

It's nearly 1,500 feet and a Category 2 climb to the top of what is left of an ancient volcano that exploded 600,000 years ago, creating the Yellowstone Caldera in one of the biggest explosions ever. Mount Washburn marks the north end of the caldera and Mount Sheridan the south end.

# MOUNT WASHBURN • DUNRAVEN PASS TO CANYON • SEVENMILE HOLE

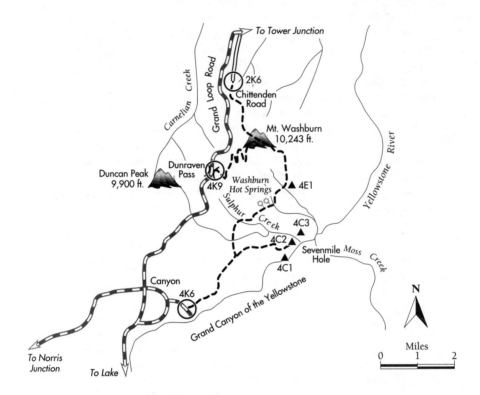

The slope of the gravel road (made for vehicles, of course) makes for easy walking. Very few vehicles use the road, so it seems like a big, wide trail.

You hike amid the open slopes of 10,243-foot Mount Washburn the entire way. If you don't see bighorn sheep on the way up, you'll almost assuredly see them on the summit where a small herd resides most of the summer. (Please don't approach them or feed them!)

Also, expect to be hiking through a virtual wildflower bouquet the entire way. Mount Washburn yearly hosts an incredible abundance and diversity of alpine wildflowers. After

*Bighorn sheep are commonly seen on top of Mount Washburn.*

*Advanced sightseeing from the viewing platform on top of Mount Washburn.*

hiking all of Yellowstone, I didn't find another place that matched the wildflower showcase found on Mount Washburn. However, please observe the wildflowers from the trail. Off-trail use can flatten this delicate alpine vegetation.

At the summit, you might be surprised to find a major structure conservatively referred to as a lookout. It has an interpretive center, 20-power telescopes for wildlife viewing, drinking fountain, bathrooms, and even a pay phone.

Watch the weather. You don't want to get caught on this mountain in a thunderstorm. This makes a morning trip safer than waiting until the afternoon when one of those common "Yellowstone rollers" can come rolling through and light up the mountain with lightning.

**Options:** You can get to the summit of Mount Washburn by two other routes—from Dunraven Pass and from Glacier Boulder Trailhead in Canyon. The Dunraven Pass route (refer to the first part of the Dunraven Pass to Canyon hike) is about the same intensity as the Chittenden Road route, but the Glacier Boulder route is a Category H climb and a real lung-buster.

**Side trips:** If you have some extra time on top, you can walk along the ridge toward Dunraven Pass for about a half mile without losing much elevation. You can also hike the first part of the spur trail to Canyon, which heads off to the east through a major wildflower garden. If you want to identify every flower along the way, you'll need several hours.

157

# 53  SEVENMILE HOLE

| Type of hike: | Out-and-back. |
|---|---|
| Type of trip: | Day hike or overnighter. |
| Total distance: | 10 miles or 16.1 kilometers (round-trip). |
| Difficulty: | Difficult. |
| Elevation gain: | 1,200 feet. |
| Maps: | Trails Illustrated (Tower/Canyon); Canyon Village and Mount Washburn USGS quads. |
| Starting point: | Glacier Boulder Trailhead (4K6). |

See Map on Page 156

**Finding the trailhead:** Drive east from the Canyon Junction for 0.9 miles and park on the left (north) side of the one-way drive, next to large boulders and dense lodgepole forest and just before the Inspiration Point viewpoint.

## Key Points:
- 1.0 (1.6)  View of Silver Cord Cascade.
- 2.0 (3.2)  Junction with the Washburn Mountain Trail.
- 5.0 (8.0)  Sevenmile Hole and spur trails to backcountry campsites 4C1 (4★), 4C2 (4★), and 4C3 (3★).

**The hike:** Most hikes start uphill and finish on a downhill, but this one starts on the rim of the Grand Canyon of the Yellowstone and drops to the river below. Local hikers sometimes refer to it as Sevenmile Hole because it feels like 5 miles down and 7 miles up. Actually and officially, it's named for the distance below Lower Falls, about 7 miles.

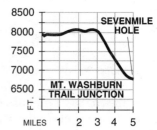

Even though it's a tough hike up from the river, this trail offers up some of the core wonders of Yellowstone—the brilliant colors of the canyon, thermal areas, waterfalls, and scenic campsites. You won't find any water sources along this trail except the Yellowstone River in Sevenmile Hole, so be sure to bring plenty of water.

The trail starts in unburned lodgepole forest on a flat grade. Several views through the trees of the canyon pass by before Silver Cord Cascade is visible on the south side of the canyon. That water comes from Ribbon Lake, just back in the trees, and drops 1,200 feet to the Yellowstone River.

When you reach the junction with the Mount Washburn Spur Trail, take a right (east) and continue along the rim of the river. The trail stays high and in the timber for about another half mile before dropping over the rim and descending on steep switchbacks to the river. On the way down, you pass a geyser and a sulfur thermal area. Just before reaching Sevenmile Hole, the trail splits. Camp 4C1 is on the right, while 4C2 and 4C3 are on the left.

The trail is heavily used and in great shape the entire way. After your fairly easy 5-mile hike in, take a nice rest and listen to the mighty river rush by for awhile before facing the Category 2 climb out of the canyon that magically adds 2 miles to the distance.

*Silver Cord Cascade.*

# 54   *CASCADE LAKE*

|  |  |
|---|---|
| **Type of hike:** | Out-and-back. |
| **Type of trip:** | Day hike or overnighter. |
| **Total distance:** | 5 miles or 8 kilometers (round-trip). |
| **Difficulty:** | Easy. |
| **Elevation gain:** | Minimal. |
| **Maps:** | Trails Illustrated (Tower/Canyon); Mammoth Hot Springs and Crystal Falls, Cook Peak, Canyon Village, and Mount Washburn USGS quads. |
| **Starting point:** | Cascade Lake Picnic Area Trailhead (4K5). |

See Elevation Profile on Page 161
See Map on Page 116

**Finding the trailhead:** Drive 1.3 miles north of Canyon Junction and park in the parking area on the west side of the road.

**Key points:**
2.0 (3.2)   Junction with Cascade Creek Trail.
2.3 (3.7)   Spur Trail to 4E4 (2★).
2.4 (3.8)   Junction with trail to Observation Peak and 4E3 (3★).
2.5 (4.0)   Cascade Lake.

**The hike:** This is a great choice for the beginning backpacker looking for one of his or her first nights in the wilderness. This also makes a nice day hike after an enjoyable picnic at the trailhead.

*Approaching Cascade Lake.*

It's a short 2.5 miles to the large, deep lake, and the trail is in excellent condition the entire way and even double wide near the picnic area. It's a nice flat hike through scattered forest and meadows until you get close to the lake and enter a huge meadow. In June and July, the meadows along the way are ablaze with wildflowers—and full of bison, too, so be careful.

The 36-acre lake has a heathly population of cutthroat and grayling, so expect to see a few anglers.

**Side trips:** If you have time, you can hike from the lake 3 miles up (one way) to the summit of Observation Peak. You can also take the 2.5-mile hike (one way) over to Grebe Lake.

**Options:** You can also get to Cascade Lake from the Cascade Creek Trailhead (4K4). It's about the same distance and gradient, but this route receives heavy use from commercial horse parties. If you're looking for an easy overnighter, Cascade Lake is a good choice.

# 55  OBSERVATION PEAK

| | | |
|---:|:---|:---|
| **Type of hike:** | Out-and-back. | See Map on Page 116 |
| **Type of trip:** | Day hike or overnighter. | |
| **Total distance:** | 11 miles or 17.7 kilometers (round-trip). | |
| **Difficulty:** | Moderate. | |
| **Elevation gain:** | 1,400 feet. | |
| **Maps:** | Trails Illustrated (Tower/Canyon); | |
| | Mammoth Hot Springs and Crystal Falls, Cook Peak, | |
| | Canyon Village, and Mount Washburn USGS quads. | |
| **Starting point:** | Cascade Lake Picnic Area (4K5). | |

**Finding the trailhead:** Drive 1.3 miles north of Canyon Junction and park in the parking area on the west side of the road.

**Key points:**
- 2.0 (3.2)  Junction with Cascade Creek Trail.
- 2.3 (3.7)  Spur Trail to 4E4 (2★).
- 2.4 (3.8)  Junction with trail to Observation Peak and 4E3 (3★).
- 5.5 (8.8)  Summit of Observation Peak.

**The hike:** The trail into Cascade Lake is flat and easy, but that abruply changes when you turn right (north) just before the lake and head for Observation Peak.

It's a steady, Category 2 climb to the summit. From the top, you get a wonderful view of the Central Plateau area and the Hayden Valley.

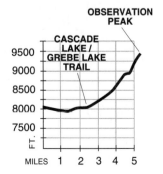

161

The trail to the summit isn't in as good of shape as the first 2.5 miles into Cascade Lake, but it's still well-defined and easy to follow—and not as steep as it looks on the map. It gets a little rocky in places as you switchback through mostly burnt forest to the summit. You don't get much of a view on the way up, but on top, you can see it all.

Be sure to bring plenty of water. There are no water sources on this trail.

**Options:** You can also start this hike at the Cascade Creek Trailhead (4K4), but this route receives heavy use from commercial horse parties. If you're interested in enjoying the view at sunrise and sunset or a closer view of the stars, you can stay overnight at 4P1 on the summit of Observation Peak, but bring all the water you need.

---

## 56 CLEAR LAKE LOOP

| | | |
|---|---|---|
| **Type of hike:** | Loop. | |
| **Type of trip:** | Day hike or easy overnighter. | *See Map on Page 143* |
| **Total distance:** | 5.5 miles or 8.8 kilometers. | |
| **Difficulty:** | Easy. | |
| **Elevation gain:** | Minimal. | |
| **Maps:** | Trails Illustrated (Tower/Canyon); Canyon Village USGS quad. | |
| **Starting point:** | Clear Lake Trailhead. | |

**Finding the trailhead:** Drive south 2.3 miles from the Canyon Junction, turn left (east) crossing the Chittenden Bridge, and go another 0.6 mile before parking on your left (west) in the Uncle Tom's Trail parking lot. The trail starts on your right (east) just as you enter the lot.

**Key Points:**

| | |
|---|---|
| 0.4 (0.6) | Junction with cutoff trail to Wapiti Lake Trail. |
| 0.6 (0.9) | Clear Lake. |
| 1.6 (2.6) | Junction with Wapiti Lake Trail. |
| 2.6 (4.2) | Ribbon Lake and 4R1 (3★) and  4R2 (4★). |
| 3.2 (5.1) | Junction with Wapiti Lake Trail. |
| 4.6 (7.4) | Junction with Sour Creek Trail. |
| 4.9 (7.9) | Junction with cutoff and return to Clear Lake Trailhead. |
| 5.1 (8.2) | Junction with Clear Lake Trail. |
| 5.5 (8.8) | Clear Lake Trailhead. |

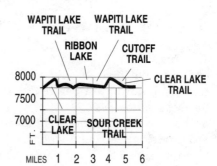

162

**The hike:** This trail could be hiked from several starting points, including Artist Point, but this route avoids most of the larger crowds and lets the hiker explore this entire area so close to the Grand Canyon of the Yellowstone. This route also avoids any hiking on the paved road. Highlights of this trail include thermal areas, Ribbon Lake, Silver Cord Cascade, and views up the Hayden Valley.

From the trailhead, the trail gently climbs through Douglas-fir and grassy meadows. About a half mile up the trail, you'll see Clear Lake on your left and shortly thereafter the junction with the cutoff trail to Wapiti Lake Trailhead. Go left (east) at this junction and follow the trail through more meadows and along the east shore of Clear Lake to a junction with the Ribbon Lake Trail.

Clear Lake is a bluish color and surrounded by lodgepole pine and Douglas-fir. The trail skirts the east side of the lake to a gurgling mud pot, one of the several thermal areas along this section of trail.

At the junction with the Ribbon Lake Trail from Artist Point, go right (northeast). Going left will take you back to the road, on which hikers have to compete with tour buses chasing bison. After this junction the trail is flat and in the trees until Ribbon Lake. At Ribbon Lake, a spur trail veers left to 4R1, 4R2, and Silver Cord Cascade overlook, a must-see side trip with an incredible view of the cascade and the Grand Canyon of the Yellowstone.

After enjoying the viewpoint, follow the trail through unburned forest around Ribbon Lake to the junction with the Wapiti Lake Trail. Turn right (southwest) here, exit the forest, and head back out into the open buffalo prairie. At the Sour Creek Trail junction, go right (southwest) and onto the junction with the cutoff trail to Clear Lake. This junction might not show up on your map, but it's definitely there. Turn right (north) and hike to Clear Lake, where you turn left (west) and return to the trailhead.

## 57  WRANGLER LAKE

| | | |
|---|---|---|
| **Type of hike:** | Out-and-back. | |
| **Type of trip:** | A day hike or intermediate overnighter. | See Map on Page 192 |
| **Total distance:** | 8.8 miles or 14.0 kilomters (round-trip). | |
| **Difficulty:** | Moderate. | |
| **Elevation gain:** | Minimal. | |
| **Maps:** | Trails Illustrated (Tower/Canyon); Canyon Village USGS quad. | |
| **Starting point:** | Wapiti Lake Trailhead (4K7). | |

**Finding the trailhead:** Drive south 2.3 miles past Canyon Junction and turn left crossing the Chittenden Bridge. Just after crossing the bridge, turn right into the parking lot for the Wapiti Lake Trailhead.

**Key Points:**

| | |
|---|---|
| 1.2 (1.9) | Clear Lake junction. |
| 1.5 (2.4) | Junction with Sour Creek Trail, stay right. |
| 2.0 (3.2) | Junction with Wrangler Lake Trail, stay left. |
| 4.4 (7.0) | Wrangler Lake and 4W1 (3★). |

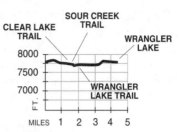

**The hike:** This trail doesn't lead to extended trips, but for an intermediate overnighter to a Yellowstone lake, this is hard to beat. In June and July, Wrangler Lake doubles as a mosquito breeding haven, so I recommend a late-season trip. Getting to Wrangler Lake involves fording Sour Creek, which in June is at least a precarious waist deep.

From the trailhead, take the left trail past the trailhead sign. The path passes a couple trees then rises up on rolling prairie with many bison in sight in this part of the Hayden Valley.

At 1.2 miles is the junction with the cutoff trail to Clear Lake (not shown on some maps). Stay right (east) and continue through the buffalo prairie.

The next junction is just after a lodgepole pine stand. Again turn right (south) for Wrangler Lake and Sour Creek. The trail passes in and out of small groves of trees and by a thermal area just after crossing a small creek.

At about 2 miles is the junction with the Wrangler Lake Trail. Turn left (east) to reach Wrangler Lake. The trail continues across the prairie until crossing a tributary of Sour Creek, which may be a hefty ford in early season.

*Fording Sour Creek on Wrangler Lake or Hayden Valley trails.*

If this one is deep, expect the next to be worse. After this ford, the trail crosses the flood plain of Sour Creek, which is flat and sometimes wet. The ford across Sour Creek is on a wide, deep meander, but don't let the calm surface fool you, there is definitely a current.

After fording Sour Creek, the trail gets faint as it goes through several meadows and stands of lodgepole. Upon reaching 35-acre, fishless Wrangler Lake, you might hear a low humming sound. No, that isn't the interstate highway in the distance. It's the swarm of flesh-loving mosquitoes waiting for you. It might be time for some Deet. This is frog, mosquito, and lilypad heaven, but it's also a nice mountain lake nestled in an unburned lodgepole forest.

## 58 ALUM CREEK

|  |  |
|---|---|
| **Type of hike:** | Out-and-back. |
| **Type of trip:** | Day hike. |
| **Total distance:** | Up to 10 miles or 16.1 kilometers (round-trip). |
| **Difficulty:** | Moderate. |
| **Elevation gain:** | Minimal. |
| **Maps:** | Trails Illustrated (Mammoth Hot Springs or Old Faithful); Canyon Village and Crystal Falls USGS quads. |
| **Starting point:** | Alum Creek Trailhead at the north end of Hayden Valley. |

See Elevation Profile on Page 204
See Map on Page 205

*Hiking Alum Creek.*

**Finding the trailhead:** Drive 4.4 miles south from Canyon or 11.6 miles north from Fishing Bridge Junction and park in a pullout on the east side of the road. The trail starts directly across the road from the parking area. This trailhead does not show on any of the four Trails Illustrated maps covering the park. All four maps show parts of the Alum Creek Trail, but none of them show the beginning of the Alum Creek Trail.

**The hike:** This hike is ideal for avid wildlife watchers. It goes along the north edge of the wildlife-rich Hayden Valley, and you can almost always see a variety of wildlife along the trail, including the grizzly bear.

The trail starts right at the north edge of Hayden Valley, and follows Alum Creek (which has several interesting thermal areas along its course) through the northern edge of the valley. The trail stays in the open all the way and stays marshy throughout the summer and fall, so be prepared for wet feet. Also, bison use this area extensively, so stay alert so you don't get off the official trail and onto a bison trail.

For those hikers who really want to see grizzly bears, get up early and hike Alum Creek. The great bear is often sighted along this trail, but be very careful not to disturb or get too close to any bear you see—both for your safety and the bear's.

Alum Creek is the eastern section of the Mary Mountain Trail that goes by Mary Lake and comes out Nez Perce Creek north of Old Faithful. However, many hikers take Alum Creek out and back to make this a shorter hike and to avoid the problematic shuttle of vehicles.

You can go as far as you choose before turning back, but most people go about 4 to 5 miles into the west end of the open valley, where you can see the trail start to head off to the west into heavy timber.

**Options:** You can also hike Alum Creek as part of the Mary Mountain shuttle hike.

# 59 *REPUBLIC PASS*

|  |  |
|---|---|
| **Type of hike:** | Shuttle. |
| **Type of trip:** | Backpacking trip. |
| **Total distance:** | 23.1 miles or 37.9 kilometers, plus 1 mile if you don't have a four-wheel-drive vehicle. |
| **Difficulty:** | Difficult. |
| **Elevation gain:** | 2,350 feet from Cooke City, Montana, 1,950 feet from the end of four-wheel-drive road. |
| **Maps:** | Trails Illustrated (Tower/Canyon); Cooke City, Pilot Peak, Abiathar Peak, Wahb Springs, and Opal Creek USGS quads. |
| **Starting point:** | About 1 mile south of Cooke City, just outside the park's Northeast Entrance. |

**Finding the trailhead:** In Cooke City, turn south on Republic Lane and cross Ellen's Bridge. After the bridge, veer right and then take a left and follow the steep, four-wheel-drive road for about 1 mile until it ends near some old mines at the boundary line of the Shoshone National Forest. If you don't have a four-wheel drive, park just before the bridge and hike up the road to the trailhead.

**Key points:**

| | | |
|---|---|---|
| 1.5 | (2.4) | Republic Meadows. |
| 4.5 | (7.2) | Republic Pass and park boundary. |
| 9.3 | (13.6) | 3C4 (3★). |
| 10.1 | (14.5) | Cache Creek patrol cabin. |
| 10.5 | (14.9) | Thunderer Cutoff Trail. |
| 13.6 | (21.8) | 3C3 (3★). |
| 15.4 | (24.7) | 3C2 (3★). |
| 19.0 | (30.6) | Wahb Springs and Death Gulch. |
| 21.0 | (33.8) | Junction with Lamar River Trail, trail to 3L1 (4★) and 3L2 (3★). |
| 22.7 | (36.5) | Junction with Specimen Ridge Trail. |
| 24.1 | (38.8) | Lamar River Trailhead. |

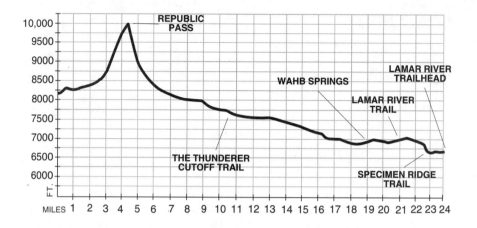

**Recommended itinerary:** Three-day trip, staying at 3C4 and 3C2.

**The hike:** This is the only hike in this book that starts outside of the park. But this doesn't detract from it. The scenery outside the park equals or surpasses that inside the park. Republic Pass is a tough hike from either direction, but it's a gorgeous and seldom-seen corner of the Yellowstone backcountry and well worth the effort.

*On Republic Pass.*

# REPUBLIC PASS • THE THUNDERER
## • WAHB SPRINGS

From the end of the road, the trail gradually climbs through unburnt timber along Republic Creek and through beautiful Republic Meadows. The rocky trail is not well-marked, but you can stay on it if you stay alert. Right below the pass, the trail more or less disappears. Angle off to the right and climb up to the pass. Plan on putting out a major sweat to get to the 9,987-foot pass, especially over the murderous last mile where you gain about 1,000 feet in elevation (Category H).

From the pass (which has a sign), you can take a short stroll to the south up to an unnamed, 10,440-foot peak, less than a quarter mile south of the pass.

When you head down the pass, the trail continues to be nearly invisible, so stay alert and keep your topo map and compass out. A few scattered blazes and cairns reveal the faint route. After the pass, you go into burnt forest, but before you do, you get a great view of Amphitheater Mountain to the north. After about 1 mile, you drop into Cache Creek, and the trail is well defined the rest of the way. Once in Cache Creek, put the compass away and enjoy a gradual downhill walk for 18.6 miles to the Lamar River Trailhead.

At the Thunderer Cutoff Trail junction, go left (south). Here, you might want to take a break from your overnight pack (be sure to hang it out of reach of bears) with a short climb to 8,827-foot Chaw Pass, but only if you have extra time and energy. It's a tough, 1,100-foot, Category 1 climb over about 1.5 miles of trail, a real calf stretcher.

When you get to Wahb Springs, hang your pack and take the short off-trail side trip down to the remarkable thermal area. Well-named Death Gulch comes into the springs from the south.

*Amphitheater Mountain from the Republic Pass Trail.*

It doesn't appear to be a problem today, but in the early days of Yellowstone, certain climatic conditions apparently created a hazardous inversion around the springs that allowed the gases to build up to lethal levels. That may sound weird when you read it, but when you're standing at Wahb Springs, it makes sense.

When you reach the Lamar River Trail, turn right (north) and follow the heavily used Lamar River Trail through the open splendor of the Lamar Valley back to the Northeast Entrance Road.

**Options:** You could make this a shorter (14.8 miles) shuttle by taking the Thunderer Cutoff Trail back to the Northeast Entrance Road. You can take this trip in reverse, but it's still a deadly climb to get up to Republic Pass.

**Side trips:** A must-see side trip would be the short off-trail trip to Wahb Springs and aptly named Death Gulch.

# 60  PEBBLE CREEK

| | |
|---|---|
| **Type of hike:** | Shuttle. |
| **Type of trip:** | Overnighter or long day hike. |
| **Total distance:** | 12 miles or 19.3 kilometers. |
| **Difficulty:** | Moderate. |
| **Elevation gain:** | 700 feet. |
| **Maps:** | Trails Illustrated (Tower/Canyon); Cutoff Mountain and Abiathar Peak USGS quads. |
| **Starting point:** | Warm Creek Picnic Area (3K4). |

**Finding the trailhead:** Drive 27.5 miles east of Tower Junction or 1.5 miles west of the Northeast Entrance and park on the south side of the road at the Warm Creek Picnic Area. The trail starts on the opposite side of the road about 100 yards west of the parking area.

**Key points:**

| | | |
|---|---|---|
| 1.5 | (2.4) | Top of ridge. |
| 2.3 | (3.7) | First ford. |
| 2.5 | (4.0) | 3P5 (3★). |
| 3.3 | (5.3) | 3P4 (2★). |
| 4.0 | (6.4) | Second ford. |
| 5.4 | (8.7) | 3P3 (4★). |
| 5.5 | (8.8) | Junction with Bliss Pass Trail. |
| 6.0 | (9.6) | 3P2 (4★). |
| 6.5 | (10.4) | Third ford. |
| 7.5 | (12.0) | Fourth ford. |
| 9.0 | (14.5) | 3P1 (4★). |
| 11.8 | (19.0) | Trail forks (right to campground, left to highway). |
| 12.0 | (19.3) | Pebble Creek Campground. |

# PEBBLE CREEK • TROUT LAKE

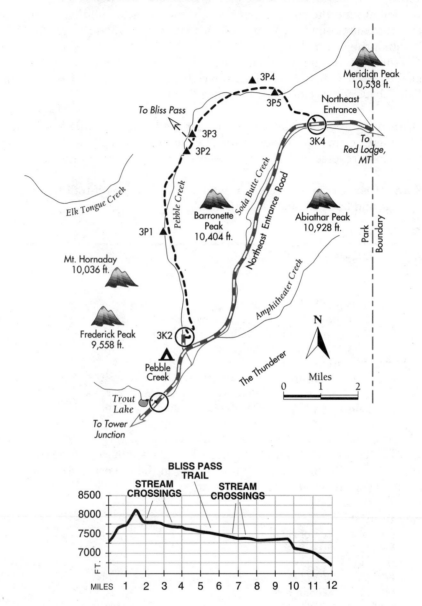

**Recommended itinerary:** A two-day trip, staying overnight at 3P3 or 3P2.

**The hike:** On the map, it looks like the Pebble Creek Trail follows the Northwest Entrance Road, but it's actually hidden from view. It goes through spectacular meadows along a totally natural stream, and it's a mostly downhill, 12-mile hike.

The trail starts out in an ominous manner, climbing seriously for about 1.5 miles to the top of a ridge. However, once you put out the effort to get over this Category 3 hill, it's all downhill for 10.5 miles.

The trail is well-defined and maintained the entire way. However, you have to ford Pebble creek four times—all are safe crossings unless you go during the high run-off period in June or early July.

Once you reach Pebble Creek, follow the stream through wildflower-filled meadows (especially heavy with lupine) for another 2.5 miles to the second ford. This stretch treats the hiker with some of the best mountain scenery in Yellowstone. After this ford, you go into a short stretch of burned forest broken by a few meadows. Watch for moose and elk.

After the Bliss Pass Trail junction, where you go left (south), the trail is not quite as scenic. It goes through a mostly unburned forest, again broken by a few large meadows, all the way back to Pebble Creek Campground. Ford the stream twice more along the way. Within sight of the campground, the trail forks—go right for the campground, left for the trailhead along the highway, depending on where you left your vehicle.

Fishing in Pebble Creek doesn't match up to its famous neighbor, Slough Creek, but it can be excellent in late summer especially in the lower stretches where the stream gets larger. Don't forget your park fishing permit or the catch-and-release regulations.

**Options:** Hiking in reverse means 10.5 miles of gradual uphill instead of 10.5 miles of gradual downhill. Beginning backpackers might want to hike into 3P5, stay overnight, and return to the Warm Springs Picnic Area. This also works well if you can't arrange the shuttle. Serious hikers will consider this 12-mile trip a moderate day hike.

# 61  SLOUGH CREEK

|  |  |
|---|---|
| **Type of hike:** | Out-and-back. |
| **Type of trip:** | Moderate backpacking trip or long day hike. |
| **Total distance:** | Up to 22 miles or 35.4 kilometers (round-trip). |
| **Difficulty:** | Moderate. |
| **Elevation gain:** | 400 feet. |
| **Maps:** | Trails Illustrated (Tower/Canyon); Lamar Canyon, Mount Hornaday, and Roundhead Butte USGS quads. |
| **Starting point:** | Slough Creek Trailhead (2K5). |

**Finding the trailhead:** Drive 5.8 miles east of Tower Junction or 23.2 miles west of the Northeast Entrance and turn north onto the unpaved road to the Slough Creek Campground. Go 1.5 miles and park at the trailhead, which is on your right just before the campground.

# SLOUGH CREEK

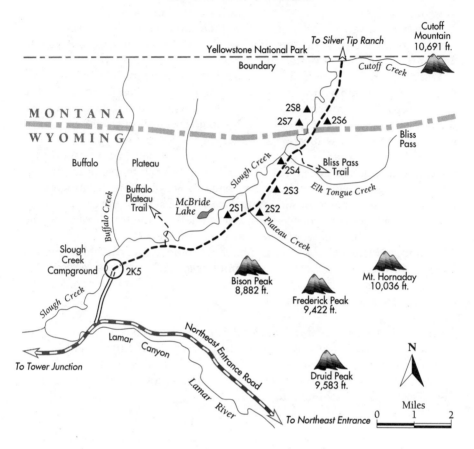

## Key points:

| | | |
|---|---|---|
| 2.0 | (3.2) | Junction with Buffalo Plateau Trail (Buffalo Fork Trail on sign). |
| 3.5 | (5.6) | Junction with spur trail to 2S1 (5★). |
| 4.0 | (6.4) | 2S2 (3★). |
| 6.5 | (10.4) | 2S3 (4★). |
| 7.5 | (12.0) | 2S4 (3★). |
| 8.0 | (12.8) | Junction with Bliss Pass Trail. |
| 9.0 | (14.5) | 2S6 (5★). |
| 11.0 | (35.4) | Park boundary. |

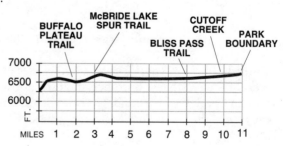

**Recommended itinerary:** Hike into 2S4 or 2S6, stay overnight, fish, and return the next day.

**The hike:** This is an unusual hike through an unusual valley. The trail is actually an old wagon road leading to the Silver Tip Ranch, just north of the park. Non-motorized access to the ranch is guaranteed, so you might meet a horse-drawn wagon on the trail. And, of course, the wagon road makes a superb hiking trail, which only gains 400 feet elevation over 11 miles, most of that in a little hill shortly after leaving the trailhead. If you meet the wagon, please step well off the trail and stand still to avoid spooking the stock animals.

Slough Creek is a slow-moving, meandering stream that goes though an expansive, treeless valley. Elk, deer, bison, and other large mammals graze the slopes of Slough Creek in large numbers, and now the park's growing wolf population has followed this smorgasbord to Slough Creek.

If you're a flycaster, you probably have a soft spot in your heart for Slough Creek, now world-famous for its fat but difficult-to-catch cutthroats. Actually, some biologists have called this the best natural cutthroat stream in the world. Don't plan on having the stream to yourself, however. Instead, expect to see a dozen or more anglers stalking the wily trout on any summer day. Don't forget the park fishing permit and note the catch-and-release fishing regulations.

If you plan to stay overnight, be sure to take advantage of the park's advance reservation system—and reserve as early as possible. The campsites in Slough Creek rank among the park's most popular, and the summer can be completely booked a month in advance.

**Options:** Since this is an out-and-back hike with no exact destination (e.g. mountain summit or lake), you have the option of going as far up the creek as you choose.

**Side trips:** If you have time, it's worth the effort to take the short, off-trail side trip to McBride Lake. There is no maintained trail to the lake, and you have to ford Slough Creek to get there. Keep your map and compass out to make sure you don't miss the lake.

|                    |                                                      |
|--------------------|------------------------------------------------------|
| **Type of hike:**  | Shuttle.                                             |
| **Type of trip:**  | Backpacking trip.                                    |
| **Total distance:**| 19.5 miles or 33.1 kilometers.                       |
| **Difficulty:**    | Difficult.                                           |
| **Elevation gain:**| 2,750 feet.                                          |
| **Maps:**          | Trails Illustrated (Tower/Canyon); Cutoff Mountain, Abiathar Peak, Roundhead Butte, Mount Hornaday, and Lamar Canyon USGS quads. |
| **Starting point:**| Slough Creek Trailhead (2K5).                        |

**Finding the trailhead:** Drive 5.8 miles east of Tower Junction or 23.2 miles west of the Northeast Entrance and turn north onto the unpaved road to the Slough Creek Campground. Go 1.5 miles and park at the trailhead, which is on your right just before the campground.

## Key points:

|            |        |                                                |
|------------|--------|------------------------------------------------|
| 2.0        | (3.2)  | Junction with Buffalo Plateau Trail.           |
| 3.5        | (5.6)  | Junction with trail to 2S1 (5★).               |
| 4.0        | (6.4)  | 2S2 (3★).                                      |
| 6.5        | (10.4) | 2S3 (4★).                                      |
| 7.5        | (12.0) | 2S4 (3★).                                      |
| 8.0        | (12.8) | Junction with Bliss Pass Trail.                |
| 12.0       | (19.3) | Bliss Pass.                                    |
| 14.0       | (22.5) | Junction with Pebble Creek Trail and 3P3 (4★). |
| 16.4       | (26.4) | 3P4 (2★).                                      |
| 17.3       | (27.8) | 3P5 (3★).                                      |
| 19.5       | (33.1) | Warm Creek Trailhead.                          |

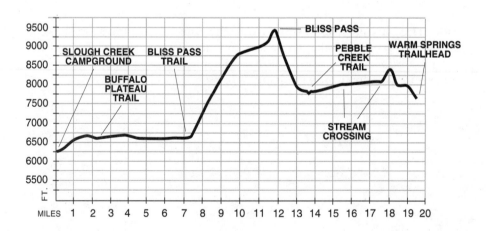

# BLISS PASS

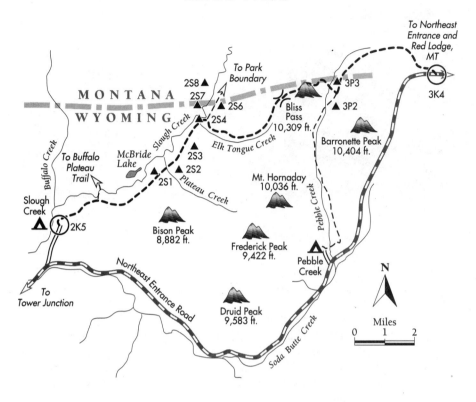

**Recommended itinerary:** Three-day trip staying at 2S3 or 2S4, and 3P3 or 3P5. This leaves extra time for fishing in Slough and Pebble creeks.

**The hike:** The hike starts on the wagon road going along Slough Creek to the Silver Tip Ranch. Once past a small hill in the first mile of trail, this is relatively easy, flat hiking all the way to the junction with the Bliss Pass Trail going up Elk Tongue Creek. The trail goes in and out of the unburned timber for the first few miles. Then, it breaks out into the sweeping openness of Slough Creek. Watch for wildlife, including wolves, which frequent the area.

Plan on seeing lots of hikers carrying rod cases along the first 8 miles[1]. Slough Creek is world-renown for its flyfishing. The oversized cutthroat

---

[1]The mileage on the first part of this hike seems exaggerated. Even though trail signs and NPS records indicate that it's 8 miles to the Bliss Pass Trail junction, you'll probably agree that it doesn't seem nearly that far.

*Looking west from Bliss Pass.*

have seen so many artificial flies that beginning flycasters might have a hard time catching them.

At the Bliss Pass junction, go right (east) and follow Elk Tongue Creek all the way to Bliss Pass where you'll find two marshy ponds—and perhaps a moose or two. Although this rates as a Category 1 climb, it doesn't seem that difficult. The trail passes through intermittently burned timber and is in great shape the entire 4 miles to the pass. The view on the pass is limited by the trees right on the pass, but from the east side of the pass, you get a spectacular view down into Pebble Creek.

From the pass, the trail switchbacks down 1,300 feet to Pebble Creek, which you ford just before reaching the trail. When you reach the Pebble Creek Trail, go left (north) and head into Upper Pebble Creek. You ford the stream twice more—easy crossings (except in June). If you go early in the year, check with a ranger on the condition of the stream crossings before heading for the trailhead.

Upper Pebble Creek is a miniature version of Slough Creek—open, lush, and filled with wildlife and wildflowers. The fishing is good, too, but the native cutthroats are much smaller than in Slough Creek.

Although you are technically going uphill along Pebble Creek, it's so gradual that you probably won't notice. You'll notice the small climb to get up to the ridge at the end of the valley, but it's much easier and shorter than coming up the other side of the ridge (just in case you decided to do this trip in reverse).

**Options:** Upon reaching Pebble Creek, you can go south instead of north. If you do, it's downhill all the way to Pebble Creek Campground, but 1 mile longer, and you miss the gorgeous meadows along Upper Pebble Creek.

Hiking this trip in reverse means climbing two big hills (one to get into Upper Pebble Creek and the east side of Bliss Pass) instead of one big hill (the west side of Bliss Pass and one little hill to the top of the ridge at the end of the hike).

**Side trips:** If you have time, you'll be rewarded by trying the short, off-trail side trip to McBride Lake.

---

## 63  LAMAR RIVER

| | | |
|---|---|---|
| **Type of hike:** | Out-and-back. | |
| **Type of trip:** | Easy to moderate | See Map on Page 197 |

backpacking trip or moderate to long day hike, depending on distance.

| | |
|---|---|
| **Total distance:** | Up to 32 miles or 51.5 kilometers (round-trip). |
| **Difficulty:** | Moderate to difficult, depending on distance. |
| **Elevation gain:** | Maximum of 600 feet. |
| **Maps:** | Trails Illustrated (Tower/Canyon); Opal Creek, Wahb Springs, and Little Saddle Mountain USGS quads. |
| **Starting point:** | Lamar River Trailhead (3K1). |

**Finding the trailhead:** Drive 14.4 miles east of Tower Junction or 14.6 miles west of the Northeast Entrance and park in the Lamar River Trailhead parking area on the south side of the road. The parking lot for horse trailers is about 100 yards west of the trailhead parking area.

## Key points:

| | | |
|---|---|---|
| 1.4 | (2.2) | Junction with Specimen Ridge Trail. |
| 3.1 | (5.0) | Junction with Cache Creek Trail. |
| 3.4 | (5.4) | 3L1 (4★). |
| 3.5 | (5.6) | Ford Cache Creek. |
| 3.6 | (5.8) | Spur trail to 3L2 (4★). |
| 5.0 | (8.0) | 3L3 (3★). |
| 5.7 | (9.1) | 3L4 (4★). |
| 9.2 | (14.8) | Junction with Miller Creek Trail and ford Miller Creek. |
| 10.5 | (16.9) | 3L7 (4★). |
| 11.1 | (17.8) | 3L8 (4★). |
| 13.4 | (21.5) | 3U1 (2★). |
| 14.5 | (23.3) | 3U2 (4★). |
| 14.7 | (23.6) | 3U3 (3★), |
| 16.0 | (25.7) | Junction with Cold Creek and Frost Lake trails and 3T1 (4★). |

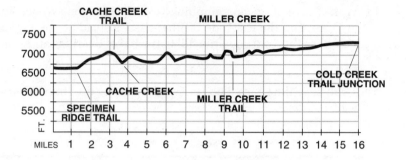

**Recommended itinerary:** Three-day trip staying two nights at 3L1, 3L2, 3L3, or 3L4, with side trips to Wahb Springs and farther up the river.

**The hike:** The Lamar River area was burnt heavily in 1988, but it's still excellent fishing and a popular hiking and horsepacking trail.

You can do as much of the Lamar as you choose. You can hike 3.5 miles into Cache Creek and stay at one of the campsites there. You can go the full 16 miles to where the trail splits into the Frost Lake Trail and the Cold Creek Trail. Or you can do anything in-between. You can also make this a long day hike, but most people prefer to stay at least one night to fish the Lamar.

The trail is as well-defined as trails get, mainly because of the heavy horse traffic and outfitter use in the area. At the trailhead after July 1, you might see as many as ten horse trailers. If you want to avoid the horse groups, stay at one of the first campsites. Most of the stock parties go farther up the Lamar.

At the trailhead, you cross over Soda Butte Creek on a sturdy bridge, but that's the last bridge on this trip. The first 1.4 miles of trail goes through the flat bottomland surrounding the confluence of the Lamar River and Soda Butte Creek. At the junction with the Specimen Ridge Trail, go left (south) and continue hiking through open sagebrush and grassland all the way to Cache Creek Trail junction where you take a right (south) and head down a hill to ford Cache Creek.

If you're staying overnight pick one of the campsites here or go 1 or 2 miles more down the trail to reach two more campsites. Then, spend the next day fishing and exploring the Lamar River Valley or going to Wahb Springs before retracing your steps to the trailhead.

**Side trips:** Wahb Springs, a must-see side trip, can be reached from the Cache Creek Trail or by bushwhacking up Cache Creek, a preferred route for anglers when they find that just below Wahb Springs, Cache Creek becomes suddenly devoid of fish. You can also hike farther up the Lamar River from your camp.

|                    |                                                                                      |
| ------------------ | ------------------------------------------------------------------------------------ |
| **Type of hike:**  | Shuttle.                                                                             |
| **Type of trip:**  | Long day hike.                                                                       |
| **Total distance:**| 18.8 miles or 30.2 kilometers.                                                       |
| **Difficulty:**    | Difficult.                                                                           |
| **Elevation gain:**| 3,300 feet.                                                                          |
| **Maps:**          | Trails Illustrated (Tower/Canyon); Opal Creek, Amethyst Mountain, and Lamar Canyon USGS quads. |
| **Starting point:**| Specimen Ridge Trailhead (2K4).                                                      |

**Finding the trailhead:** Drive 2.5 miles east of Tower Junction and park in a small parking area on the north side of the road.

**Key points:**
| | | |
|---|---|---|
| 1.2 | (1.9) | Junction with trail to picnic area. |
| 3.0 | (4.8) | Junction with Agate Creek Trail. |
| 11.5 | (18.5) | Summit of Amethyst Mountain. |
| 17.0 | (27.3) | Lamar River Ford. |
| 17.4 | (27.3) | Junction with Lamar River Trail. |
| 18.8 | (30.2) | Lamar River Trailhead. |

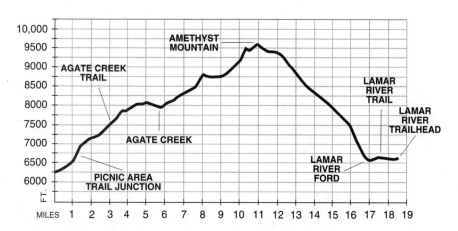

**The hike:** The scenery on Specimen Ridge rivals anything in the park, and most hikers would say it's worth the long, gradual climb to get on the ridge. You gain a whopping 3,300 feet in elevation, but it's spread out over 11 miles so it doesn't seem punishing.

Nonetheless, this hike is not for the beginner. Conditioning is critical, and it helps to have route-finding skills because the trail can be hard to find in places. Also, you can run short of water. In July, you'll find snow and snowmelt rivulets, but in August and September, the ridge can be dry. So be sure to carry ample water with you from the trailhead.

# SPECIMEN RIDGE • AGATE CREEK

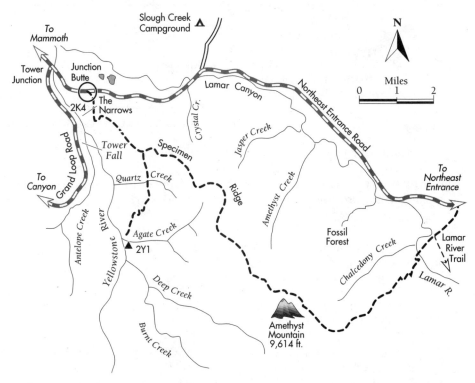

*Route finding skills are required on the open terrain of Specimen Ridge.*

The trail starts out in the sagebrush and grass meadows, and stays there until the junction with the Agate Creek Trail, where you go left (east). From here, the trail goes in and out of scattered stands of timber until you break out on the top of the ridge.

The NPS has marked the trail with posts with orange markers, but in many cases, bison and weather flatten the posts. Therefore, it can be a route-finding experience just to stay on the trail.

The vistas are fantastic—the Beartooths and Absarokas to the north, Mount Washburn and the Grand Canyon of the Yellowstone to the south. Wild-flower fans will be in heaven with the entire ridge a virtual carpet of color as you gradually climb toward Amethyst Mountain.

When you reach the grassy summit of Amethyst Mountain, the trail starts a sharp descent to the northeast. You'll be glad you aren't coming up this hill which would be a Category H climb. You switchback down to the Lamar River ford which can be waist-deep in July. Check with a ranger on the condition of this ford before hitting the trail. During high water, this ford can be dangerous—and you don't want to hike 17 miles and then have to turn back!

From the ford, hike through the openness of the Lamar Valley to the junction with the Lamar River Trail. Go left (northeast) here, and hike the flat 1.4 miles to the Lamar River Trailhead.

**Options:** You can take this trip in reverse, but the climb to the summit of Amethyst Mountain is murderous. You could also start this hike at the Yellowstone River Picnic Area which would lengthen the hike about 1 mile, but would add some great scenery over the first 2 miles.

---

# 65  *AGATE CREEK*

| | | |
|---|---|---|
| **Type of hike:** | Out-and-back. | See Map on Page 182 |
| **Type of trip:** | Long day hike or overnighter. | |
| **Total distance:** | 15 miles or 24.1 kilometers (round-trip). | |
| **Difficulty:** | Difficult. | |
| **Elevation gain:** | 1,100 feet. | |
| **Maps:** | Trails Illustrated (Tower/Canyon); Tower Junction, Lamar Canyon, and Amethyst Mountain USGS quads. | |
| **Starting point:** | Specimen Ridge Trailhead (2K4). | |

**Finding the trailhead:** Drive 2.4 miles east of Tower Junction and park on the north side of the road. The trail starts on the south side of the road across from the parking area.

**Key points:**

| | | |
|---|---|---|
| 1.2 | (1.9) | Junction with trail to Yellowstone River Picnic Area. |
| 3.0 | (4.8) | Junction with Specimen Ridge Trail. |
| 7.5 | (12.0) | Yellowstone River and 2Y1 (2★). |

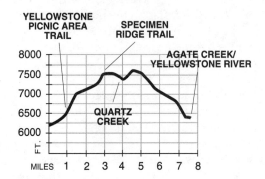

**The hike:** The trail starts out across the flat, lower section of Specimen Ridge, but then starts a gradual climb up to the top of a small hill, where you find the junction with the trail coming in from the Yellowstone River Picnic Area. Go left (southeast) at this junction and start a more serious climb. About a quarter mile past this junction, you can look down into Bannock Ford. This is a historic crossing on the Great Bannock Trail possibly used by John Colter during his famous trip to what would later become Yellostone National Park.

From here, the trail climbs for about a half mile then levels off on the easternmost section of Specimen Ridge and stays there until you get to the Agate Creek Trail junction, where you turn right (south). From here, the trail goes over a few small hills and then drops down into Quartz Creek and over another ridge before dropping abruptly into Agate Creek. You get a spectacular view of the Yellowstone River from the ridge above Agate Creek.

The trail goes all the way to the river and ends in a beautiful, shady spot where Agate Creek disappears into the big river. The trail goes through open country most of the way and is in great shape over the entire distance. Water is scarce, so carry an extra bottle.

**Options:** You could start this hike at the Yellowstone River Picnic Area, which would add 0.8 mile each way (1.6 miles total), but would be a more scenic route over the first 2 miles of trail.

|  |  |
|---|---|
| **Type of hike:** | Loop. |
| **Type of trip:** | Backpacking trip. |
| **Total distance:** | 20 miles or 32.2 kilometers. |
| **Difficulty:** | Difficult. |
| **Elevation gain:** | 1,218 feet. |
| **Maps:** | Trails Illustrated (Mammoth Hot Springs); |
|  | Tower Junction and Specimen Creek USGS quads. |
| **Starting point:** | Hellroaring Trailhead (2K8). |

> **See Map on Page 153**

**Finding the trailhead:** Drive 14.5 miles east from Mammoth or 3.5 miles west from Tower and pull into the Hellroaring Trailhead. The actual trailhead is about a half mile down an unpaved service road.

## Key points:

|  |  |  |
|---|---|---|
| 0.8 | (1.3) | Junction with trail to Tower. |
| 1.0 | (1.6) | Suspension bridge over Yellowstone. |
| 1.6 | (2.6) | Junction with trails to Coyote Creek and Buffalo Plateau. |
| 2.1 | (3.3) | Junction with trail to Buffalo Plateau Trail. |
| 6.0 | (9.6) | 2C1 (4★). |
| 6.4 | (10.3) | 2C2 (4★). |
| 6.7 | (10.7) | Park boundary. |
| 7.2 | (11.5) | USFS Poacher Trail No. 98. |
| 9.5 | (15.3) | USFS Coyote Creek Trail No. 97. |
| 9.8 | (15.7) | Hellroaring Bridge. |
| 10.2 | (16.4) | Hellroaring Guard Station and Horse Creek Bridge. |
| 10.4 | (16.7) | Junction with USFS trail to Jardine. |
| 13.0 | (20.9) | Park Boundary. |
| 15.8 | (25.4) | 8H9 (3★). |
| 16.3 | (17.9) | Junction with trail to 8H8 (4★), trail down west side to creek and to 8H5 (4★), 8H3 (5★), and 8H1 (5★), a footbridge, and the trail down the east side of Hellroaring Creek. |
| 17.8 | (28.6) | 8H6 (4★). |
| 18.1 | (29.1) | Junction with Yellowstone River Trail and spur trail to 8H4(4★) and 8H2 (5★). |
| 18.4 | (29.6) | Junction with trail to Coyote Creek and Buffalo Plateau. |
| 19.0 | (30.6) | Suspension Bridge over Yellowstone. |
| 19.2 | (30.9) | Junction with trail to Tower. |
| 20.0 | (32.2) | Hellroaring Trailhead. |

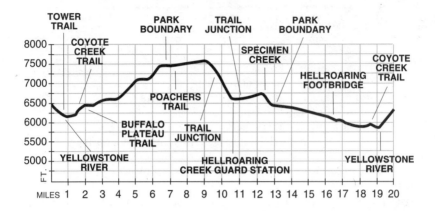

**Recommended itinerary:** To leave time for fishing and exploring, try a three-day trip staying the first night at 2C1 or 2C2 and the second night at one of the nine excellent campsites along Hellroaring Creek. This loop trip could be shortened to a two-day powerhike by staying overnight outside the park or could be a long day trek for fit hikers who like to travel light.

**The hike:** This hike differs from every other trip in this book because it combines trails in the park with those outside of the park in the Gallatin National Forest managed by the U.S. Forest Service (USFS). This makes a nice loop out of two trips (Coyote and Hellroaring creeks) that would normally

*Big dry meadows along Coyote Creek.*

186

be out and back. The trail loops around a grassy butte called Bull Mountain, easily viewed from the Coyote Creek Trail.

This is a low-altitude, dry section of the park where you can hike in June on most years without walking through snowbanks. But go before September, when hundreds of big game hunters mob the area, most using horses and some staying at large outfitter camps just north of the park. In summer months, however, the area is amazingly devoid of people.

The trail starts out with a steep drop through mostly open hillside to the suspension bridge over the Yellowstone River. From here, go another 0.6 mile to the junction with the Coyote Creek and Buffalo Plateau trails.

Some maps for this area have not been updated. The outdated maps show the Coyote Creek Trail coming up from Hellroaring Creek instead of branching out from the Buffalo Plateau Trail 0.5 mile after taking a right (north) at this junction.

From the Yellowstone River to the park boundary, the trail goes through open, dry terrain. Start early in the day because there's little shade to comfort you on a hot summer afternoon. About a half mile after leaving the Yellowstone River Trail, the Buffalo Plateau Trail goes off to the right. You go left (north) on the Coyote Creek Trail. In another half mile or so, you might see the abandoned trail coming up from Hellroaring Creek (abandoned but still visible on the ground and shown on many maps).

Before and after the park boundary, the trail goes into a partially burned forest and stays there for about 1 mile. I couldn't help noticing that during this forested leg of the trip, the trail seemed to serve as a fireline, with the trees on the west side of the trail green and unburnt, while those on the east side appeared to be victims of the 1988 fires.

After you go left (north) at the junction with the Poacher Trail (about a half mile north of the park), the trail breaks out on the east edge of a huge, marshy meadow. This is a very easy place to get on the wrong trail. Note on the map that the trail crosses this meadow and goes up the west side even though an excellent trail (not on most maps) continues up the east side of the meadow, tempting you to follow it. If you do, you won't be completely lost, but you'll add about 1 mile to your trip. Both trails intersect with the USFS Coyote Creek Trail No. 97 about a half mile apart. Whichever trail you follow, turn left (west) when you reach the Coyote Creek Trail.

This section of the trip goes through a more lush forest than the lower stretches of Coyote and Hellroaring creeks. Just before crossing Hellroaring Creek, the trail drops steeply for about a half mile, making you happy you didn't do the trip in reverse. Hellroaring is a huge stream even this far from its eventual merger with the Yellowstone, and the USFS has constructed a great bridge to handle the heavy horse traffic this area gets during the hunting season.

After the bridge, you pass through a large meadow and by the Hellroaring Guard Station. If you're staying overnight outside of the park, pick from the many nice campsites in this area. Four USFS trails take off to the north and west from this area, but you keep turning left at all the junctions and follow

Hellroaring Creek back to the park. After the guard station, the trail stays out of sight of the creek up on the west hillside and passes through mature, unburned lodgepole—or at least it was unburned when we came through in August, 1996.

After the park boundary, until just after 2H9, the trail stays away from the creek in timber. However, when we hiked this trail, we came through a live forest fire burning on both sides of the trail, including 2H9. Later, this fire burned north up to Hellroaring Guard Station. Since this lightning-caused fire was a natural part of the Yellowstone ecosystem (just like rain and wind), the NPS rightfully let it burn.

After breaking out into a series of large meadows, you reach the junction with the stock bridge over Hellroaring Creek. Unless you want to ford Hellroaring Creek, take a left (east) here. On the other side of the bridge, a spur trail to 2H8 goes off to the left and you go right (south), following the stream for 1.5 miles back to the Yellowstone River Trail, where you go left (east) and retrace your steps back to the trailhead.

The trail is in excellent shape the entire way, but the many trail junctions (some not on maps) can be confusing, especialy when you're outside of the park.

**Options:** You can do this loop in reverse, but it might be slightly more difficult because of the hill east of the Hellroaring Guard Station. You can also skip the loop option and go out and back into either Coyote or Hellroaring creeks.

# 67  *DUNRAVEN PASS TO CANYON*

| | |
|---|---|
| **Type of hike:** | Shuttle. |
| **Type of trip:** | Day hike or overnighter. |
| **Total distance:** | 11.3 miles or 17.8 kilometers. |
| **Difficulty:** | Difficult. |
| **Elevation gain:** | 1,400 feet. |
| **Maps:** | Trails Illustrated (Tower/Canyon); Mount Washburn and Canyon Village USGS quads. |
| **Starting point:** | Dunraven Pass (4K9). |

See Map on Page 156

**Finding the trailhead:** Drive 4.7 miles north of Canyon Junction or 13.3 miles south of Tower Junction and park at the Dunraven Pass parking area on the east side of the road.

## Key points:

| | | |
|---|---|---|
| 3.0 | (4.8) | Junction with Chittenden Road. |
| 5.7 | (9.1) | 4E1 (2★). |
| 8.0 | (12.8) | Washburn Hot Springs. |
| 8.8 | (14.1) | Junction with Sevenmile Hole Trail. |
| 10.3 | (16.5) | View of Silver Cord Cascade. |
| 11.3 | (17.8) | Glacier Boulder Trailhead. |

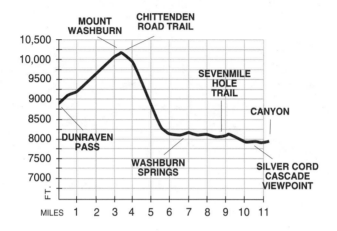

*The trail to Canyon leaving the Chittenden Road.*

*Washburn Hot Springs.*

**The hike:** The trail is actually an old road abandoned many years ago by the NPS. This might seem sort of hard to believe while hiking up this Category 2 hill, but stagecoaches and Model T Fords used to make the trip on the road built in 1905. In fact, the Model T drivers had to back up the hill because the forward gears weren't low enough to make the grade.

The old roadbed makes for easy uphill walking as you switchback up to the ridge before the summit. From the ridge, you get a great view of the Yellowstone River Valley. The trail stays on the ridge for about a half mile before reaching the Chittenden Road, which is another route to the top of Mount Washburn. Although maps show this road as a trail, official vehicles use it to reach the Mount Washburn Lookout. The road is also open to mountain bikers.

At this junction, you'll see the trail to Canyon going off to the east, but before you start hiking it, take the half mile side trip to the lookout. Along the way, you'll probably see, at close range, the bighorn sheep herd that hangs out on Mount Washburn during the summer. Please don't try to approach or feed the sheep. This disrupts natural patterns and can lead to a shorter life for the sheep.

From the lookout, you can get a view of, it seems, the entire park. There is also an interpretive display of how Mount Washburn was formed, a 20-power telescope, bathrooms, and even a pay phone.

When you leave the lookout and start down the trail to Canyon, you find yourself in the midst of a wildflower garden. After hiking the entire park, we found no place with as rich an abundance of wildflowers as Mount Washburn.

The trail stays high and scenic for about 1.5 miles from the summit. Then, it drops very steeply into the timbered east slope of Mount Washburn. You'll be so happy that you didn't hike this shuttle trip in reverse because this is a Category H climb on a trail apparently built before the advent of switchbacks. Some sections are too steep to walk down comfortably.

You might still see the old sign pointing to the Howard Eaton Trail to Tower Falls. This trail was abandoned long ago to protect key grizzly habitat, and is now officially closed to all travel.

Shortly after this abandoned trail junction, you see 4E1 off to your left and then cross a stream—sorry, no footbridge even though the map indicated there is one. About 1.5 miles later, you go through Washburn Hot Springs, an interesting thermal area with several boiling pools and caldrons.

Then, you reach the Sevenmile Hole Trail. Take a right (west) and go another 2.5 miles to the Glacier Boulder Trailhead. About 1 mile before the trailhead, you're treated to a stunning view of the Silver Cord Cascade plummeting into the Grand Canyon of the Yellowstone.

The trail down from Mount Washburn gets faint in a few places, but it's fairly easy to follow. The Sevenmile Hole Trail is heavily used and well-defined.

**Options:** You can also start this hike at the Chittenden Road Trailhead (2K6) If you want to see the view from Mount Washburn but don't want a long hike, you can hike from Dunraven Pass to Chittenden Road or out and back on either trail. You can make this an overnighter by staying at 4E1 or one of the three campsites at Sevenmile Hole.

**Side trips:** You definitely want to take the short side trip to the lookout.

---

# 68 WAPITI LAKE

| | |
|---|---|
| **Type of hike:** | Out-and-back. |
| **Type of trip:** | Base camp. |
| **Total distance:** | 32 miles or 15.5 kilometers (round-trip). |
| **Difficulty:** | Difficult. |
| **Elevation gain:** | 1,200 feet. |
| **Maps:** | Trails Illustrated (Tower/Canyon); Canyon Village and White Lake USGS quads. |
| **Starting point:** | Wapiti Lake Trailhead (4K7). |

# WAPITI LAKE • WRANGLER LAKE

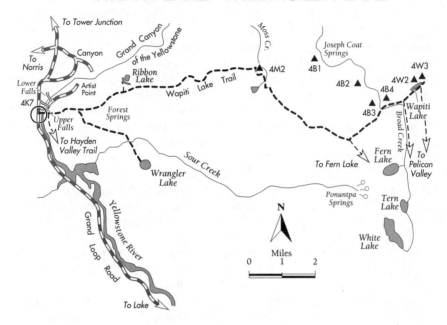

**Finding the trailhead:** From Canyon, drive south for 2.4 miles and turn left (east) at the Artist Point Junction, cross the Yellowstone just above Upper Falls on the Chittenden Bridge, and in 0.2 mile, turn right (east) into the Wapiti Lake Trailhead, a large, paved parking lot with toilet facilities and picnic tables.

## Key points:

| | | |
|---|---|---|
| 0.5 | (0.8) | Junction with Sour Creek Trail. |
| 0.7 | (1.1) | Junction with Wrangler Lake Trail. |
| 3.0 | (4.8) | Junction with Ribbon Lake Trail. |
| 7.5 | (12.0) | 4M2. |
| 13.0 | (20.9) | Junction with Fern Lake Trail. |
| 15.0 | (24.1) | Broad Creek and off-trail route to 4B3 (3★), 4B2 (2★), and 4B1 (2★). |
| 15.5 | (24.9) | Junction with Broad Creek Trail to 5B2 and 5B1. |
| 16.0 | (51.5) | Wapiti Lake and 4W2 (4★) and 4W3 (3★). |

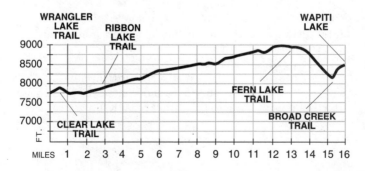

**Recommended itinerary:** Wapiti Lake is a great destination, but getting there is a long haul on a less-than-ideal trail, so make it a base camp and stay a day or two before heading back. I recommend a five- or six-day trip, taking two days to get to Wapiti Lake, staying at least two nights to allow time for exploring, and then two days for the return trip, staying at 4M2 both on the way in and the way out.

**The hike:** It's a long, hot hike to Wapiti Lake, and getting there isn't really that nice of a hike. However, the Wapiti Lake/Broad Creek/Fern Lake area is a wild, remote place with lots of thermal areas, lakes, streams, and scenery to make getting there worth the extra effort.

The first section of this trail goes through the north edge of the open Hayden Valley where you'll probably see wildlife. Also, keep your map out, as you go by three junctions in the first mile before leaving the valley and starting to climb through thick lodgepole. The first (and last) segment of this hike has several trail junctions and some mileages listed on signs (and in maps and guidebooks) don't match up, but don't worry about the miles because it really doesn't matter.

At the 3-mile mark, go right (east) at the junction with the trail to Ribbon Lake. From here, the trail keeps gradually climbing through unburned forest for another 10 miles to the junction with the Fern Lake Trail where you go left (east). This is the highest point of the trip, and the trail drops abruptly (which can be difficult if the trail hasn't been cleared) into open and marshy Broad Creek where several bazillion mosquitoes greet you (unless you waited until August to do this hike).

After going past the Broad Creek junction, where you go left (east), climb about 300 feet through burned timber to shallow, 11-acre Wapiti Lake. This is a charming mountain lake with marshy edges and a good waterfowl population. The campsites are a little too close together at the far end of the lake. Spend a day or so exploring the Broad Creek/Fern Lake area before retracing your steps back to Canyon.

The trail is in good shape and definable the entire way to Broad Creek, but if you go early in the year, you might have to climb over numerous downed trees. In the Broad Creek area, the trail gets boggy and indistinct in a few spots, especially around 4B3 and 4B4.

**Options:** Instead of taking the last pitch up to Wapiti Lake, you could camp at one of the two campsites near where you cross Broad Creek. You can also make a long shuttle hike by leaving a vehicle or arranging to be picked up at the Pelican Valley Trailhead and hiking south from Wapiti Lake either on the Pelican Creek or Astringent Creek trails.

**Side trips:** From Wapiti Lake, you can make a nice loop around to see Fern Lake and add a short foray to the south to explore Tern Lake and White Lake. The trail from Fern Lake through Ponuntpa Springs and north to the

Wapiti Lake Trail gets faint, boggy, and hard to follow in several spots. You can also hike the off-trail route up Broad Creek. And just south of Wapiti Lake you might be able to find an off-trail route over to Wapiti Hot Springs, where geologists have determined that the magma is only 1 kilometer below the surface.

# 69   MIST CREEK PASS

| | |
|---|---|
| **Type of hike:** | Shuttle. |
| **Type of trip:** | Long backpacking trip. |
| **Total distance:** | 34.2 miles or 55 kilometers. |
| **Difficulty:** | Difficult. |
| **Elevation gain:** | 800 feet. |
| **Maps:** | Trails Illustrated (Tower/Canyon); Lake Butte, Mount Chittenden, Pelican Cone, Little Saddle Mountain, Wahb Springs, and Opal Creek USGS quads. |
| **Starting point:** | Pelican Valley Trailhead (5K3). |

**Finding the trailhead:** Drive 3.5 miles east of the Fishing Bridge Junction, turn north on a gravel road, and follow it about a half mile until it ends at the trailhead.

## Key points:
| | | |
|---|---|---|
| 0.5 | (0.8) | Abandoned road and trail to Turbid Lake. |
| 3.4 | (5.4) | Junction with Astringent Creek Trail and Pelican Creek Bridge. |
| 7.2 | (11.6) | Pelican Springs Cabin and junction with Pelican Cone Trail. |
| 9.0 | (14.5) | Mist Creek Pass. |
| 11.5 | (18.5) | 3T3 (5★). |
| 12.5 | (20.1) | 3T2 (5★). |
| 18.1 | (29.1) | 3T1 (4★) and ford Lamar River. |
| 18.2 | (29.3) | Junction with Lamar River Trail. |
| 19.5 | (31.7) | 3U3 (3★). |
| 20.5 | (33.1) | 3U2 (4★). |
| 21.5 | (34.7) | 3U1 (2★). |
| 23.3 | (37.5) | 3L8 (4★). |
| 24.5 | (39.1) | 3L7 (4★). |
| 25.4 | (40.8) | Ford Miller Creek and junction with Miller Creek Trail. |
| 28.4 | (45.7) | 3L4 (4★). |
| 29.2 | (47.0) | 3L3 (3★). |
| 30.5 | (49.1) | 3L2 (4★). |
| 30.6 | (49.2) | Ford Cache Creek. |
| 30.7 | (49.4) | 3L1(4★). |
| 31.1 | (50.0) | Junction with Cache Creek Trail. |
| 32.8 | (52.8) | Junction with Specimen Ridge Trail. |
| 34.2 | (55.1) | Lamar River Trailhead. |

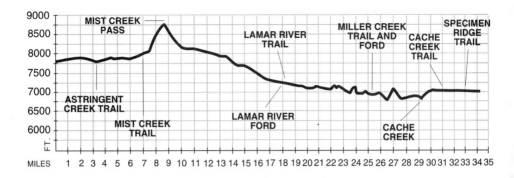

MILES  1 2 3 4 5 6 7 8 9 10 11 12 13 14 15 16 17 18 19 20 21 22 23 24 25 26 27 28 29 30 31 32 33 34 35

**Recommended itinerary:** Four-day trip staying at 3T3 or 3T2 the first night, 3U3, 3U2, or 3U1 the second night, and 3L4 or 3L3 the third night.

**The hike:** The Pelican Valley is a fantastic slice of wild nature, and that's why the grizzly bear likes it, too. The area is a favorite haunt of the big bear, and the NPS has imposed special regulations to reduce the impact of human use on grizzly behavior. This is great for the bear, but it limits the options for backpackers.

Regulations prevent any overnight camping in the area. The area remains closed until July 15, and after that, you can only be in Pelican Valley between 9 a.m. and 7 p.m. with parties of four or more hikers recommended.

*The Pelican Bridge.*

# MIST CREEK PASS

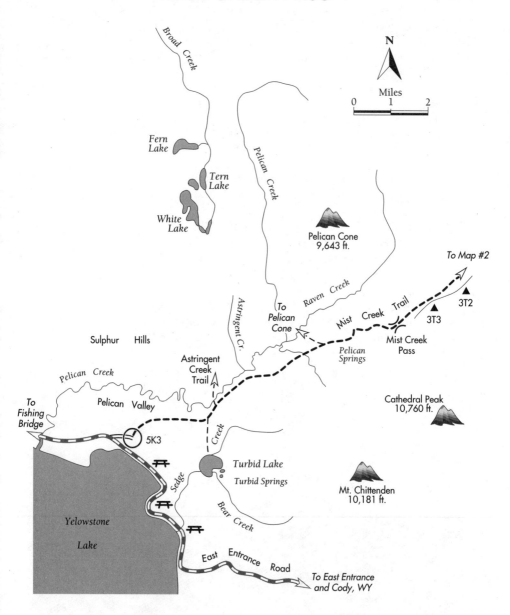

Broad Creek

Fern Lake

Tern Lake

White Lake

Pelican Creek

N

Miles
0      1      2

Pelican Cone
9,643 ft.

To Map #2

Raven Creek

Mist Creek Trail

3T2

3T3

To
Pelican
Cone

Mist Creek
Pass

Astringent Cr.

Pelican
Springs

Sulphur   Hills

Astringent
Creek
Trail

Pelican   Creek

Pelican   Valley

Cathedral Peak
10,760 ft.

To
Fishing
Bridge

5K3

Creek

Turbid Lake

Turbid Springs

Sedge

Mt. Chittenden
10,181 ft.

Yelowstone

Lake

Bear Creek

East   Entrance   Road

To East Entrance
and Cody, WY

# MIST CREEK PASS • LAMAR RIVER

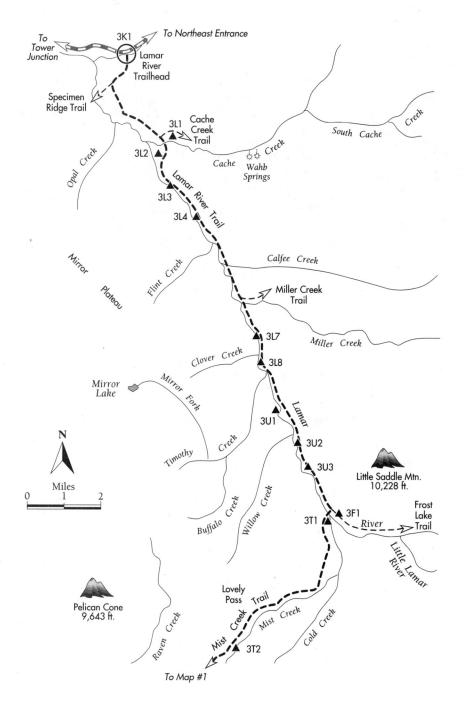

To Tower Junction

3K1
Lamar River Trailhead

To Northeast Entrance

Specimen Ridge Trail

Opal Creek

3L1
Cache Creek Trail

3L2

Cache
Wahb Springs

Creek

South Cache
Creek

3L3
Lamar River Trail

3L4

Mirror Plateau

Flint Creek

Calfee Creek

Miller Creek Trail

Miller Creek

3L7

Clover Creek

3L8

Mirror Lake

Mirror Fork

Timothy Creek

Lamar

3U1

3U2

3U3

Little Saddle Mtn.
10,228 ft.

N

Miles
0    1    2

Buffalo Creek

Willow Creek

3T1

3F1

River

Frost Lake Trail

Little Lamar River

Pelican Cone
9,643 ft.

Lovely Pass

Mist Creek Trail

Mist Creek

Cold Creek

Raven Creek

3T2

To Map #1

*Mist Creek Meadows.*

This means a minimum of 11.5 miles the first day, and that includes a Category 3 climb over Mist Creek Pass.

The first 7.2 miles to the patrol cabin is a well-defined, flat trail through the broad, open Pelican Valley. Watch for elk and bison grazing the high-altitude grassland. There's no shade in the valley, so hope for an overcast day. Because of the time restrictions, you have no choice but to hike through the shadeless valley in mid-day.

At the 3.4-mile mark, the Astringent Creek Trail heads north over the Pelican Bridge (which looks ready to collapse). Go right (east) at this junction.

The Pelican Cone junction is right at the patrol cabin. You go right (east) again. The trail is confusing right at the cabin. It splits to go around the cabin, and a few social trails go here and there. Follow the orange markers to be sure you're on the correct route.

After the cabin, the trail enters the timber and stays in intermittently burned forest over the pass and down into the headwaters of Mist Creek where you break out into a huge, wet meadow. 3T3 is off to your right, and 3T2 is at the other end of the meadow, 1 mile down the trail.

The trail disappears for 100 yards or so right across from 3T3, but after this little marshy area, the trail reappears and remains easy to follow the rest of the way. You get a nice view of Lovely Pass from the meadows as well as Little Saddle Mountain, Saddle Mountain, and Hague Peak on the eastern horizon.

After the meadows, the trail goes through heavily burned forest, which blocks out most of the scenery all the way to the Lamar River. Since you can't get into Pelican Valley until mid-July because of bear regulations, you shouldn't have any trouble crossing the Lamar.

Immediately after the ford, you see the Lamar River Trail[1]. Go left (north) here and start a 16-mile gradual downhill hike (okay, there are a few little hills as the trip goes up and down gullies left by feeder streams) all the way to the trailhead. The 1988 fires scorched most of the Lamar Valley, but you can now see nature coming back in full force. Somehow, the NPS always finds a good spot in a stand of live trees for the numerous campsites along the way. You also ford both Miller Creek and Cache Creek, but they should only be knee-deep after July 15. Go left at both the Miller Creek and Cache Creek junctions.

Try to plan out your trip so you have some extra time on the last day for a side trip up to Wahb Springs and Death Gulch, 2 miles up the Cache Creek Trail. For most of the trip, the trail stays in the fairly narrow Lamar Valley, but over the last 3 miles, it goes through the sagebrush flats and angles away from the river.

**Options:** Hiking this trip in reverse might be just as easy. You can avoid the first killer day with your heaviest pack, but you have more uphill miles getting up Mist Creek Pass.

**Side trips:** Pelican Cone is a great side trip, but because of the limited time regulations for Pelican Valley, it might as well be on the moon for most backpackers. If you're one of the super-fit, you can hang your pack (10 feet off the ground and 4 feet from any object) and dash up to the lookout and back to the cabin with enough daylight to get over to 3T3 or 3T2 before nightfall. You get a great view of the Pelican Valley from the lookout.

# 70  HAYDEN VALLEY

| | |
|---|---|
| **Type of hike:** | Shuttle. |
| **Type of trip:** | Long day hike. |
| **Total distance:** | 14 miles or 22.5 kilometers. |
| **Difficulty:** | Difficult. |
| **Elevation gain:** | Minimal. |
| **Maps:** | Trails Illustrated (Tower/Canyon); Yellowstone Lake, Lake Butte, and Canyon Village USGS quads. |
| **Starting point:** | Fishing Bridge Trailhead (5K2). |

---

[1]Plan on seeing lots of horses on the Lamar River Trail. We counted 47 animals in the last 6 miles of trail, as well as nine horse trailers at the trailhead.

**Finding the trailhead:** You might be able to knock a half mile off your hike by driving to the end of the road behind the Fishing Bridge store, but to make life easier, park on the north side of the road just over Fishing Bridge and start hiking there.

## Key points:

| | | |
|---|---|---|
| 2.0 | (4.8) | Le Hardys Rapids. |
| 11.0 | (17.7) | Ford Sour Creek. |
| 12.0 | (19.3) | Junction with trail to Wrangler Lake. |
| 12.5 | (20.1) | Junction with Wapiti Lake Trail. |
| 12.8 | (20.6) | Junction with cutoff trail to Clear Lake. |
| 14.0 | (22.5) | Wapiti Lake Trailhead. |

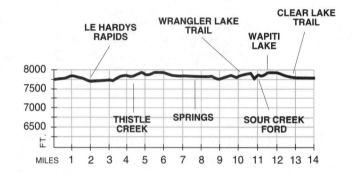

*Le Hardys Rapids from the Hayden Valley Trail.*

# HAYDEN VALLEY

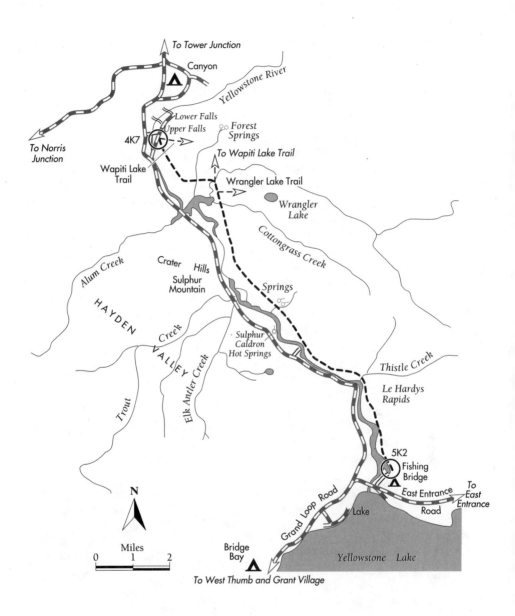

To Tower Junction

Canyon

Yellowstone River

Lower Falls
Upper Falls

Forest Springs

4K7

To Wapiti Lake Trail

Wapiti Lake Trail

Wrangler Lake Trail

Wrangler Lake

Cottongrass Creek

Alum Creek

Crater Hills

Sulphur Mountain

Springs

To Norris Junction

H A Y D E N   V A L L E Y   Creek

Elk Antler Creek

Sulphur Caldron Hot Springs

Thistle Creek

Le Hardys Rapids

Trout

5K2

Fishing Bridge

East Entrance

To East Entrance

Road

N

Miles
0    1    2

Grand Loop Road

Lake

Bridge Bay

Yellowstone Lake

To West Thumb and Grant Village

**The hike:** Although this trail loses elevation overall, it's not that easy. You have to climb over several ridges leading down into the Yellowstone which can make this a difficult hike, especially on a hot day. However, you would be wise to avoid the afternoon heat by starting at dawn. This also maximizes wildlife watching opportunities. The Hayden Valley is a mecca of wildlife watching, and an early start helps you see as many wild animals as possible.

Along with the other wildlife comes the likelihood of seeing a grizzly bear on this trail. Because of the high population of bears in the area, the NPS prohibits off-trail travel along this trail and recommends parties of four or more hikers.

The trail stays in the unburned, open forest for the first 6 miles. About a half mile after leaving the road, the trails splits. Take the right fork instead of the left fork, a social trail heavily used by anglers going down to sample the oversized cutthroats of the Yellowstone River.

At the 3-mile mark, you climb up to a nice viewpoint over the Le Hardys Rapids. This is an unfenced overlook, so be careful. There is no trail down to the rapids.

The first half of this trail is well-traveled by bison, so be sure to promptly yield if you see bison coming down the trail.

After the rapids, the trail continues to be in great shape and easy to follow through mature forest intermingled with large meadows. Finally, you break out of the trees into the openness of the Hayden Valley. Here, the trail is not so easy to follow as it fades away here and there, but you can stay on the trail with some vigilance. About 1 mile after the trail opens up, watch for a big spring coming in from the east, a great water source and place for lunch.

*Hiking the wildlife-rich Hayden Valley.*

Sour Creek can be a serious ford in June and July—at least waist deep with a deceptively strong current. After fording the creek, watch for the Wrangler Lake Trail going off to the right (east). You go left (north), and go another half mile to the Wapiti Lake Trail, where you go left (west) again and stay on this trail to the trailhead.

**Options:** This trail can be hiked in reverse, but you would face a small elevation gain instead of hiking downhill.

**Side trips:** If you had extra time, you could take the short side trip to Wrangler Lake.

# 71  *MARY MOUNTAIN TRAIL*

| | |
|---|---|
| **Type of hike:** | Shuttle. |
| **Type of trip:** | Long day hike. |
| **Total distance:** | 20 miles or 32 kilometers. |
| **Difficulty:** | Difficult. |
| **Elevation gain:** | 400 feet. |
| **Maps:** | Trails Illustrated (Mammoth Hot Springs or Old Faithful); and Canyon Village, Crystal Falls, and Lower Geyser Basin USGS quads. |
| **Starting point:** | Alum Creek Trailhead at the north end of Hayden Valley. |

**Finding the trailhead:** Drive 4.4 miles south from Canyon or 11.6 miles north from Fishing Bridge Junction and park in a pullout on the east side of the road. The trail starts directly across the road from the parking area. Leave your vehicle at the Mary Mountain Trailhead (OK7), which is 6.6 miles south of the Madison Junction or 9.4 miles north of Old Faithful. The trailhead does not show on any of the four Trails Illustrated maps covering the park, but it does show on the Trails Illustrated map for the entire park and on the USGS Canyon Village quad.

**Key points:**
| | | |
|---|---|---|
| 4.0 | (6.4) | Violet Creek. |
| 6.0 | (9.6) | Abandoned trail to Trout Creek. |
| 9.0 | (14.5) | Highland Hot Springs. |
| 10.0 | (16.1) | Mary Lake. |
| 10.2 | (16.4) | Abandoned Trail from Cygnet Lakes. |
| 14.0 | (22.5) | Cowan Creek. |
| 20.0 | (32.2) | Old Faithful Road. |

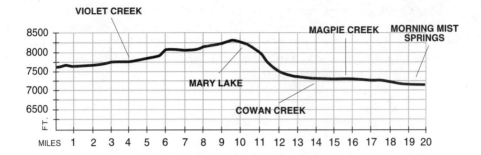

**The hike:** The trail starts right at the north edge of Hayden Valley and follows Alum Creek (which has several interesting thermal features along its course) along the forest edge on the northernmost reaches of the wildlife-rich valley. The trail stays in the open all the way. The first few miles of the trail are not well-defined, but you can follow orange markers to stay on course. For some reason, this trail stays marshy all summer, so be prepared for wet feet.

Also, bison use this area extensively, so the bison trails are often better than the official trail. Watch for orange markers, and if you don't see them, you're probably off the main trail.

This is prime grizzly habitat, which is why you can't stay overnight in this area. It's also why you should be especially careful not to disturb or get too close to any bear you see—both for your safety and the bear's welfare.

After hiking through the open Hayden Valley along Alum Creek for about 7 miles, the trail heads into unburned timber on the Central Plateau for about 3 miles until you reach Mary Lake. At about the 6-mile mark, you may see a sign showing a trail going south down Trout Creek to the Canyon Road. This trail has been abandoned by the NPS because of heavy bear use in the area. Just before Mary Lake, you pass through several thermal areas.

Mary Lake is a charming, forest-lined lake, but has no fish. Again, because of heavy bear use, the NPS prohibits camping at the 20-acre lake. The trail goes around the north shore of the lake. You might see a sign showing a trail going north to Cygnet Lakes, but this trail has also been abandoned by the NPS.

After the lake, the trail descends rather suddenly for about 1 mile and keeps going downhill for another 2 to 3 miles until you reach the headwaters of Nez Perce Creek. You'll see that this is still a "bison freeway," used heavily by bison going back and forth between the Hayden Valley to the Old Faithful area. Be sure to yield if you see any bison on the trail in this forest-lined corridor.

At about the 14-mile mark at the bottom of a hill, the trail gets boggy. You might notice a historic sign in the middle of the marshy meadow. This marks the location of a confrontation between the Nez Perce and the U.S. Army. The sign says: "On this spot (August 26, 1877), the Nez Perce Chiefs held a council to decide the fate of the Cowan Party who had been captured that

# MARY MOUNTAIN TRAIL • ALUM CREEK
## • NEZ PERCE CREEK

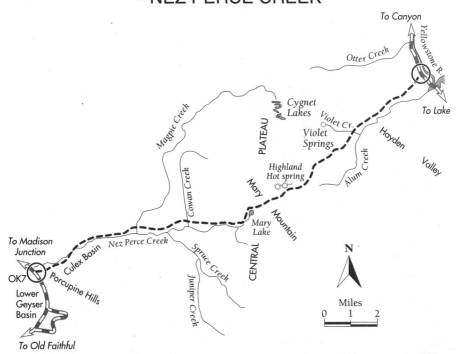

The "bison freeway" east of Mary Lake.

morning in the Lower Geyser Basin. The party was released but afterwards recaptured and taken back about a half mile east of the council ground and there attacked by the Indians. Cowan was left for dead. Carpenter and the two ladies were taken along as prisoners and the rest escaped."

From here to the Old Faithful Road, the trail follows beautiful Nez Perce Creek. At the upper end, the trail goes through meadows interspersed with a few stands of unburned timber, but the last 5 miles is totally open, similar to the Hayden Valley where you started the hike. You might see anglers throwing artificial flies in Nez Perce Creek which supports nice populations of brown and rainbow trout. You have to ford Nez Perce about 2 miles from the trailhead—sorry, no bridge.

**Options:** You can start hiking at Nez Perce Creek with only a minor increase in difficulty because of the hill just east of Mary Lake.

## BACKCOUNTRY CAMPSITES

These campsites serve backpacking trips in the northeast section of the park and are on the Tower/Canyon Trails Illustrated map. Stock-party-only sites are not covered.

Please keep in mind that the rating serves as a general guide only. We only visited these campsites once, and it might have been an especially good or especially bad day. For example, campsites clouded with bugs in July may be bug-free in September, and campsites without a view on a rainy day might have a good view on a clear day.

All campsites in Yellowstone allow campfires unless otherwise indicated. Likewise, all campsites are supposed to have bear poles, but just in case, be prepared to improvise.

As this book goes to print, the NPS is in the process of moving campsites previously located along the trail. Bears use the trails as travel corridors, which increases the chance of an encounter.

**Coyote Creek:** 2C1 (4★) is a private, hiker-only site right along Coyote Creek. Good water source and tent sites. Protected from the elements. Marginal view.

2C2 (4★) is similar to 2C1 with a slightly better view but less privacy (only about 50 yards off trail).

**Hellroaring Creek:** All nine campsites along Hellroaring Creek are excellent hiker-only sites. On the Trails Illustrated map it's difficult to see this, but the odd-numbered campsites are on the west side of the stream and the even-numbered on the east side. All of the sites are close to Hellroaring Creek, with the stream serving as a readily accessible water source. None of the campsites allow campfires, but these campsites (as well as others farther down the river) prove that you can have a five-star camping experience without a campfire.

2H1 (5★) is at the confluence of Hellroaring Creek and the Yellowstone and has all the elements of a great campsite.

2H2 (5★) is also right at the confluence and even has a beach for lounging on a hot day. Tent sites are somewhat limited, so you might be tempted to pitch your tent on the beach, which would be a bad idea if it rained up in the headwaters of Hellroaring Creek.

2H3 (4★) is about a quarter mile from the main trail and has a great view from the food area under a spreading spruce tree. Even though there is a trail going around the campsite, hikers going to 2H1 might pass through your camp.

2H4 (4★) is on your left as you approach Hellroaring Creek. In fact, the trail naturally goes downstream toward 2H4 and 2H2, so you might accidentally see this site when you're looking for the ford. It's a private site except for people going to 2H2 who come right through your camp.

2H5 (4★) is similar to 2H6, but it doesn't have quite as nice of a food area or view, and you have to labor down a very steep slope to get there.

2H6 (4★) is on your right about a half mile up Hellroaring Creek. It's private, and the food area and the view are slightly better than 2H5 which is just upstream on the other side of the creek.

2H7 (4★) is not quite as private as other campsites along Hellroaring Creek (about 100 yards off trail), but it is similar to the other sites in most respects. It lacks a well-defined food area.

2H8 (4★) is a private, hiker-only site about a half mile north of the Hellroaring footbridge on a good spur trail right at the confluence of Hellroaring and Coyote creeks. Good water source. No campfires allowed.

2H9 (3★) was closed when we hiked Hellroaring Creek because a lightning fire had burned right through the campsite. However, the NPS plans to keep it open. It's a hiker-only site about 50 feet off the trail on the west bank of Hellroaring Creek. Good water source and fair view, but a little too close to the trail.

**Pebble Creek:** 3P1 (4★) is a very private, hiker-only site at the bottom of a huge meadow along the creek about a quarter-mile from the trail. Easy access to water, good tent sites, and a good view.

3P2 (4★) and 3P3 (4★) are private, hiker-only sites used heavily by backpackers making a two-day trip out of Pebble Creek or coming over Bliss Pass. Both are on a forested bench on the south side of Pebble Creek about 200 yards from the trail. Both have fair views, good tent sites, and easy water access. 3P2 can accommodate a larger group than 3P3.

3P4 (3★) is a private, mixed site in the meadows of Upper Pebble Creek. It has a great view of this gorgeous valley and has lots of tent sites, but it's a bothersome distance to water. Used by horse outfitters.

3P5 (4★) is a private, hiker-only site on the north bank of Pebble Creek just after the ford at the upper end of the valley (coming in from the Warm Springs Trailhead). Well-suited for an easy, out-and-back overnighter from Warm Springs. Fair view, good tent sites, and easy access to water.

**Slough Creek:** All the campsites in Slough Creek are very popular, so get your reservation in early. Even though the NPS has placed an above-average number of campsites here, they still go months in advance. Only campsite 2S1 is mixed (private horse parties only; no commercial outfitters). The other four sites are hiker-only, but regulations prohibit large parties at any of them. 2S1 and 2S6 are probably the nicest, but it's unlikely you'll be disappointed with any of the sites.

2S1 (5★) is a private site right along Slough Creek about a half mile off the main trail on a defined spur trail. It's a short bushwhack and a ford of the creek to reach McBride Lake. Nice view, good water source, and lots of tent sites.

2S2 (3★) is a not-so-private site on Plateau Creek and about 1 mile from Slough Creek. It has a good water source, but limited tent sites and marginal view.

2S3 (4★) is a not-so-private site on an unnamed tributary of Slough Creek, which is about 1 mile away. Great view of entire valley, good water source and tent sites.

2S4 (2★) is a private site at the confluence of Elk Tongue Creek and Slough Creek. Limited view and tent sites, and marginal water source.

2S6 (5★) is a semi-private site on a bench above the trail with a great view of the Slough Creek valley. Good water source and tent sites.

**Agate Creek:** 2Y1 (2★), a hiker-only site, is closed until July 15. A quarter mile or so from the river but close to the creek. The banks of the creek are too steep to get water so you have to haul water from the river. Marginal view. Adequate tent sites. The trail goes right through the campsite.

**Cache Creek:** All three campsites are private, mixed sites along Cache Creek with good water sources and plenty of tent sites.

3C2 (3★) also has a good view of the valley, but it's farther south than indicated by some maps.

3C3 (3★) has a nice view of the Cache Creek valley.

3C4 (3★) is a lightly used site with a great view of the Thunderer and almost unused tent sites, but difficult to find (no sign when we were there).

**Lamar River:** All campsites along the Lamar River Trail allow campfires unless special regulations are in effect. Some campsites have been moved in recent years, and the high water of 1996 affected some sites, so check with the ranger before heading out.

3L1 (4★) is a private, hiker-only campsite on the north side of Cache Creek about a quarter mile east of the main trail on a marked route. Fair view, adequate tent sites, good water source. Campfires allowed.

3L2 (4★) is a private, hiker-only site on the south side of Cache Creek about a half mile off the main trail on a good spur trail and close to the confluence between Cache Creek and the Lamar River. Good view and water source, but the alluvial gravel in the area makes for rocky tent sites.

3L3 (3★) is a private, hiker-only site about a quarter mile on a good spur trail west of the main trail and close to the Lamar River. Marginal view, good water source, but the obviously well-used tent site is too close to the cooking area and bear pole, so set up the tent on the bench above the cooking area. This site was partially flooded in 1996.

3L4 (4★) is a private, hiker-only site about a half mile off the trail on an off-trail route that is a little difficult to follow. Right along the river (good water source), but exposed. Great view and adequate tent sites.

3L7 (4★) is a private, hiker-only site about a quarter mile from the main trail on a good spur trail. Right along the river, but you can't see it from the cooking area. Good water source and tent sites nicely separated from cooking area.

3L8 (4★) is a private, mixed site right along the river about a half mile from the trail on an off-trail route. Exposed site with a great view but "nature calls" are a problem because you can see everything for 1 mile around. The high water took out the bear pole in 1996, but the NPS plans to get it back in service. Adequate tent sites and good water source.

3U1 (2★) is a very private, mixed site on the west side of the river. You have to ford the river to get to this site. Although a mixed site, it looks mainly set up for stock parties. The cooking area is away from the river with a marginal view and a fair distance to water. Room for 50-100 tents, but only 20 people allowed.

3U2 (4★) is a private, hiker-only site about a quarter mile off the trail in a grove of live trees (not many green trees along this section of trail!) on a little point in the river offering a great view. A little difficult to find. Good water source and tent sites.

3U3 (3★) is a hiker-only site about 100 yards off the main trail on a route marked with orange markers. Good water source and tent sites and a fair view.

**Mist Creek Pass:** All campsites along the Mist Creek Pass Trail allow campfires.

3T1 (4★) gets a high rating mainly because of its wonderful location at the confluence of Cold Creek and the Lamar River. It's about 100 yards south of the Mist Creek Trail on a rough, off-trail route, located right at the confluence. Terrific view and good water source, but marginal tent sites.

3T2 (5★) is a private, hiker-only site on a bench on the east end of Mist Creek Meadows, perfect set up for wildlife watching from camp. Slightly nicer than 3T3. Terrific view west across the meadows and up to Mist Creek Pass. Fair water source and good tent sites.

3T3 (5★) is a private, mixed site about a half mile south of the trail on an off-trail route in a grove of live trees on the south edge of Mist Creek Meadows. Not quite as nice as 3T2, but still a great campsite. Great view from the cooking area. Good water source and tent sites.

**Broad Creek:** All six campsites along Broad Creek are mixed with good water sources. Go for 4B1 or 4B2 only if you like to get very secluded and don't mind bushwhacking. No bearpoles at 4B1, 4B2, or 4B3 when we were there.

4B1 (2★) is a totally secluded site that can be hard to find. Off-trail route and no sign when we were there. Overgrown, and apparently receives very little use. Adequate tent sites and fair view. Nearby thermal features.

4B2 (2★) is also totally secluded but easier to find that 4B1. Adequate view and marginal tent sites.

4B3 (3★) is a private site not far from trail. Decent view but marginal tent sites.

4B4 (2★) is a not-so-private site right along the trail. Nice view and plenty of good tent sites.

5B1 (5★) is a private site about 400 yards off the trail on the other side of the stream. Not quite as good a view as 5B2 and a slightly longer walk to water.

5B2 (4★) is a not-so-private site along Broad Creek and right along the trail. Nice view. Good tent sites.

**Wapiti Lake:** The two campsites at Wapiti Lake are quite close together.

4W2 (4★) is a mixed site right next to the trail. Good water source (the lake), adequate tent sites. Good view of lake.

4W3 (3★) is also a mixed site right by the trail similar to 4W2 except the view is marginal. Can see into the other campsite. Good water source and tent sites.

4M2 (3★) is fairly private, mixed site along Moss Creek. About 100 feet to water. No view. Good tent sites.

**Mount Washburn:** 4E1 (2★) is a private, mixed site on the edge of a meadow. No view. Good tent sites. Good water source, a small stream right through camp.

**Sevenmile Hole:** All three campsites at Sevenmile Hole are private, hiker-only sites that use the river as a water source.

4C1 (4★) is about 40 feet above the river, which makes getting water a little treacherous. Tent sites are on course gravel. Terrific veiw.

4C2 (4★) is more in the trees so you don't get the great view right from camp, but you can with a short walk. Excellent tent sites.

4C3 (3★) Similar to the other two sites but more private.

**Ribbon Lake:** 4R1 (3★) is a not-so-private, hiker-only site. Close enough to the trail to get a fair amount of use from day hikers. Good water source. Good view of the lake. Adequate tent sites.

4R2 (4★) is a more private, hiker-only site at the far end of the lake. The lake is more marshy at this site. Good tent sites and view.

**Wrangler Lake:** 4W1 (3★) is a mixed site on the left side of the lake. Marginal view. About 200 feet to water. Adequate tent sites closer to the lake.

## *SHORT HIKES*

## 72   *SENTINEL MEADOWS*

|  |  |
|---|---|
| **Type of hike:** | Out and back. |
| **Type of trip:** | Day hike or overnighter. |
| **Total distance:** | 3.8 miles or 6.1 kilometers (round-trip). |
| **Difficulty:** | Moderate. |
| **Elevation gain:** | Minimal. |
| **Maps:** | Trails Illustrated (Old Faithful); |
|  | Lower Geyser Basin USGS quad. |
| **Starting point:** | Sentinel Meadows Trailhead (OK6). |

*See Map on Page 214*

**Finding the trailhead:** Drive 6.1 miles south of Madison Junction or 9.9 miles north of Old Faithful and turn west onto Fountain Flat Drive, and park in a large parking area about a half mile from the main road. At this point, Fountain Flat Drive is barricaded, so walk on the road for about another quarter mile to the official trailhead on your right (west), just after crossing the Firehole River Bridge.

**Key points:**

|  |  |
|---|---|
| 0.2 (0.3) | Ojo Caliente Spring. |
| 0.3 (0.5) | Firehole River Bridge and Sentinel Meadows Trailhead (OK6). |
| 1.0 (1.6) | OG1 (3★). |
| 1.5 (2.4) | Junction with trail from Imperial Meadows Trailhead (OK8). |
| 1.9 (3.0) | Sentinel Meadows and Queens Laundry. |

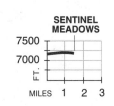

**The hike:** The first 0.3 mile of this hike is on the closed section of Fountain Flat Drive. Just before crossing the Firehole River, you go by Ojo Caliente Spring (Spanish for "hot spring"), which is only one of the interesting thermal areas along this trail.

The trail stays in great shape (flat, and easy to follow) all the way to the junction with the trail coming in from Imperial Meadows. Watch for bison on the trail and give them a wide berth.

At the junction, the trail starts to deteriorate rapidly. In short order, it disappears into the massive Sentinel Meadows just past a major thermal area called Queens Laundry, where early explorers bathed and, yes, did their laundry. Please don't try either today. Regulations prevent this, and early use of the area destroyed some colorful terraces. You might also see the remains of an old bathhouse build in 1881 and rumored to be the first building meant to serve the public ever built in any national park.

At this point, retrace your steps to the trailhead. After Queens Laundry, the trail melts into a huge marsh. Even in August, you can't cross anywhere without walking through water and muck.

**Options:** You can make a loop out of this trip by turning on the Imperial Meadows Trail and coming out at the end of the Fountain Flats Drive. However, this section of trail is difficult to follow, so you're likely to end up essentially going off-trail until you hit the closed section of Fountain Flat Drive.

# 73  FAIRY FALLS

| | |
|---|---|
| **Type of hike:** | Out and back. |
| **Type of trip:** | Day hike. |
| **Total distance:** | 3.6 miles or 5.8 kilometers (round-trip). |
| **Difficulty:** | Easy. |
| **Elevation gain:** | Minimal. |
| **Maps:** | Trails Illustrated (Old Faithful); |
| | Lower Geyser Basin USGS quad. |
| **Starting point:** | Fairy Falls Trailhead (OK5). |

See Map on Page 214

**Finding the trailhead:** Drive 5.5 miles south of Madison Junction or 10.5 miles north of Old Faithful and pull into the parking area on the west side of the road, just south of the Grand Prismatic Spring. The trail starts across the bridge on the old Fountain Freight Road, which was recently turned into a trail (also open to bicycles).

**Key points:**

0.8 (1.2)  Junction with Fairy Falls Trail.
1.4 (2.2)  Spur trail to OD1 (1★).
1.6 (2.5)  Fairy Falls.

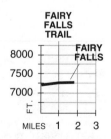

**The hike:** This is a short, easy hike to a falls more mystic than Mystic Falls.

From the trailhead, walk on Fountain Flats Drive as it crosses the Firehole River on a bridge and skirts the west side of the Midway Geyser Basin, with Grand Prismatic Spring off to the right (east). In less than 1 mile, the Fairy Falls Trail turns left (west) off the road. The trail is well-traveled and easy to follow as it goes through burnt lodgepole.

Fairy Falls is a delicate, 197-foot waterfall named for its graceful beauty. There's a bridge below the falls, and a short spur trail allows you to get an even closer look at the falls and the deep pool it has carved out.

After enjoying a nice break at the falls, retrace your steps to the trailhead.

**Options:** Although the above route may be the easiest route to Fairy Falls, there are three other routes:

1. Hike the Fairy Creek hike in reverse. But this option is for experienced hikers only.

2. Start at the north end of the Fountain Freight Road Trail (0K6) at the end of Fountain Flats Drive, a paved section of road south of Nez Perce Picnic Area. It's 0.6 mile from the picnic area to the trailhead at the end of the paved road. Fountain Freight Road is open to bicycles between 0K6 and 0K5, but all spur trails are closed to bicycles. From 0K6, hike south for about 0.4 mile to the junction with the Sentinel Meadows Trail. Continue straight (south) on the Fountain Freight Road Trail for another 1.1 miles to the second junction with the Sentinel Meadow Trail. Turn right (west) here and after 0.1 mile the trail forks with the right (northwest) fork going to Sentinel Meadows and the left (south) fork going to Fairy Falls on what is now called the Imperial Meadows Trail. After 1.1 miles, you reach the main trail to Fairy Falls. Turn left (east) and hike 0.4 mile to the well-named falls, which is particularly spectacular in the spring (the best time to take this hike).

   Before going to the falls, however, go left for about 0.25 mile to see Imperial and Spray Geysers, two of the hidden geothermal jewels that make hiking the Yellowstone backcountry so renowned. Imperial Geyser (the first geyser you see) goes off every few minutes. Spray Geyser (another 0.1 mile to the west) spouts constantly from a beautiful and colorful hot pool.

   Instead of retracing your steps to the trailhead, you can turn this into a "lollipop" loop by going east from Fairy Falls on the Fairy Falls Trail for 1.4 miles to the junction with the Fountain Freight Road Trail. Turn left (north) here and go 1.5 miles until you reach the junction with the Sentinel Meadows Trail you were at earlier in the day. From here, retrace your steps along the Fountain Freight Road Trail north back to your vehicle.

3. Your can also take the Sentinel Meadows Trail and make the loop described in Option 2 into a larger, "figure 8" route, by taking the Sentinel Meadows Trail to the northwest and then back east to the Fountain Freight Road Trail.

# MYSTIC FALLS • UPPER GEYSER BASIN • FAIRY CREEK • FAIRY FALLS • SENTINEL MEADOWS

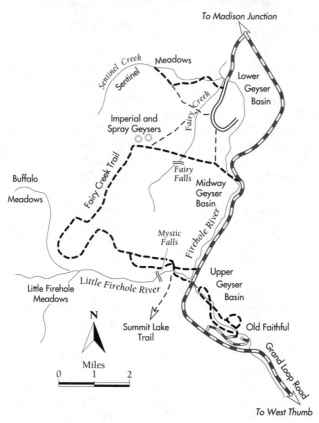

---

## 74 MYSTIC FALLS

|                    |                                                                                                                           |
| ------------------ | ------------------------------------------------------------------------------------------------------------------------- |
| **Type of hike:**  | Loop.                                                                                                                     |
| **Type of trip:**  | Short day hike.                                                                                                           |
| **Total distance:**| 4 miles or 6.4 kilometers (round-trip).                                                                                   |
| **Difficulty:**    | Easy.                                                                                                                     |
| **Elevation gain:**| 700 feet.                                                                                                                 |
| **Maps:**          | Yellowstone Association's Old Faithful map/ brochure; Trails Illustrated (Old Faithful); Old Faithful USGS quad.          |
| **Starting point:**| Biscuit Basin Trailhead (OK4).                                                                                            |

**Finding the trailhead:** Drive 2 miles north of Old Faithful or 14 miles south of Madison Junction and park in the Biscuit Basin Boardwalk parking area on the west side of the road.

*Mystic Falls.*

## Key points:

0.6 (1.0)   Junction with Summit Lake Trail.
0.8 (1.2)   Junction with Mystic Falls Trail.
1.1 (1.8)   Mystic Falls.
1.7 (2.7)   Junction with Fairy Creek Trail.
2.5 (4.0)   Overlook.
3.2 (5.1)   Junction with Mystic Falls Trail.
3.8 (6.1)   Junction with Summit Lake Trail.
4.0 (6.4)   Biscuit Basin Trailhead.

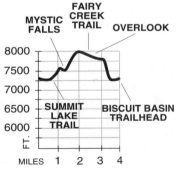

**The trail:** Mystic Falls is a popular day hike destination from Old Faithful and receives heavy use. It's a short, easy, and beautiful hike with incredible views of a cascading, 100-foot waterfall, Biscuit Basin, and the Old Faithful area.

From the parking area follow the Biscuit Basin Boardwalk around to the right until you reach the Little Firehole Meadows Trail. Go left (west) here, and stay right (west) again when you pass the junction with the trail to Summit Lake about a quarter mile down the trail. Next is the junction with the Mystic Falls loop trail that joins from the right. Stay left for the quickest route to the falls. You can return on the overlook route.

At 1.1 miles is Mystic Falls where the Little Firehole River suddenly leaves the Madison Plateau and drops into Biscuit Basin. Past Mystic Falls, the trail climbs abruptly to the junction with the trail from Fairy Creek.

Turn right (east) here and hike another quarter mile or so to a fenced over-look and sweeping view to the east of Old Faithful and the Firehole River.

After soaking in the view for awhile, continue east of the overlook, drop-ping steeply, until you rejoin the Mystic Falls Trail. Then, retrace your steps to the trailhead.

## 75 UPPER GEYSER BASIN

| | |
|---|---|
| **Type of hike:** | Loop. |
| **Type of trip:** | Day hike. |
| **Total distance:** | Varies from 1.5 (2.4 kilometers) to 5 miles (8 kilometers), depending on which loop you hike. |
| **Difficulty:** | Easy. |
| **Elevation gain:** | Minimal, unless you go to geyser hill, an easy, 250-foot climb. |
| **Maps:** | Yellowstone Association's Old Faithful map/brochure; Trails Illustrated (Old Faithful); Old Faithful USGS quad. |
| **Starting point:** | Old Faithful Visitor Center. |

See Map on Page 214

**Finding the trailhead:** Drive 16 miles south of Madison Junction or 17 miles west of West Thumb and take the Old Faithful exit. Follow the signs to the visitor center.

*Walking the boardwalk trail through the Upper Geyser Basin.*

*View of Upper Geyser Basin and Old Faithful from Geyser Hill.*

**The hike:** When you hear people talking about day hiking in Yellowstone, they usually talk about geysers and other thermal areas, and they are probably talking about this hike. This trail goes by an almost unimaginable number of fascinating thermal features, but don't expect to be alone in the wilderness. This may also be the most heavily used trail in the park.

Be sure to spend a quarter at the visitor center for a well-done brochure and map of the area published by The Yellowstone Association. This brochure is much better than any other map of the area.

Unlike most other hikes, this loop offers several options in length to suit your physical ability and mood of the day. Also, much of the trail is on boardwalks and paved walkways accessible to wheelchairs. The trail and walkway on the south side of the Firehole River is open to bicycles.

The longest route includes the Geyser Hill Loop and goes from the visitor center to the Biscuit Basin Trailhead, along the Grand Loop Road for less than a quarter mile and then back on the other side of the Firehole River.

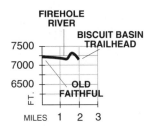

This long route includes about 2 miles of regular trails in addition to the boardwalks and paved walkways.

You can shorten the loop by crossing over the Firehole River on bridges near the Morning Glory Pool (2.8-mile trip) or Grand Geyser or Castle Geyser (1.4-mile loop). Adding the Geyser Hill loop lengthens the trip by 1.3 miles.

All Upper Geyser Basin hikes start out with a bang—the eruption of Old Faithful, which erupts an average of every 79 minutes, more frequently than any other big geyser. You can view this famous phenomenon from benches in front of the visitor center, or if you have time, you can get a more distant view from Geyser Hill. If you carefully plan your hike, you can do both.

It pays to study the map carefully before taking off. The entire trip is on superb trails, walkways, or boardwalks. Even the trip up to the Geyser Hill Viewpoint is in excellent shape with well-planned switchbacks, making the small climb seem easy.

Regardless of how much of the area you choose to hike, set aside much more time than you would normally allow for a hike of this length. Speed is not an issue on this hike. Instead, the NPS has provided an incredible educational experience with frequent interpretive signs, brochures, and guided tours. Interpretive rangers normally hike the area and can answer your questions. If you're interested in a ranger-led tour, inquire in the visitor center for the schedule.

**Options:** You can start this loop hike at the Biscuit Basin Trailhead.

## 76  ROBINSON LAKE

| | |
|---|---|
| **Type of hike:** | Out and back. |
| **Type of trip:** | Day hike. |
| **Total distance:** | 4 miles or 6.4 kilometers (round-trip). |
| **Difficulty:** | Easy. |
| **Elevation gain:** | Minimal. |
| **Maps:** | Trails Illustrated (Old Faithful); Bechlser Falls USGS quad. |
| **Starting point:** | Bechler Ranger Station Trailhead (9K1). |

See Map on Page 257

**Finding the trailhead:** You can reach the ranger station by two routes, both of which are shown on an overview map at the beginning of the book. The rough, scenic route goes from Flagg Ranch just south of the park on the Ashton-Flagg Road, past Grassy Lake Reservoir. Watch for a signed junction where you turn right (north) to the Cave Falls Road and right again (east) when you reach the Cave Falls Road. After about 2 miles on an unpaved section of Cave Falls Road, you reach a junction where the pavement starts, and you can turn left (north) to the ranger station.

You can also get to the Bechler Ranger Station from the west from either Ashton, Idaho, or West Yellowstone, Montana, by getting on Idaho Highway 47 and turning on the Cave Falls Road.

**The hike:** This is a short, easy hike through a thick forest, It can be a day hike, or you can go past the lake and stay overnight at one of two designated campsites. Even though this is a short walk in the woods, you can feel isolated because few hikers use this trail. The trail is in good shape the entire way.

Robinson Lake is a shallow, forest-lined, 35-acre lake with no fish. The lake is usually covered with lilypads.

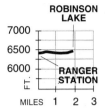

## MODERATE HIKES

## 77  MALLARD LAKE

| | |
|---|---|
| **Type of hike:** | Out and back with shuttle and loop options. |
| **Type of trip:** | Day hike or overnighter. |
| **Total distance:** | 7 miles or 11.2 kilometers (round-trip). |
| **Difficulty:** | Moderate. |
| **Elevation gain:** | 825 feet. |
| **Maps:** | Trails Illustrated (Old Faithful); Lower Geyser Basin USGS quad. |
| **Starting point:** | Mallard Lake Trailhead (OK3). |

**Finding the trailhead:** Drive south from Madison Junction on the Grand Loop Road for 16 miles and take the Old Faithful exit. Cross over the divided highway and stay on the main road past the Old Faithful Inn turnoff, continuing on about 1.25 miles to the Old Faithful Lodge. Circle around the large parking area on a one-way road, and at the lodge entrance, watch for a small sign for Mallard Lake Trail at a service road on the right that goes down to a group of cabins. Park off the road in the spaces provided. The trail is well marked with a sign and departs from the service road on the northeast side of the cabins. If you get lost in the Old Faithful area, stop at the visitor center and ask for directions to the trailhead.

**Key points:**
0.3 (0.5)  Evidence of hot springs on left as trail begins climbing gently.
0.5 (0.8)  Trail enters burn.
1.0 (1.6)  Trail switchbacks northwest with views of Old Faithful.
2.5 (4.0)  A small divide before the descent to Mallard Lake.
3.3 (5.3)  Junction with Mallard Creek Trail.
3.5 (5.6)  Mallard Lake.

**The hike:** This trail wanders through areas of forest where wild fires caused varying degrees of damage. In places, a few Douglas-fir and lodgepole pine survived, while other sections were devastated.

The trail is well maintained, with most deadfall cut from the treadway annually. Expect to encounter a few rocky sections, but generally the trail is dry and well marked. The first half of the hike to Mallard Lake is a popular day hike for people staying overnight in the Old Faithful area. But few people camp at the lake and fewer people continue hiking along the Mallard Creek Trail.

# MALLARD LAKE

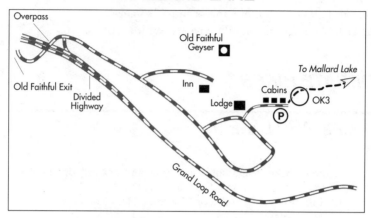

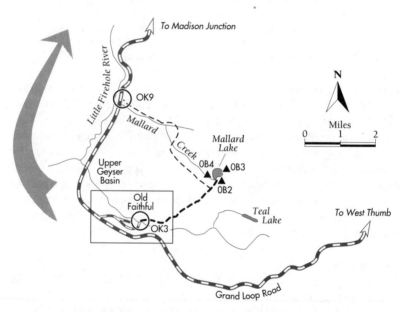

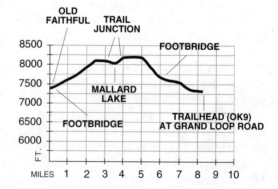

Within a half mile of the trailhead, the route begins to feel like Yellowstone backcountry, leaving the hubbub of tourists and the commercialism of the Old Faithful Inn and Lodge area. The sandy trail climbs gently and enters burned lodgepole for-

*Mallard Lake.*

est where wildflowers are often abundant during early summer. At about 0.75 mile, the terrain levels slightly and crosses an unnamed creek. Switchbacks ascend gentle hills that offer glimpses of Old Faithful through the silvery snags left from the fire. The trail then wanders through a shallow gorge with rock outcrops along the trail to a meadow area and over a small divide about 2.5 miles. Along the descent from the divide toward the lake, the Mallard Creek Trail takes off to the left (north), 0.2 mile from the lake. Turn right (east) and continue toward the lake.

The 32-acre, fishless lake has no visible outlet except for a dry gulch that descends toward the west. Evidence of old rock slides at the head of the gulch may have buried the outlet stream, Mallard Creek, which eventually surfaces a couple miles downstream.

**Options:** If continuing on to Mallard Creek, leave a vehicle at the parking area for trailhead OK9 for a shuttle, or finish the loop by continuing another 5 miles along the Powerline Trail to the lodge.

To do the shuttle or loop option, take the main trail back uphill from the lake to the Mallard Creek Trail junction. Go right (north) and ascend to the summit of the ridge above the southwestern shore of the lake. The trail follows the ridge for about another 1.25 miles before descending to cross the intermittently dry creek bed of Mallard Creek. The trail continues to follow the creek, crossing it once on a bridge, to the Grand Loop Road and OK9 trailhead parking area near the Little Firehole River. It's 5 miles along Mallard Creek from the lake to the road.

| | | |
|---|---|---|
| **Type of hike:** | Out and back. | See Elevation Profile on Page 204 |
| **Type of trip:** | Day hike. | See Map on Page 205 |
| **Total distance:** | Up to 12 miles or | |
| | 19.3 kilometers. | |
| **Difficulty:** | Moderate. | |
| **Elevation gain:** | Minimal. | |
| **Maps:** | Trails Illustrated (Old Faithful); | |
| | Lower Geyser Basin USGS quad. | |
| **Starting point:** | Mary Mountain Trailhead (OK7). | |

**Finding the trailhead:** Drive 6.6 miles south of Madison Junction or 9.4 miles north of Old Faithful and park in the parking area on the east side of the road just south of the Nez Perce Creek Bridge.

**The hike:** This is the western section of the long shuttle hike over Mary Mountain, but it's one of the most scenic sections of the longer trail. You can hike as far as you wish into Nez Perce Creek and then return. It's about 2 miles to the ford (sorry, no bridge) and about 6 miles to Cowan Creek where the trail starts climbing up to Mary Lake. Cowan Creek is where the Nez Perce attacked the Cowan party.

*Nez Perce Creek.*

Nez Perce is a big, open valley with an idyllic mountain stream running through it. Nez Perce is not only beautiful, but it hosts a healthy trout population (rainbow and brown). At the beginning of the hike, you can explore several thermal areas and hot springs off to the north.

The trail is in great shape the entire way. In June and July, however, it can get marshy in several areas near the east end of the valley around Cowan Creek. The trail stays in the nearly treeless valley the entire way, with the exception of a few short sections after 5 miles.

**Options:** You can also hike Nez Perce Creek as part of the Mary Mountain Trail, a long shuttle hike.

# 79 LONE STAR GEYSER

| | |
|---|---|
| **Type of hike:** | Out and back with loop option. |
| **Type of Trip:** | Day hike. |
| **Total distance:** | 4.6 miles or 7.4 kilometers (round-trip). |
| **Difficulty:** | Easy. |
| **Elevation gain:** | Minimal. |
| **Maps:** | Trails Illustrated (Old Faithful); Old Faithful USGS quad. |
| **Starting point:** | Lone Star Trailhead (OK1). |

See Map on Page 224

**Finding the trailhead:** Drive 3.5 miles east of the Old Faithful interchange and park at the Lone Star Trailhead on the south side of the road.

**The hike:** This is a fairly level hike to a well-known and heavily visited geyser. The trail to Lone Star Geyser is an old service road that is paved but closed to vehicles (but open to mountain bikers). Even though you might see a few bikers and more than a few hikers on this trail, it's still a pleasant hike along the Upper Firehole River. About a half mile before the geyser, stay right (south) at the junction with the Spring Creek Trail,

continuing on the paved path. The pavement ends about a 100 feet before the geyser and is blocked by downed trees to discourage bicycle traffic beyond this point.

Lone Star Geyser was named for its isolated location (5 miles south of Old Faithful with no other geysers in the neighborhood). The name has no link to Texas, the Lone Star State. The geyser erupts 30-50 feet every 2-3 hours or so for about 10-15 minutes. Gurgling sounds come from the geyser's large cone between eruptions.

**Option:** If you don't want to hike on a paved trail with mountain bikers, you can hike into Lone Star Geyser, out and back, from Fern Cascades Trailhead (OK2), which is about 1.7 miles north of the Lone Star Trailhead. This lengthens the round-trip to 6.4 miles.

You can also make an almost-a-loop shuttle out of this by starting at Fern Cascades Trailhead and coming out at Lone Star Trailhead or vice versa. This requires two vehicles or a 1.7-mile walk on the highway to get back to your vehicle. Total distance of the loop is 7.2 miles.

## 80 DIVIDE MOUNTAIN

|  |  |
|---|---|
| **Type of hike:** | Out and back. |
| **Type of trip:** | Day hike. |
| **Total distance:** | 5 miles or 8 kilometers (round-trip). |
| **Difficulty:** | Moderate. |
| **Elevation gain:** | 735 feet. |
| **Maps:** | Trails Illustrated (Old Faithful); Craig Pass USGS quad. |
| **Starting point:** | Divide Mountain Trailhead. |

**Finding the trailhead:** Drive 10.5 miles west of West Thumb Junction or 6.5 miles east of Old Faithful and park in a pullout on the south side of the road.

## DIVIDE MOUNTAIN • LONE STAR GEYSER

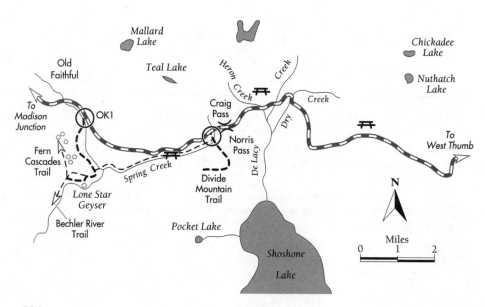

**The hike:** This is a well-defined path through un-burned forest to the top of a ridge above Craig Pass on the Continental Divide. Right after the trailhead, be sure to take a left on the trail to the summit instead of following the better trail along Spring Creek to the Lone Star Geyser Trailhead.

The view from the summit is well worth the short, Category 4 climb. You get an especially expansive view of Shoshone Lake just to the south.

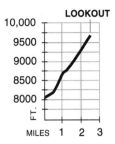

---

## 81  BEULA LAKE

|  |  |
|---|---|
| **Type of hike:** | Out and back. |
| **Type of trip:** | Day hike or overnighter. |
| **Total distance:** | 6 miles or 9.6 kilometers (round-trip). |
| **Difficulty:** | Easy. |
| **Elevation gain:** | Minimal. |
| **Maps:** | Trails Illustrated (Old Faithful); |
|  | Grassy Lake Reservoir USGS quad. |
| **Starting point:** | Beula Lake Trailhead. |

**Finding the trailhead:** Drive 10 miles west of Flagg Ranch (2 miles south of the park on U.S. 287) on a mostly unpaved road to Grassy Reservoir. The

*Beula Lake.*

# BEULA LAKE

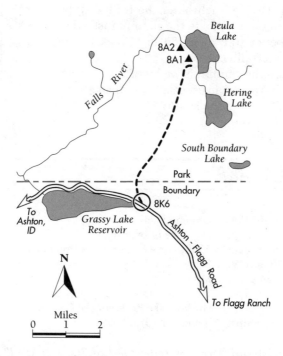

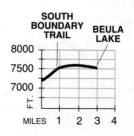

trailhead is not marked, but it's a steep pullout on the north side of the road at the east end of the reservoir.

**The hike:** From the trailhead, the trail gradually climbs over a small ridge and drops into Beula Lake. The trail is in superb condition the entire way. It goes though partly burned forest, but the lakeshore itself has not been burned.

About a half mile from the trailhead, the trail crosses the South Boundary Trail. When we hiked this trail, there was no sign at this junction, so be careful not to turn either way on the South Boundary Trail. Instead, go straight (north) to Beula Lake.

Beula Lake (named after a mystical land of sunshine and delight) is a fairly large (107 acres) lake with two designated campsites. It hosts a healthy cutthroat population and is popular with anglers.

**Side trips:** It's a half-mile, off-trail trek over to Herring Lake, which is smaller (60 acres), but also has a healthy cutthroat population.

226

## 82  BECHLER SHORT LOOP

| | |
|---|---|
| **Type of hike:** | Loop. |
| **Type of trip:** | Day hike or overnighter. |
| **Total distance:** | 7 miles or 11.2 kilometers. |
| **Difficulty:** | Moderate. |
| **Elevation gain:** | Minimal. |
| **Maps:** | Trails Illustrated (Old Faithful); Bechler Falls USGS quad. |
| **Starting point:** | Bechler Ranger Station Trailhead (9K1). |

See Map on Page 257

**Finding the trailhead:** You can reach the ranger station by two routes, both of which are shown on an overview map at the beginning of the book. The rough, scenic route goes from Flagg Ranch just south of the park on the Ashton-Flagg Road, past Grassy Lake Reservoir. Watch for a signed junction where you turn right (north) to the Cave Falls Road and right again (east) when you reach the Cave Falls Road. After about 2 miles on an unpaved section of Cave Falls Road, you reach a junction where the pavement starts, and you can turn left (north) to the ranger station.

You can also get to the Bechler Ranger Station from the west from either Ashton, Idaho, or West Yellowstone, Montana, by getting on Idaho Highway 47 and turning on the Cave Falls Road.

**Key points:**
| | | |
|---|---|---|
| 1.5 | (2.4) | Junction with Boundary Creek Trail. |
| 2.5 | (4.0) | Junction with cutoff trail to Bechler River Trail. |
| 3.2 | (5.1) | 9C1 and junction with Bechler River Trail. |
| 6.0 | (9.6) | Trail to Bechler Falls and Cave Falls Trailhead. |
| 7.0 | (11.2) | Bechler Ranger Station. |

**The hike:** This is a convenient loop hike from the Bechler River Ranger Station. The trail is in great shape all the way—and unlike most trails in the area, you don't have to ford any major rivers. Like other hikes in the Bechler area, though, wait until at least mid-July (and preferably later) for the trails to dry out.

Even though the loop trail goes all around Lilypad Lake, you can't see it from the trail. You might not want to bushwhack over to the lake because the terrain around the lake stays quite marshy, even into late August. The shallow, 58-acre lake is fishless and almost completely covered with lilypads.

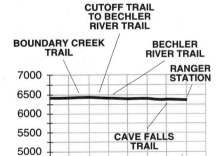

227

The trail alternates between unburned forest and meadows most of the way, and this is, in short, a very nice, moderate hike that allows you to experience the Bechler River country.

**Options:** You can take the loop in either direction with no extra difficulty.

## LONG HIKES

## 83 SUMMIT LAKE

|  |  |
|---|---|
| **Type of hike:** | Out and back. |
| **Type of trip:** | Long day hike or overnighter. |
| **Total distance:** | 15 miles or 24 kilometers (round-trip). |
| **Difficulty:** | Difficult. |
| **Elevation gain:** | 1,266 feet. |
| **Maps:** | Trails Illustrated (Old Faithful); |
|  | Old Faithful and Summit Lake USGS quads. |
| **Starting point:** | Biscuit Basin Trailhead (OK4). |

**Finding the trailhead:** Drive 14 miles south of Madison Junction or 2 miles north of Old Faithful Village and turn into the Biscuit Basin parking area on the west side of the road.

**Key points:**
0.6  (0.9)  Junction trail to Mystic Falls Trail.
7.5 (12.0)  Summit Lake and OE1 (3★).

**The hike:** The trail starts out on a boardwalk, but quickly leaves it behind as it turns into a well-defined and well-used trail to Mystic Falls. In the first half mile, you go by two junctions. Go left (southwest) at both unless you want to take a short trip to Mystic Falls.

After the junction, you go through a big meadow. The trail

gets faint, but orange markers show the way. After the meadow, the trail heads into a burned forest and starts climbing. This is a Category 3 climb, gaining about 900 feet in 2 miles. Once you're up on the plateau, the grade gets almost flat as you continue through partially burned forest and along an unnamed stream all the way to Summit Lake, which you'll see just after going through a large marshy section of trail.

# SUMMIT LAKE

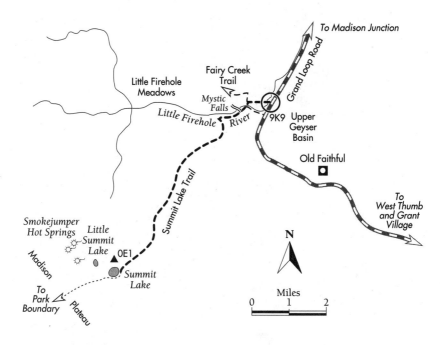

Most of the trail is in fair condition but gets rocky in places. Also, expect to be climbing over some downfall.

**Side trips:** The short side trip to Mystic Falls is worth the effort.

# 84  FAIRY CREEK

| | | |
|---|---|---|
| **Type of hike:** | Loop. | |
| **Type of trip:** | A long day hike or overnighter. | See Map on Page 214 |
| **Total distance:** | 12.5 miles or 20.1 kilometers (not including walk on road). | |
| **Difficulty:** | Difficult. | |
| **Elevation gain:** | 800 feet. | |
| **Starting point:** | Fairy Falls Trailhead (OK5). | |

See Map on Page 214

**Finding the Trailhead:** Drive 5.5 miles south of Madison Junction or 10.5 miles north of Old Faithful and turn into the parking area on the west side of the road just south of the Grand Prismatic Spring. The trail starts across a bridge on Fountain Flats Drive, which is closed to moter vehicles but open to mountain bikes.

**Key points:**

| | | |
|---|---|---|
| 0.8 | (1.2) | Fairy Creek Trail turns off Fountain Flats Drive. |
| 1.4 | (2.2) | Spur trail to OD1 (1★). |
| 1.8 | (2.9) | Spur trail to Fairy Falls. |
| 2.0 | (3.2) | Junction with trail to Imperial Meadows Trailhead. |
| 2.3 | (3.7) | Imperial Geyser. |
| 8.9 | (14.3) | OD2 (5★). |
| 9.4 | (15.1) | OD3 (4★). |
| 11.2 | (18.0) | Junction with Mystic Falls Trail. |
| 11.5 | (18.5) | Overlook. |
| 11.7 | (18.8) | Junction with Little Firehole Meadows Trail. |
| 11.9 | (19.1) | Junction with Summit Lake Trail. |
| 12.5 | (20.1) | Biscuit Basin Boardwalk. |

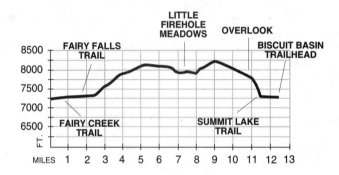

**The trail:** This is a great hike to Fairy Falls, Imperial Geyser, Mystic Falls, and the Little Firehole Meadows, but it isn't for beginners. Parts of the trail require advanced route-finding skills.

From the trailhead, follow Fountain Flats Drive (closed to vehicles) as it crosses the Firehole River on a bridge and skirts the west side of the Midway Geyser Basin. You can see large numbers of people viewing Grand Prismatic Spring. In less than 1 mile, turn left (west) off the road onto the Fairy Falls Trail. The trail is well-traveled and easy to follow through burnt lodgepole.

Fairy Falls is a 197-foot, thin stream of water. The colors of the cliff make the falls seem medieval or fantasy-like, but the waterfall was actually named for its graceful beauty. Gooseberry and raspberry plants surround the bridge over Fairy Creek below the falls.

The trail continues west on marshy log crossings to the junction with the Fairy Creek Trail. Turn left (south) and head for Imperial Geyser. At this point, the NPS has put up a warning sign about the condition of the trail and advises people not to attempt the loop unless you're an "expert navigator" and prepared to spend the night out.

On your right (north) just after the junction is little Spray Geyser, which erupts about every 5 minutes, to a height of 10 feet—not terribly impressive, but entertaining. At 0.3 mile past the junction is Imperial Geyser. This geyser used to be one of the largest in the park, but it has been mostly dormant since the late 1920s. Now, the only evidence of a geyser is a large thermal pool.

From here, the trail grows increasingly faint as it goes through severely burned forest. Many downed trees and a few faint orange markers (some on fallen trees) lead the way, but it requires expert route-finding skills to navigate the route, especially in a heavily burned stretch where the trail climbs up to the Madison Plateau on switchbacks. Many markers are difficult to see because of downed timber. This route climbs steadily along Fairy Creek over a small ridge and then levels out as it enters the beautiful valley of the Little Firehole River. After a gradual descent, the trail disappears into the Little Firehole Meadows. The trail hugs the northeast side of the meadow to OD2.

After OD2, the trail gets more distinct and swings to the left following the Little Firehole River in unburned forest. The river is a clear, slow-water fishery, but speeds up as you near OD3, which is between the trail and the river.

After OD3, the trail climbs through burned and unburned lodgepole. Here, the trail is easy to follow and well used.

At about 11 miles is the junction with the loop trail around Mystic Falls. You can go either way at this point. If you turn right, you head to the base of the falls. The left fork takes you to an overlook for a view of the Old Faithful area.

After Mystic Falls, you'll see the other part of the Mystic Falls loop joining the main trail and less than a quarter mile later, you'll see the Summit Lake Trail joining from the right (south). Keep going east on the well-traveled trail to the Biscuit Basin Trailhead. If you left a vehicle here, you can avoid the 2-mile walk along the road back to your vehicle at the Fairy Falls Trailhead.

**Options:** If you don't want to risk losing your way on the difficult section of this trail, but would like to see the beautiful Little Firehole Meadows, you can hike out and back from Biscuit Basin Trailhead, viewing Mystic Falls along the way. However, you'll miss Fairy Falls. You could also stay overnight at OD2 or OD3, both nice campsites.

|                   |                                                  |
|-------------------|--------------------------------------------------|
| **Type of hike:** | Loop.                                            |
| **Type of trip:** | Multi-day backpacking trip.                      |
| **Total distance:** | 28.3 miles or 45.5 kilometers.                 |
| **Difficulty:**   | Difficult.                                       |
| **Elevation gain:** | Overall minimal elevation gain, but several short, steep hills around the lake. |
| **Maps:**         | Trails Illustrated (Old Faithful); Craig Pass, Shoshone Geyser Basin, and Lewis Falls USGS quads. |
| **Starting point:** | DeLacy Creek Trailhead (7K2).                  |

**Finding the trailhead:** Drive 8.4 miles west of West Thumb Junction (0.25 mile past the DeLacy Creek Picnic Area) or 8.6 miles east of Old Faithful and park in a pullout on the south side of the road.

**Key points:**

| | | |
|---|---|---|
| 3.0 | (4.8) | Shoshone Lake. |
| 3.5 | (5.6) | 8S2 (2★). |
| 4.0 | (6.4) | 8S3 (2★). |
| 7.7 | (12.4) | 8R2 (3★). |
| 7.8 | (12.5) | 8R3 (3★). |
| 8.3 | (13.3) | Patrol cabin. |
| 11.0 | (17.7) | 8R5 (5★). |
| 11.3 | (18.2) | Junction with Shoshone Lake Trail to Old Faithful. |
| 11.5 | (18.5) | Shoshone Geyser Basin. |
| 12.2 | (19.6) | Junction with horse bypass trail. |
| 12.4 | (19.9) | 8T1 (2★). |
| 16.3 | (26.2) | Moose Creek and 8M2 (3★). |
| 18.8 | (30.2) | 8M1 (3★). |
| 21.1 | (33.9) | Lewis Channel ford. |
| 21.3 | (34.3) | Junction with Lewis Channel Trail. |
| 21.5 | (34.6) | 8S1 (4★) and patrol cabin. |
| 25.3 | (40.7) | Junction with DeLacy Creek Trail. |
| 28.3 | (45.5) | DeLacy Creek Trailhead. |

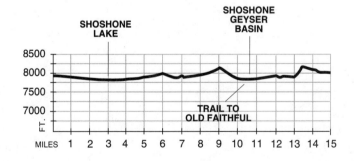

# SHOSHONE LAKE • LEWIS CHANNEL LOOP

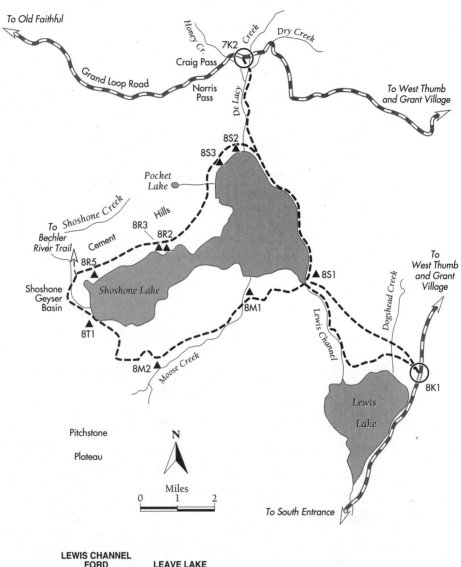

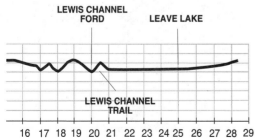

**Recommended itinerary:** A three-night, four-day trip with an easy first day, which leaves time for driving to the trailhead. Camp the first night at 8S2 or 8S3, second night at 8R5 or 8T1, and the third night at 8S1 (preferred) or 8M1 or 8M2.

**The hike:** Shoshone Lake is one of the most popular backpacking destinations in Yellowstone. In addition, paddlers come up the Lewis Channel and camp at the lake, which actually has more boat-access campsites (not covered in this book) than trail-access campsites.

This is a very large (8,050 acres), very deep (205 feet maximum, with most of the lake over 90 feet deep), forest-lined mountain lake. The shoreline commonly drops off like a cliff, and the lake supports good populations of brown, brook, and lake trout. If you want to avoid an overpopulation of mosquitoes, wait until late August.

The trail starts out with a gentle descent into DeLacy Creek and then follows the stream grade about 200 feet to the lake. The first mile goes through unburned forest right along the creek. Then, the creek widens in a slow-moving, marshy stream, and the trail opens up into a series of meadows. The trail to the lake is in great shape and stays dry, distinct, and easy to follow all the way to the lake.

When you reach the Shoshone Lake Trail (assuming you chose the counterclockwise route described here), take a right (west). You walk along a beach for a short distance and ford DeLacy Creek before you go into the

*Shoshone Lake.*

timber and to 8S2 and 8S3, where you probably want to spend your first night.

The trail stays near the lake for another mile or so, after the campsites, before heading away from the lake for about 3.5 miles, climbing over several small but sometimes steep ridges until you come back to the lakeshore around 8R2 and 8R3 and the patrol cabin. Although well defined, this section of trail gets rocky in places.

After the patrol cabin, the trail goes out of sight of the lake again and stays there until you reach the junction with the trail to Lone Star Geyser and Old Faithful. Again, this section of trail goes up and down over several small ridges and stays in unburned timber.

At the junction, turn left (south), and the trail opens up into Shoshone Geyser Basin which has dozens of interesting thermal features. In the basin, you face two marshy fords of an unnamed creek and Fall Creek and near the end of the basin, one more ford of Cold Mountain Creek. In July, the entire basin stays marshy, one reason horses are not allowed in the basin. About halfway through the basin, you'll see the horse bypass trail coming in from the right (west). Keep going straight (south) along the lake.

Just after the Cold Mountain Creek ford, the trail gets faint. Watch for markers on the end of the timber. Once you get in the trees, the trail is well defined. From here, the trail climbs steeply up 300 feet to a ridge above the lake and then drops steeply into Moose Creek. The trail then follows Moose Creek (with one ford just before 8M1) all the way to the Lewis Channel going over two small ridges just before reaching the channel.

The Lewis Channel (the outlet of Shoshone Lake) is a big stream and fording it can get your pulse rate up. In late season, however, it isn't difficult. After the ford, go about a quarter mile along the lakeshore to the junction with Lewis Channel Trail to Dogshead Trailhead. Go left (north) here and in another quarter mile, you reach the patrol cabin and 8S1.

From here, it's 4 miles to DeLacy Creek, where you came in. This section of trail goes right along the lakeshore the entire way, even dipping down to walk on the rocky beach in several places. You get terrific views of the lake all along this stretch of trail. At DeLacy Creek, take a right (north) and retrace your steps to the trailhead.

**Options:** You can take this trip in reverse with the same degree of difficulty. You can also reach Shoshone Lake from the Fern Cascades, Lone Star Geyser, and Dogshead trailheads, and still make a loop (but a longer loop) out of the trip. You can also make it a shuttle hike by going in at DeLacy Creek and out to the Dogshead Trailhead or vice versa.

|                    |                                          |
|--------------------|------------------------------------------|
| **Type of hike:**  | Loop.                                    |
| **Type of trip:**  | Day hike or overnighter.                 |
| **Total distance:**| 11.7 miles or 18.8 kilometers.           |
| **Difficulty:**    | Moderate.                                |
| **Elevation gain:**| Minimal.                                 |
| **Maps:**          | Trails Illustrated (Old Faithful);       |
|                    | Mount Sheridan and Lewis Falls USGS quads. |
| **Starting point:**| Dogshead Trailhead (8K1).                |

See Map on Page 233

**Finding the trailhead:** Drive 5.1 miles south of Grant Village or 14.1 miles north of South Entrance and park in the pullout on the west side of the road.

**Key points:**

|            |        |                                                  |
|------------|--------|--------------------------------------------------|
| 3.5  | (5.6)  | Lewis Channel.                                   |
| 6.9  | (11.1) | Ford Summit Creek.                               |
| 7.0  | (11.2) | Shoshone Lake and junction with Dogshead Trail.  |
| 11.7 | (18.8) | Dogshead Trailhead.                              |

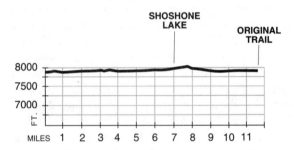

**The hike:** This is a convenient loop trail that goes to Shoshone Lake and follows the scenic Lewis Channel for 3.5 miles. This route follows the clockwise route, so take the trail on the left (south) side of the trailhead.

The first section of the trail is flat and easy as it goes through partly burned forest for about 2.5 miles north of Lewis Lake (but mostly out of view of the lake). Then, the trail turns north for about 1 mile to the Lewis Channel. It follows the picturesque channel for another 3.5 miles to Shoshone Lake.

The trail is in great shape except a couple of places in the meadows along Lewis Channel, where it gets faint, and a few boggy spots in the last mile before the lake. This section of trail is heavily used by anglers casting their lines in the Lewis Channel for brown trout. You might also see paddlers negotiating their canoes or kayaks up or down the Lewis Channel between Lewis Lake and Shoshone Lake.

Just before the lake, you'll see the Dogshead Trail coming in from the right. From here, it's less than a quarter mile to the lake.

*The flat water of the Lewis Channel allows paddlers to go upstream to Shoshone Lake.*

The way back on the Dogshead Trail is shorter (4.7 miles from lake to trailhead), but not nearly as scenic as the Lewis Channel Trail. The trail is in good shape the entire way and goes through burned forest most of the way with a small ridge.

**Options:** This loop can be done in either direction with no additional difficulty. Some people like the scenic south leg of the loop so much better than the north leg that they go out and back along Lewis Channel. You can stay overnight at 8S1 and make this a nice overnighter. You can also make this a long backpacking trip by going around Shoshone Lake.

## 87  UNION FALLS

|  |  |
|---|---|
| **Type of hike:** | Out and back. |
| **Type of trip:** | Day hike or overnighter. |
| **Total distance:** | 15.6 miles or 24.6 kilometers (round-trip). |
| **Difficulty:** | Difficult (because of length). |
| **Elevation gain:** | 600 feet. |
| **Maps:** | Trails Illustrated (Old Faithful); Grassy Lake Reservoir USGS quad. |
| **Starting point:** | Grassy Lake Trailhead (9K5). |

**Finding the trailhead:** About 2 miles south of the park on U.S. 287 and just before Flagg Ranch, turn west on what is called the Ashton-Flagg Road. This also goes to Flagg Ranch Village. After about a quarter mile, turn right (west) as the left fork goes to the campground. The road stays paved for about 2 more miles before turning into a gradually worsening gravel road. The trail starts just after crossing over the spillway at the west end of Grassy Lake Reservoir, which is just south of the park, 10 miles west of Flagg Ranch. If you have a two-wheel-drive vehicle, you should park at the top of the dam and walk to the trailhead. Many people have driven down to the trailhead parking area with two-wheel-drive vehicles and then not been able to get back up the hill.

**Key points:**

| | | |
|---|---|---|
| 1.0 | (1.6) | Junction with Cascade Creek Trail and ford Falls River. |
| 1.2 | (1.9) | 9C5 (4★) and trail to Pitchstone Plateau. |
| 5.0 | (8.0) | Proposition Creek. |
| 5.9 | (9.5) | Junction with Mountain Ash Creek Trail. |
| 6.4 | (10.3) | 9C4 (3★). |
| 7.8 | (12.5) | Union Falls. |

**The hike:** Union Falls is definitely one of the most spectacular waterfalls in the park and well worth the long, out-and-back hike to see it. This trail gets fairly heavy use and is in excellent shape the entire way.

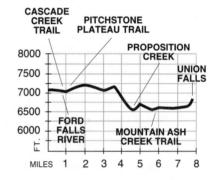

The first mile is flat and easy as it follows the stream leaving Grassy Lake Reservoir and then the Falls River. Just before the ford, a trail heads off to the left (west) to the Cascade Creek Trailhead, where you could also start this hike. The ford is long, but only knee-deep in August.

Immediately after the ford, the trail to Pitchstone Plateau takes off to the right (east). You go left (north). The trail goes through mature, unburned forest for about 4 miles over a small ridge and drops into Proposition Creek, an easy ford. From here, go about 1 mile more to the major junction with the Mountain Ash Creek Trail which goes off to the left (west). Turn right (north).

The trail continues through unburned forest along Mountain Ash Creek until the stream splits and the trail goes past a little A-frame patrol cabin and onto a small ridge between the two forks to Union Falls. The last 2 miles of trail to Union Falls have been seriously pounded with heavy horse traffic. Just before the falls, there is a small clearing where trail riders have

# UNION FALLS

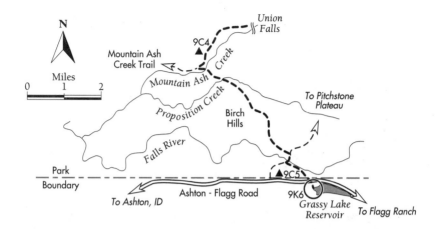

to leave their horses and walk the last half mile to the falls on a small upgrade made easy with switchbacks.

At this point, a major trail goes off to the left and is marked "North Fork Trail." This short spur trail goes down to a naturally heated "swimming hole" just below a small waterfall in Mountain Ash Creek. Locals also refer to this as the "Scout Pool" because numerous scout troops hike to Union Falls and take a dip in this warm water pool.

*Remote and massive Union Falls, the second highest waterfall in Yellowstone.*

You can hear Union Falls from a mile away in September (when we were there), so it must really be loud in June and July. The falls is actually two streams coming together and forming a "union" at the same spot. The sensational, 265-foot waterfall is the second-highest in the park, only surpassed by 308-foot Lower Falls of the Yellowstone. The trail ends at a great viewpoint. Don't try to get down to the base of the falls; it's much too dangerous.

**Options:** You can also reach Union Falls from Cascade Creek Trailhead (a slightly shorter route) or Fish Lake Trailhead (a much longer route, used by many stock parties, that requires a four-wheel-drive vehicle).

**Side trips:** If you're feeling ambitious, you could take side trips along Mountain Ash Creek or take the Cascade Creek Trail to Terraced Falls.

# 88  PITCHSTONE PLATEAU

|  |  |
|---|---|
| **Type of hike:** | Shuttle. |
| **Type of trip:** | Long day hike or overnighter. |
| **Total distance:** | 20.2 miles or 32.5 kilometers. |
| **Difficulty:** | Difficult. |
| **Elevation gain:** | 963 feet. |
| **Maps:** | Trails Illustrated (Old Faithful); Lewis Canyon and Grassy Lake Reservoir USGS quads. |
| **Starting point:** | Grassy Lake Trailhead (9K5). |

**Finding the trailhead:** About 2 miles south of the park on U.S. 287 and just before Flagg Ranch, turn west on what is called the Ashton-Flagg Road (also called Grassy Lake Road). This also goes to Flagg Ranch Village. After about a quarter mile, turn right (west) as the left fork goes to the campground. The road stays paved for about 2 more miles before turning into an uneven gravel road. The trail starts just after crossing over the spillway at the west end of Grassy Lake Reservoir, which is just south of the park, 10 miles west of Flagg Ranch. At the east end of the trail, leave a vehicle or arrange to be picked up at the Phantom/Pitchstone Trailhead (8K4), which is 14 miles south of West Thumb or 6 miles north of the South Entrance. The trailhead is a pullout on the south side of the road, barely big enough for about three vehicles. If you have a two-wheel-drive vehicle, you should park at the top of the dam and walk down to the trailhead. Many people have driven a two-wheel-drive to the trailhead parking lot and not been able to get back up the hill.

## Key points:

| | | |
|---|---|---|
| 1.0 | (1.6) | Junction with Cascade Creek Trail and ford Falls River. |
| 1.2 | (1.9) | 9C5 (4★) and junction with Union Falls Trail. |
| 13.0 | (20.9) | 8P1 (3★) and 8P2 (3★). |
| 14.2 | (22.8) | Phantom Fumarole. |
| 20.2 | (32.5) | South Entrance Road. |

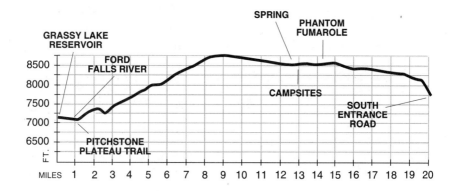

# PITCHSTONE PLATEAU

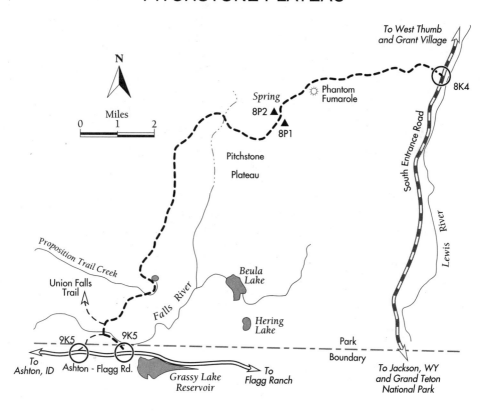

**The hike:** This hike traverses some of the greatest scenery in Yellowstone, but it's not for beginning hikers. It's a rugged hike, requiring route-finding skills. Be sure to take plenty of water because reliable sources are scarce late in the summer.

If you start at Grassy Lake Reservoir, the first mile is flat and easy. It follows the stream that leaves the reservoir and then the Falls River.

At the 1-mile mark, a trail goes off to the left (west) to Cascade Creek Trailhead just before you ford the Falls River. It's a long ford, but only knee-deep in August. You probably shouldn't try this trail until at least mid-July because the Pitchstone Plateau gets lots of snow. If snow covers the cairns, you'll have a hard time finding the route.

Right after the ford, you'll see 9C5 and then a few feet later the trail to Pitchstone Plateau, both on your right. The trail you're on (which goes to Union Falls) is much better, so be careful not to walk by this junction, where you go right (east).

From this junction to the Pitchstone Plateau, the trail becomes indistinct for several miles, but it's marked fairly well with cairns and orange markers. It goes through burnt forest for about 3 miles and then unburned timber on a more defined trail for another 3 miles to the plateau.

When you get up on Pitchstone Plateau, the trail disappears, but frequent cairns show the way. This section of trail goes through a series of gorgeous, high-altitude meadows with spectacular views in all directions, including a choice view of the Tetons off to the south. Pitchstone is glassy, black, igneous rock that resembles hardened pitch, and this will be easy to observe. The Pitchstone Plateau is one of the most recent examples of volcanic flows in the area, and the black volcanic rock is strewn everywhere across the plateau.

From the campsites, the trail continues as a chain of cairns, mostly through open country. About 1 mile past the campsites, you go by impressive Phantom Fumarole, a colorful and quite active mudpot that puts out lots of steam. It earns its name because it was hard to find, except on cold days when early explorers could spot the steam cloud above it. After the fumarole, you hike back into the timber for the last 3 miles before reaching the South Entrance Road. This section of trail was heavily burned in 1988[1].

**Options:** The shuttle can be done from either direction, depending on what logistics are most convenient. At the south end, you can start or end at the Cascade Creek Trailhead (9K5). This is a slightly shorter route, but it involves a half mile walk on a four-wheel-drive road that starts 1.5 miles east of the dam at Grassy Lake Reservoir. If you don't have a four-wheel-drive vehicle and have to walk the road, it's shorter to start or end at Grassy Lake Reservoir. Also, the Grassy Lake Reservoir Trailhead is easier to find.

---

[1]The signs at opposite ends of the trail have discrepancies in the mileages, but it looks like the longer distance is more correct.

**Side trips:** Because of the open terrain, you can hike off-trail on the Pitchstone Plateau, but you should talk to rangers about your plans and make sure you're proficient with map and compass.

# 89  BECHLER RIVER

|   |   |
|---|---|
| **Type of hike:** | Shuttle. |
| **Type of trip:** | Multi-day backpacking trip. |
| **Total distance:** | 30.3 miles or 48.8 kilometers. |
| **Difficulty:** | Difficult because of the length and river fords, but easy otherwise. |
| **Elevation gain:** | 980 feet (over the Continental Divide twice). |
| **Maps:** | Trails Illustrated (Old Faithful); Old Faithful, Shoshone Geyser Basin, Trischman Knob, Cave Falls, and Bechler Falls USGS quads. |
| **Starting point:** | Lone Star Trailhead (OK1). |

**Finding the trailhead:** Drive east of Old Faithful 3.5 miles and park at the Lone Star Trailhead. Leave a vehicle or arrange to be picked up at the Bechler Ranger Station in the far southwestern corner of the park.

You can reach the Bechler Ranger Station by two routes. Refer to the overview map in the front of the book.

The rough, scenic route goes from Flagg Ranch just south of the park on the Ashton-Flagg Road, past Grassy Lake Reservoir. Watch for a signed junction where you turn right (north) to the Cave Falls Road and right again (east) when you reach the Cave Falls Road. After about 2 miles on an unpaved section of Cave Falls Road, you reach a junction where the pavement starts and you can turn left (north) to the ranger station. Allow 2.5 hours to drive to Bechler from Flagg Ranch.

You can also get to the Bechler Ranger Station from the west, from either Ashton, Idaho, or West Yellowstone, Montana, by getting on Idaho Highway 47 and turning on the Green Timber Road which turns into the Cave Falls Road. Allow about an hour to drive the 22 miles from Ashton, Idaho.

**Key points:**

| | | |
|---|---|---|
| 1.6 | (2.5) | Junction with Spring Creek Trail. |
| 2.4 | (3.8) | Lone Star Geyser and end of paved trail. |
| 2.7 | (4.3) | Junction with trail to Fern Cascades Trailhead and Old Faithful. |
| 3.0 | (4.8) | OA1 (3★). |
| 3.5 | (5.6) | OA2 (3★). |
| 4.0 | (6.4) | OA3 (3★). |
| 7.0 | (11.2) | Grants Pass (Continental Divide). |
| 7.5 | (12.0) | Shoshone Lake Trail and 8G1. |
| 9.6 | (15.4) | Second crossing of the Continental Divide. |
| 9.8 | (15.7) | 9D4 (3★). |

# BECHLER RIVER

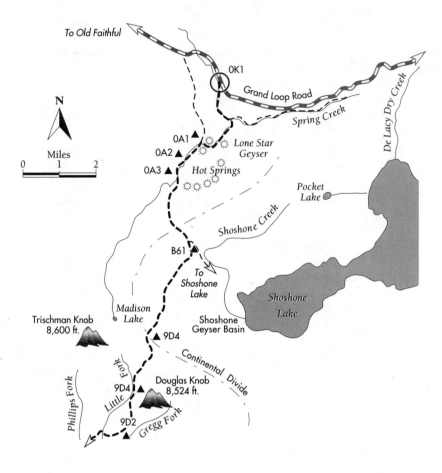

To Old Faithful

OK1

Grand Loop Road

Spring Creek

De Lacy Dry Creek

N

Miles
0   1   2

0A1
0A2
0A3

Lone Star Geyser

Hot Springs

Pocket Lake

Shoshone Creek

B61

To Shoshone Lake

Trischman Knob
8,600 ft.

Madison Lake

Shoshone Lake

Shoshone Geyser Basin

9D4

Continental Divide

Little Fork

Phillips Fork

9D4

Douglas Knob
8,524 ft.

9D2

Gregg Fork

To Map #2

## Key points (contd):

# BECHLER RIVER

From Map #1

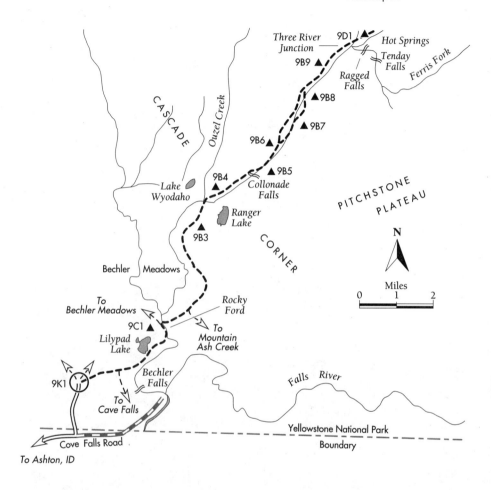

21.7 (34.9)  Ranger Lake and 9B4 (3★).
22.6 (36.3)  First cutoff Trail to Bechler Meadows Trail and 9B2 (3★).
25.6 (41.2)  Junction with Mountain Ash Creek Trail.
26.5 (42.6)  Rocky Ford of Bechler River, junction with the second cutoff trail to Bechler Meadows and 9C1(3★).
29.3 (47.1)  Junction with Cave Falls Trail.
30.3 (48.7)  Bechler Ranger Station.

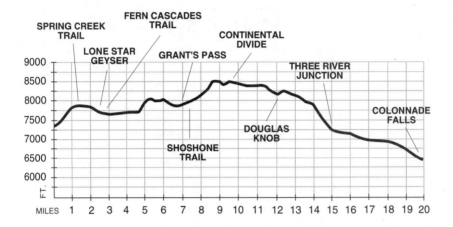

**Recommended itinerary:** A five-day trip staying at OA1 or OA3 the first night (which allows time for a leisurely drive to the trailhead the first day, as well as fishing the Upper Firehole or a side trip to Shoshone Geyser Basin), second night at 9D4 or 9D3, third night at 9B7 or 9B6, and fourth night at 9B2 or 9C1.

*Bechler River.*

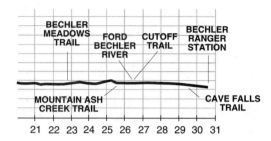

**The hike:** Along with the Thorofare and Gallatin Skyline, the Bechler River ranks among the best backpacking trips in Yellowstone. It's wild and remote, not too difficult (good trail with no monster hills), and has good fishing and matchless scenery.

In addition, this is one of the few sections of Yellowstone that escaped the fires of 1988, perhaps the only 30-mile hike you can take without walking through a burned landscape (with the exception of a 1997 fire which burned one small section of the canyon).

You can usually find water along this trail, so unlike many long hikes, you don't have to carry that extra water bottle. The only exception to this is the Bechler Meadows route (an option on this hike) which can be a desert late in the year.

If you plan to fish, be sure to get a park fishing permit and remember all of the Bechler River Valley is catch-and-release only.

A major issue on this hike is the timing of your trip. You really don't want to be in the Bechler until late July. The mosquitoes can seem life-threatening, and the water is high, which means difficult if not dangerous fords and walking in marshy trails. If you go before August, plan on having wet feet most of the time.

If you're going to be carrying a pack for five days, you might as well start out easy, right? The first leg of this backpacking adventure to Lone Star Geyser is as easy as it gets—2.4 miles on a flat, paved trail.

Lone Star is a well-known and heavily visited geyser. The trail is actually an old service road closed to motor vehicles but open to mountain bikers. Even though you might see a few bikers and more than a few hikers on this section of trail, it's still a pleasant hike along the Upper Firehole River.

At the 1.6-mile mark, stay right (south) at the junction with the Spring Creek Trail, continuing on the paved path. The pavement ends about 100 feet before the geyser and is blocked by downed trees to discourage bicycle traffic beyond this point.

*Colonnade Falls on the Bechler River.*

Lone Star Geyser was named for its isolated location (5 miles south of Old Faithful with no other geysers in the neighborhood). The name has no link with Texas, the Lone Star State. It has a great appearance and erupts 30 to 50 feet every 2 to 3 hours or so for about 10 to 15 minutes and makes gurgling sounds between eruptions.

Some maps show a little loop north of the geyser, but that loop really doesn't exist on the ground. Follow the unpaved but excellent trail past the geyser for less than a quarter mile before turning left (south) on the main trail to the Bechler River. You could have skipped the paved section and added 1 mile to your trip by starting at the Fern Cascades Trailhead near Old Faithful and getting to the same point.

From here, the trail crosses Upper Firehole River (on a footbridge) and then continues along the river for about 2 miles before veering off to the left and climbing about 300 feet up to the Continental Divide at Grants Pass. The pass is heavily forested, effectively blocking the view.

After the pass, the trail drops only slightly (about 150 feet) down to the junction with the Shoshone Lake Trail. The trail through this section is in great shape, well defined and marked.

248

At this junction, stay right (south) and head for the Bechler River. Before you drop down to the river, however, you get to go over the Continental Divide again. Once more, the climb is gentle, hardly in line with popular images of the Great Divide.

After crossing the Divide, it's all downhill for 20 miles. Hike gradually down into the Littles Fork, passing Douglas Knob on your left (south) at about the 12-mile mark and then over a small ridge into the Falls Fork and to Twister Falls which is farther downstream on the Falls Fork than shown on the maps. Twister Falls makes an unusual twist as the water drops. You can't see Twister Falls from the trail, but you can take a short spur trail to a viewpoint.

Douglas Knob is forested and visible, but not as notable as its namesake, one of the most colorful and famous rangers in the early days of Yellowstone. Witness this: In 1921, Douglas tried to walk across Yellowstone Lake from West Thumb to Lake. Two miles into his trip, he fell through the ice, but crawled out, stripped off his clothes in thirty-below-zero weather, wrung out the water and redressed himself in frozen-stiff garments. Then, a tough decision—go 2 miles back to West Thumb or 15 miles to Lake. He hiked the 15 miles, and when somebody asked him why he didn't take the 2-mile option, he replied "They'd have kidded me to death."

Another 2 miles brings you to Three Rivers Junction, a flat floodplain where three forks (Ferris, Gregg, and Phillips) merge to form the Bechler River (named after the chief topographer of the Hayden survey). Ragged Falls is off to your left (south) on Ferris Fork. There is also a patrol cabin not marked on the topo maps.

You're now in the Bechler River Canyon, which is lined with cliffs, thermal areas, hot springs, cascades, waterfalls, and generally outstanding scenery. You follow the canyon for another 7 miles. Don't be surprised to see anglers casting for the wily rainbow, which inhabits the scenic waterway.

The trail continues to be in great shape, well defined and well-marked, but a little rocky in a few places. There are more berries (huckleberries, thimbleberries, strawberries, and others species, too) in this area than most parts of Yellowstone, which means there are bears, too, so be alert.

While in the canyon, you ford the Bechler River twice. The first ford (at about the 16.5-mile mark by 9B8) is easy and knee-deep, but the second (at about the 18-mile mark just before 9B7), is hip-deep (even in August) with a fairly fast current. Kids might have a tough time with the second ford. The NPS tries to mark the ford with posts each year, but if not marked, cross slightly downstream from where the trail hits the river.

When you get to Colonnade Falls, take a break and hike the short side trip (less than a quarter mile) to see the magnificent double falls. You can't see Ranger Lake from the trail, but if you watch the map, you can take a half-mile, off-trail jaunt to see the forest-lined, 56-acre lake. You might also try to outsmart the rainbow trout living there. Hang your packs out of reach of bears before you go.

After Ranger Lake, you leave the canyon behind and head out into the incredible flat piece of wild real estate called Bechler Meadows. You basically stay on the same contour line for the last 8 miles of the hike.

At the junction with the first cutoff trail to the west over to Bechler Meadows Trail, you can go either way, but this trail description follows the Bechler River Trail, so go left (south).

From the junction, the trail stays on the east side of the massive Bechler Meadows where the Bechler River splits up into several channels. In about 3 miles, you come to the junction with the Mountain Ash Trail. Go right (south). In another mile or so, you reach the Rocky Ford of the Bechler River. If you cross right where the trail meets the river, you'll need dry underwear on the other side. If you cross about a 100 feet downstream, it's only knee-deep. The rocks are slippery, so a sturdy walking stick might prevent an embarrassing flop into the icy water.

After the ford, its an easy 3.8 miles to the ranger station. After four nights out, you might be thinking about a shower and a big steak, but you still should hang your pack for a few minutes and take the short out-and-back side trip over to see Bechler Falls, a huge cascade on the Bechler River with a nice steady roar to add an extra touch to the end of your adventure in Bechler River country.

**Options:** This trip could, of course, be done in reverse if the shuttle logistics were more convenient, but it would be a gradual upgrade most of the way.

You can finish your hike by going by the falls if you left your vehicle at the Cave Falls Trailhead instead of the ranger station. This would only shorten the hike by about a quarter mile or so. You could also shorten your trip by taking the Bechler Meadows Trail instead of staying on the Bechler River Trail, but you'd miss Rocky Ford and Bechler Falls.

Unlike many other areas of Yellowstone, there are many options for creatively building a backpacking adventure for the Bechler River area. For example, this hike can also be started or finished at the Fern Cascades, DeLacy Creek, Dogshead, Cave Falls, Fish Lake, Cascade Creek, or Grassy Lake trailheads.

**Side trips:** If you have the time, you can hang your pack and take a rewarding, 2.5-mile round-trip to Shoshone Geyser Basin on the west end of Shoshone Lake. Near the end of the trip, tack an extra hour on your last day with the short side trip to see Bechler Falls.

| | |
|---:|:---|
| **Type of hike:** | Loop. |
| **Type of trip:** | Day hike or overnighter. |
| **Total distance:** | 15.3 miles or 24.6 kilometers. |
| **Difficulty:** | Moderate. |
| **Elevation gain:** | Minimal. |
| **Maps:** | Trails Illustrated (Old Faithful); Bechler Falls and Cave Falls USGS quads. |
| **Starting point:** | Bechler Ranger Station Trailhead (9K1). |

**Finding the trailhead:** You can reach the Bechler Ranger Station by two routes. Refer to the overview map in the front of the book.

The rough, scenic route goes from Flagg Ranch just south of the park on the Ashton-Flagg Road, past Grassy Lake Reservoir. Watch for a signed junction where you turn right (north) to the Cave Falls Road and right again (east) when you reach the Cave Falls Road. After about 2 miles on an unpaved section of Cave Falls Road, you reach a junction where the pavement starts and you can turn left (north) to the ranger station. Allow 2.5 hours to drive to Bechler from Flagg Ranch.

You can also get to the Bechler Ranger Station from the west, from either Ashton, Idaho, or West Yellowstone, Montana, by getting on Idaho Highway 47 and turning on the Green Timber Road, which turns into the Cave Falls Road. Allow about an hour to drive the 22 miles from Ashton, Idaho.

**Key points:**

| | | |
|---:|---|---|
| 2.6 | (4.1) | Cave Falls Road. |
| 5.3 | (8.5) | Winegar Lake. |
| 6.0 | (9.6) | Junco Lake. |
| 6.3 | (10.1) | Junction with Falls River Cutoff Trail. |
| 8.0 | (12.8) | Ford Falls River, junction with Mountain Ash Trail and 9C2 (4★). |
| 10.9 | (17.5) | Junction with Bechler River Trail. |
| 11.8 | (18.9) | Rocky Ford of Bechler River and junction with cutoff trail to Bechler Meadows. |
| 14.3 | (23.0) | Junction with trail to Bechler Falls. |
| 15.3 | (24.6) | Bechler Ranger Station. |

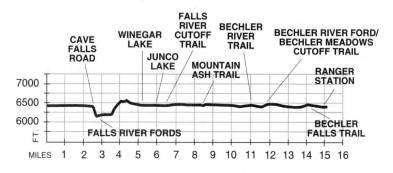

# FALLS RIVER BASIN

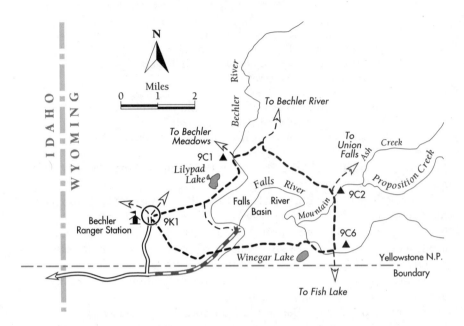

**The hike:** This route is a rare loop trip and makes a great overnighter or long day hike from the Bechler Ranger Station. You get some great scenery, can take short side trips to four lakes, and ford two major rivers as you circle the Falls River Basin. On top of that, this looks like about the flattest 15-mile hike anywhere in the Rocky Mountains. On the negative side, you wouldn't want to have a problem with fording rivers because you have to wade the Bechler River, Falls River (twice!), and Mountain Ash Creek on this trip.

From the Bechler Ranger Station, take the South Boundary Trail (well defined and forest-lined) to the Cave Falls Road. Here you cross the road and then ford the Falls River. This is a difficult ford—deep, fast, and carpeted with slick rocks—and probably too tough for kids.

After fording the Falls River, keep going east on the South Boundary Trail, which stays well-defined. After 2 miles, you get a brief glimpse of 28-acre Winegar Lake, shallow and marshy, off to the right (south). Less than 1 mile more takes you by lilypad-lined Junco Lake which is actually just outside the park in the Targhee National Forest. The trail stays in the forest all the way to the junction with the Falls River Cutoff Trail.

When you reach the junction with the Falls River Cutoff Trail, go left (north) and you immediately face another, but much easier, ford of the Falls River. After the ford, hike 1.5 miles until you see Mountain Ash Creek and another ford, but this one is knee-deep and easy in August. 9C2 is on your right just after crossing the river.

After the third ford, you head into a big meadow, and the trail appears to split, but these are merely social trails that have developed through time. Take the left fork and in about 200 yards, you'll hook up with the main Mountain Ash Trail. About 1 mile later, you ford Mountain Ash Creek, which will seem easy after fording the Falls River two times.

When you get to the Bechler River Trail, turn left (southwest) and in less than 1 mile you reach the Rocky Ford of the Bechler River. Be careful crossing. The ford is only knee-deep, but the slippery rocks make footing treacherous. Ford just downstream from where the trail hits the river.

Immediately after the ford, you see the cutoff trail going off to the west into Bechler Meadows. Go left (south) at this junction, and hike through unburned forest back to the ranger station, taking an extra hour to go over to see Bechler Falls on the way.

**Options:** This loop can be done in either direction with no extra difficulty. You could also start at Cave Falls or Fish Lake trailheads. You could make this a longer loop by going over to Bechler Meadows before heading south to the ranger station.

**Side trips:** If you're staying overnight and have extra time and energy, you can hike west on the Mountain Ash Creek Trail to Union Falls and back. The mile-long, out and back side trip to Bechler Falls is well worth the time.

# 91  BECHLER MEADOWS

| | | |
|---|---|---|
| **Type of hike:** | Loop. | See Map on Page 257 |
| **Type of trip:** | Day hike or overnighter. | |
| **Total distance:** | 12.5 miles or 20.1 kilometers. | |
| **Difficulty:** | Moderate. | |
| **Elevation gain:** | Minimal. | |
| **Maps:** | Trails Illustrated (Old Faithful); | |
| | Bechler Falls and Cave Falls USGS quads. | |
| **Starting point:** | Bechler Ranger Station Trailhead (9K1). | |

**Finding the trailhead:** You can reach the Bechler Ranger Station by two routes. Refer to the overview map in the front of the book.

The rough, scenic route goes from Flagg Ranch just south of the park on the Ashton-Flagg Road, past Grassy Lake Reservoir. Watch for a signed junction where you turn right (north) to the Cave Falls Road and right again (east) when you reach the Cave Falls Road. After about 2 miles on an unpaved section of Cave Falls Road, you reach a junction where the pavement starts and you can turn left (north) to the ranger station. Allow 2.5 hours to drive to Bechler from Flagg Ranch.

*Bechler Meadows, with the Tetons on the horizon.*

You can also get to the Bechler Ranger Station from the west, from either Ashton, Idaho, or West Yellowstone, Montana, by getting on Idaho Highway 47 and turning on the Green Timber Road which turns into the Cave Falls Road. Allow about an hour to drive the 22 miles from Ashton, Idaho.

**Key points:**
| | | |
|---|---|---|
| 1.5 | (2.4) | Junction with Boundary Creek Trail. |
| 4.0 | (6.4) | Bartlett Slough. |
| 5.0 | (8.0) | Boundary Creek (suspension bridge) and 9A1 (3★). |
| 6.0 | (9.6) | Junction with cutoff trail to Bechler River Trail. |
| 7.5 | (12.0) | Junction with Bechler River Trail. |
| 9.5 | (15.3) | 9B1 (4★). |
| 10.0 | (16.1) | Junction with second cutoff trail to Bechler River Trail. |
| 11.0 | (17.7) | Junction with Boundary Creek Trail. |
| 12.5 | (20.1) | Bechler Ranger Station. |

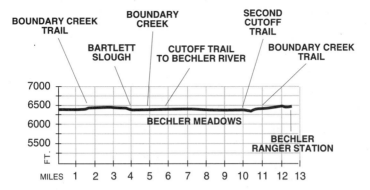

**The hike:** If you've avoided the Bechler River Trail and the Falls River Loop because you didn't like to ford big rivers, this would be a good option for seeing the Bechler River Country without getting hip-deep in it. The trail is well-defined and flat the entire way with great views from the huge meadows. However, don't try it until August. In June and July, Bechler Meadows could be called Bechler Meadows Lake, and the entire area can be under 1-2 feet of water.

The first 1.5 miles to the Bechler Meadows Trail junction goes through scattered forest and meadows and is totally flat. You can go either way at this junction, but this description takes the clockwise route, so go left (north) on the Boundary Creek Trail. Soon, you are in expansive Bechler Meadows where you cross Bartlett Slough (named after ranchers who ran cattle in the area in the late 1800s before the park was created) and Boundary Creek. Bartlett Slough is usually an easy, but thigh-deep ford on a solid bottom. Boundary Creek has a suspension bridge.

At about the 6-mile mark, you reach the junction with the trail to Buffalo Lake. Go right (southeast) and go about 1 mile until the cutoff trail joins the Bechler River Trail. Go right (south) and head back toward the ranger station, again through the scenic flatness of Bechler Meadows. You cross the Bechler River but on a bridge.

When you see the cutoff trail to Rocky Ford and the Bechler River Trail, go right (south), and hike through scattered meadows and unburned forest back to the ranger station.

**Options:** The loop can be done in either direction with no extra difficulty.

**Side trips:** You could take a short, out-and-back trip to see Silver Scarf and Dunanda falls.

|  |  |
|---|---|
| **Type of hike:** | Out and back. |
| **Type of trip:** | Multi-day backpacking trip. |
| **Total distance:** | 30 miles or 48.3 kilometers (round-trip). |
| **Difficulty:** | Difficult. |
| **Elevation gain:** | 1,300 feet. |
| **Maps:** | Trails Illustrated (Old Faithful); |
|  | Bechler Falls and Buffalo Lake USGS quads. |
| **Starting point:** | Bechler Ranger Station Trailhead (9K1). |

**Finding the trailhead:** You can reach the Bechler Ranger Station by two routes. Refer to the overview map in the front of the book.

The rough, scenic route goes from Flagg Ranch just south of the park on the Ashton-Flagg Road, past Grassy Lake Reservoir. Watch for a signed junction where you turn right (north) to the Cave Falls Road and right again (east) when you reach the Cave Falls Road. After about 2 miles on an unpaved section of Cave Falls Road, you reach a junction where the pavement starts and you can turn left (north) to the ranger station. Allow 2.5 hours to drive to Bechler from Flagg Ranch.

You can also get to the Bechler Ranger Station from the west, from either Ashton, Idaho, or West Yellowstone, Montana, by getting on Idaho Highway 47 and turning on the Green Timber Road which turns into the Cave Falls Road. Allow about an hour to drive the 22 miles from Ashton, Idaho.

**Key points:**
|  |  |  |
|---|---|---|
| 1.5 | (2.4) | Junction with Bechler Meadows Trail. |
| 4.0 | (6.4) | Bartlett Slough. |
| 5.0 | (8.0) | Boundary Creek (suspension bridge) and 9A1 (3★). |
| 6.0 | (9.6) | Junction with cutoff trail to Bechler River Trail. |
| 6.4 | (10.3) | 9A2 (3★). |
| 6.7 | (10.7) | Boundary Creek. |
| 7.8 | (12.5) | 9A3 (3★). |
| 8.0 | (12.8) | Silver Scarf Falls. |
| 8.2 | (13.2) | Dunanda Falls. |
| 11.5 | (18.5) | 9A4 (3★). |
| 15.0 | (24.1) | Buffalo Lake and 9A5 (4★). |

# BUFFALO LAKE • BECHLER SHORT LOOP
# • ROBINSON LAKE • BECHLER MEADOWS

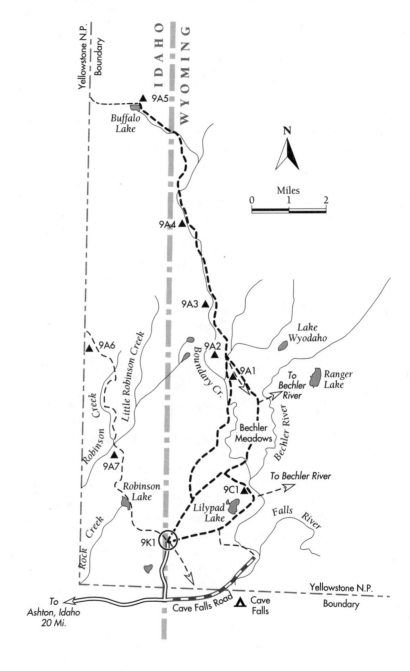

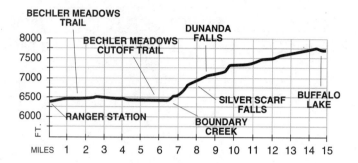

**Recommended itinerary:** A four-day trip staying at 9A2 or 9A3 the first night, 9A5 the second night, and 9A2 or 9A3 again the third night.

**The hike:** The Buffalo Lake hike will probably not rank among the most desirable hikes in the park, but it offers one thing that some Yellowstone hikes can't provide—the sense of being alone in a great wilderness. Few hikers go to Buffalo Lake, so you can find solitude. Like the Bechler River, this section of the park was not burned in 1988.

Because the Bechler Meadows area stays wet, wait until August for this hike. In July, the Bechler Meadows can still be under a foot of water.

The first 1.5 miles to the Bechler Meadows Trail junction goes through scattered forest and meadows and is totally flat. Go left (north) at the junction and take the Boundary Creek Trail into Bechler Meadows, where you cross Bartlett Slough (named after ranchers who ran cattle in the area in the late 1800s before the park was created) and Boundary Creek. Bartlett Slough is usually an easy, but thigh-deep ford on a solid bottom. The first crossing of Boundary Creek has a suspension bridge.

Watch for moose and sandhill cranes in the flat openness of Bechler Meadows. The trail is in great shape from the ranger station, through the meadows, and you get some great views of the Tetons off to the south.

At about the 6-mile mark, you reach the junction with the cutoff trail to Bechler River. Go left (north) and follow a tributary of Boundary Creek for less than 1 mile before fording it (deep in spots but slow-moving) and continuing north to Silver Scarf Falls (a 250-foot sloping cascade) and 150-foot Dunanda Falls (named for the Shoshone name for "straight down"). The trail gets steadily worse as you head for Buffalo Lake, and you frequently ford Boundary Creek (sorry, no more bridges). Watch for a few hot springs and thermal areas along this section of trail. The trail is mostly defined, with the exception of a few faint sections in meadows, but it doesn't get much use, as witnessed by small trees growing up in the trail. However, the NPS plans to fix this soon.

Buffalo Lake is a fairly shallow, forest-lined, 20-acre lake with no fish. There is a patrol cabin at the lake. After a lonely night at this remote lake,

258

retrace your steps to the trailhead. On the way back, you might want to choose a different campsite, and you can take one of two alternative routes back to the Bechler Ranger Station.

**Options:** You can take the Bechler River or Bechler Meadows trails over the first or last part of the hike, but each will lengthen your trip.

# *BACKCOUNTRY CAMPSITES*

These campsites serve backpacking trips in the southwest section of the park and are on the Old Faithful Trails Illustrated map. Stock-party-only or boater-access sites are not covered.

Please keep in mind that the rating serves as a general guide only. We only visited these campsites once, and it might have been an especially good or especially bad day. For example, campsites clounded with bugs in July may be bug-free in September, and campsites without a view on a rainy day might have a good view on a clear day.

All campsites in Yellowstone allow campfires unless otherwise indicated. Likewise, all campsites are supposed to have bear poles, but just in case, be prepared to improvise.

As this book goes to print, the NPS is in the process of moving campsites previously located along the trail. Bears use the trails as travel corridors, which increases the chance of an encounter.

**Beula Lake:** 8A1 (4★) would be a 5★ if it wasn't so close to the end of the trail where it comes into the lake, limiting privacy. Hiker-only site. Great view of the lake and easy water source from the lake. Good tent sites. Finding more than one good tent site might be a challenge. No campfires

8A2 (4★) is a similar hiker-only site a quarter mile down the lakeshore from 8A1, which gives it more privacy, but people going along the lake would still go right by your camp. Limited tent sites after rejecting the one that's too close to the food area. Bear pole nicely located away from tent sites. Great view of lake and good water source. No campfires.

**Shoshone Lake:** Shoshone Lake has lots of campsites, but more than half of them are reserved for boaters. These campsites are covered in another Falcon book, *Paddling Yellowstone and Grand Teton* (to be released in spring of 1998). No campfires at any Shoshone Lake campsites, but 8M1 and 8M2 are not on the lake and allow campfires.

8S1 (4★) is a large, two-party site open to hikers and boaters. Limit of 8 people per party. Right on trail, so limited privacy from trail users. About 100 feet from patrol cabin. Good view of lake. Good water source and tent sites. Toilet.

8S2 (3★) is open to both hikers and boaters and is right on the trail. No privacy from other trail users. Cooking area next to lake. Has a toilet and a reasonably good view of the lake. Adequate tent sites. Good water source.

8S3 (3★) is very similar to 8S2 but restricted to hikers only. No boaters.

8R2 (4★) is a private site (about a quarter mile off the trail) open to both hikers and boaters. Nice view. Cooking area on a cliff above the lake. Toilet. Good water source and adequate tent sites.

8R3(3★) is a private, hiker-only site about a quarter mile off the trail. Cooking area right on the lake with a nice view. Have to climb a hill to get to toilet and tent sites. Good water source.

8R5 (5★) is a private, hiker-only site out on a peninsula almost a half mile from the trail. Great view. Easy water source. Toilet. Nice tent sites.

8T1 (3★) is a not-so-private, hiker-only site right on the trail. The tent sites are up a small hill right next to a small waterfall. Good water source and nice view of the lake. Toilet.

8M1 (3★) is a not-so-private mixed site. Good water source. Marginal view. Adequate tent sites. Campfires allowed.

8M2 (3★) is a private, mixed site along Moose Creek, which serves as the water source. Marginal view. Lots of good tent sites. Campfires allowed.

**Pitchstone Plateau:** Both 8P1 and 8P2 are high-altitude campsites (about 8,600 feet) so be prepared for foul weather. Both use a spring for water source, which is great water only about 50 feet from camp, but in dry years, this water source can dry up. Neither site has a bear pole, so plan on making alternative food storage arrangements. Campfires allowed at both sites. Both sites are right on the trail, but privacy won't be much of a problem because of the infrequent use of the area.

8P1 (3★) is a mixed site, but the NPS recommends against stock use. Excellent view and plenty of tent sites.

8P2 (3★) is a hiker-only site with a fair view. Good tent sites.

**Bechler River:** The Bechler River has an abundance of designated camp-sites, probably a higher density than any other area in the park, which reflects the popularity of the area. Many sites are limited to one night stays, and some sites are minimum impact sites, which means no campfires.

0A1 (3★) a not-so-private, mixed site right along the trail, just past Lone Star Geyser. Reasonably good water source and plenty of tent sites. Exposed campsite. Nice view of the Upper Firehole River from camp.

0A2 (3★) is a not-so-private, hiker-only site just off the trail. Nice view. Lots of tent sites. Good water source.

0A3 (2★) is a not-so-private, hiker-only site just off the trail near Firehole Springs. No view. Tent sites on hard ground—hard to get stakes in. Good water source.

8G1 (3★) is a private, hiker-only site accessed from the Shoshone Lake Trail, not the Bechler River Trail. About a 100 yards off trail. Marginal view. Fair water source. Lots of tent sites.

9D1 (3★) is a hiker-only site right along the trail. Cooking area and bear pole on one side of the trail and tent sites and toilet on the other side. Good water source. Near hot springs. No campfires. This site is scheduled to be moved.

9D2 (3★) is a not-so-private, hiker-only site. No sign when we came through. Good water source. Fair view. Limited tent sites.

9D3 (3★) is a not-so-private, mixed site near Douglas Knob. Large campsite. Lots of tent sites, but rocky terrain. Fair view. Good water source. No campfires.

9D4 (3★) is a minimum impact, hiker-only site along the trail just after crossing the Continental Divide. Marginal view. Lots of tent sites. Good water source. No campfires.

9B2 (4★) is a mixed, two-party site right along the trail. One backpacker and one stock party allowed each night. Good view and water source. Good tent sites. Toilet. No campfires.

9B4 (4★) is a semi-private, hiker-only site about 50 feet off the trail. Good view and water source. Adequate tent sites.

9B5 (2★) is a not-so-private, hiker-only site. Marginal view. Lots of tent sites but some too close to bear pole. Good water source.

9B6 (4★) is a not-so-private, hiker-only site right along the trail. Nice view of the river. Good water source. Lots of tent sites.

9B7 (3★) is a mostly private, hiker-only site about 100 feet off the trail. Limited view. Good water source and tent sites.

9B8 (4★) is a not-so-private, hiker-only site right along the trail. Nice view of a small waterfall. Good water source and tent sites.

9B9 (5★) is a large, mixed, two-party site in the Three Rivers Meadow. Incredible view of Ragged Falls from camp—and you can hear the steady roar from camp, too. Limited tent sites. Good water source. No campfires.

**Falls River Loop:** 9C1 (3★) is a private, hiker-only site. Good water source. Marginal view. Lots of tent sites.

9C2 (4★) is a not-so-private mixed site right at the ford of the Falls River. Great view of the river and meadows. Lots of tent sites and good water source.

9C6 (4★) is a fairly private, hiker only site on the north side of the Falls River. Good water source.

**Bechler Meadows:** 9B1 (3★) is a mixed, two-party site right along the trail. One backpacker and one stock party allowed each night. Stock site on other side of creek. Nice view out into meadow. A fairly long walk to get water. Good tent sites. Toilet. No campfires.

9C1 (3★) a private, hiker-only site. Good water source. Marginal view. Lots of tent sites.

9A1 (3★) is a not-so-private, hiker-only site located right along the trail in the Boundary Creek Meadows. Great view over meadows toward the Tetons. About 150 feet to water. Good tent sites

**Buffalo Lake:** 9A5 (4★) is a private, mixed site on the north shore of remote Buffalo Lake. About a quarter mile off-trail hike to campsite. Great view of lake. Good water source but limited tent sites.

**Boundary Creek:** 9A1 (3★) is a not-so-private, hiker-only site located right along the trail in the Boundary Creek Meadows. Great view over meadows toward the Tetons. About 150 feet to water. Good tent sites.

9A2 (3★) is a large, mixed, two-party site on Upper Boundary Creek. Limited to one backpacker and one stock party each night. Maximum party size—12. The two sites are about 300 yards apart. Private—off the trail. About 200 feet to water. Nice view. Plenty of tent sites.

9A3 (2★) is a private, hiker-only site at Dunanda Falls. About 100 yards down a steep, muddy slope to water. Limited tent sites. Great view from the toilet.

9A4 (3★) is a not-so-private, mixed site. Good water source and plenty of tent sites. Fair view.

**Robinson Creek:** 9A6 (1★) is a not-so-private, mixed site on Robinson Creek. Marshy, including some tent sites and the poorly defined cooking area. Walk through marsh to get to water. Marginal view.

9A7 (2★) is a not-so-private, hiker-only site right on the trail by Little Robinson Creek. About 150 feet down a steep slope to water. Marginal view. Some tent sites too close to bear pole.

**Union Falls:** 9C4 (3★) is a large, mixed, two-party site on your left just after crossing small creek on footbridge. Private—about 100 feet off the trail. About 100 feet to water. Adequately separated from stock site. Marginal view. Nice cooking area, but no campfires allowed. Plenty of tent sites but two of the well-used sites are too close to the bear pole. Toilet.

9C5 (4★) is a hiker-only site right on the Falls River. Nice view of the river and good water source (50 yards to river). Good tent sites. Campfires allowed and lots of firewood around.

**Mountain Ash Creek:** 9C2 (4★) is a not-so-private mixed site right at the ford of the Falls River. Great view of the river and meadows. Lots of tent sites and good water source.

9C3 (2★) is a two-party site right on the trail. Not private. Stock site adequately separated on other side of creek. A fairly long trek to get water. Some tent sites too close to bear pole. Toilet. No campfires.

**Summit Lake:** OE1 (3★) is on the south side of the lake where the trail comes in. It's a mixed site with no campfires allowed. A fair view, but a bit marshy for good tent sites. Good water source.

**Fairy Falls:** OD1 (1★) is a private, hiker-only site with no view or water source. Poor tent sites. No campfires allowed. The spur trail to OD1 is marked but easy to miss.

**Little Firehole Meadows:** OD2 (5★) is a private, hiker-only campsite in the trees on the edge of the meadow with a spectacular view of the Little Firehole Meadows. Good tent sites and water source and nearby fishing opportunities for wise river trout. No campfires allowed.

OD3 (4★) is also a private, hiker-only campsite between the trail and the river and next to a small waterfall. Easy water access and good tent sites. View is good, but not quite as good as OD2, but you can have a campfire.

**Mallard Lake:** All three campsites at Mallard Lake are hiker-only, fairly private, use the lake as a handy water source, and have good views of the lake.

OB2 (3★) is in live trees, on a small peninsula, 300 yards east of where the main trail meets the lake. Well used, with a large fire ring surrounded by improvised log benches. Tent sites are too close to the bear pole. Exposed—which can be a plus during bug season.

OB3 (4★) is another 200 yards farther around the eastern shore of the lake from OB2. Located on a small point on the lakeshore. Large fire ring with improvised log seats and adequate tent sites. Numerous dead snags ominously threaten to fall on tent sites during periods of high wind.

OB4 (4★) is located on the western shore close to a rock slide/talus slope near the lake's outlet. From where the main trail meets the lake, go left and follow blazes around lake to join a well-traveled path past a bear pole and cramped cooking area. Tent sites are located another 100 yards past the bear pole. This site gets early morning sun and is surrounded by live trees. A pit toilet is located up the hill about 200 feet from the tent sites. No campfires allowed.

**Sentinel Meadows:** OG1 (3★) is a private, hiker-only site about 150 yards north of the trail. Nice view of Sentinel Meadows and the thermal features there. Watch carefully for the site which is marked with an orange marker, not a trailside sign. Good water source. Exposed. No campfires allowed.

## SHORT HIKES

## 93    PELICAN CREEK NATURE TRAIL

|  |  |
|---|---|
| **Type of hike:** | Loop. |
| **Type of trip:** | Short day hike. |
| **Total distance:** | 0.5 mile or 0.8 kilometer. |
| **Difficulty:** | Easy. |
| **Elevation gain:** | Minimal. |
| **Maps:** | Trails Illustrated (Yellowstone Lake); |
|  | Lake Butte USGS quad. |
| **Starting point:** | Pelican Nature Trail Trailhead. |

See Map on Page 271

**Finding the trailhead:** Drive 2.5 miles east of Fishing Bridge Junction and park in the small parking area on the south side of the road, just before leaving the timber and going out into a large meadow along Pelican Creek.

*Boardwalks keep your feet dry on the Pelican Creek Nature Trail.*

The hike: This is a very short hike though a marshy area, to the shore of Yellowstone Lake, and back on a different route. Boardwalks over long stretches of marsh keep your feet dry and allow you to peacefully observe wildflowers. On the lakeshore, you can relax on a sandy beach and enjoy views of Mount Sheridan and Stevenson Island, as well as the massiveness of the "inland ocean" itself—all 87,450 acres of it!

The NPS offers ranger-led nature tours along this trail. Inquire at the Fishing Bridge Visitor Center or the Lake Ranger Station.

# 94  STORM POINT

| | | |
|---|---|---|
| **Type of hike:** | Loop. | See Map on Page 271 |
| **Type of trip:** | Day hike. | |
| **Total distance:** | 1.5 miles or 2.4 kilometers. | |
| **Difficulty:** | Easy. | |
| **Elevation gain:** | Minimal. | |
| **Maps:** | Trails Illustrated (Yellowstone Lake); | |
| | Lake Butte USGS quad. | |
| **Starting point:** | Storm Point Trailhead by Indian Pond. | |

**Finding the trailhead:** Drive 3.1 miles east of Fishing Bridge Junction and park in the small parking area on the south side of the road, about a half mile after crossing Pelican Creek.

The hike: If you'd like a ranger-led interpretive hike where you can really learn about the human and natural history of the Yellowstone Lake area, check at the Fishing Bridge Visitor Center or Lake Ranger Station for a schedule of trips on the Storm Point Trail. You can, of course, also take the hike anytime you feel the urge, without an official guide—and many people do. This is a delightful

evening stroll after driving around or working all day. The nearly-level trail is in great shape.

The trail starts out by going by the west edge of Indian Pond, a popular bird-watching site in the Lake area. The pond gets its name because it served as a historic camping area for Indian tribes.

After going by the pond, the trail goes through a short section of timber before taking a swing to the right, to Storm Point, a small, rocky peninsula, named for the storms that whip it as they move northeasterly through the park.

After Storm Point, the trail follows the lakeshore, offering constant scenic views of the lake for about a half mile before turning right through timber and clouds of mosquitoes (in June and July) back to the highway.

*Approaching Storm Point.*

The trail breaks out into the same large meadow you started in just before reaching the road. Walk about a quarter mile along the road back to your vehicle.

## 95   NATURAL BRIDGE

| | |
|---|---|
| **Type of hike:** | Out-and-back. |
| **Type of trip:** | Day hike. |
| **Total distance:** | 2.5 miles or 4 kilometers (round-trip). |
| **Difficulty:** | Easy. |
| **Elevation gain:** | Minimal. |
| **Maps:** | Trails Illustrated (Yellowstone Lake);<br>Lake USGS quad. |
| **Starting point:** | Bridge Bay Marina parking lot. |

See Map on Page 271

**Finding the trailhead:** Drive 2 miles south of Lake on the Lake-West Thumb section of the Grand Loop Road and turn west into the Bridge Bay Marina. Go another 0.4 mile and turn left into the parking lot.

**The hike:** You used to be able to drive to Natural Bridge, but the NPS has converted the trip into a short day hike. This hike is the mirror image of most trails. It starts out as a super trail and gets better instead of worse. You begin on a single track, go to a double-wide trail, and finish on a paved road.

From the marina parking lot, look for a trail sign and a paved trail heading west toward the campground. Just as you reach the campground, the trail takes a sharp left (south), so be careful not to miss this turn.

From here, walk through unburned forest on an abandoned road along the west side of Bridge Bay for about a half mile to a paved road (now closed to motor vehicles, but still open to bicycles). Turn right (west) and follow the road for another half mile or so until it ends with a little loop, which goes by Natural Bridge.

An interpretive display at the end of the road explains the story of the Natural Bridge. Bridge Creek flows beneath the ground under the Natural Bridge. Through the centuries, freezing and thawing broke away sections of rock that were carried away by spring runoff, gradually creating the bridge.

There used to be a trail over the bridge, but it was abandoned for fear that the bridge might collapse. Likewise, an early proposal to build a road over the bridge was shelved—or you probably wouldn't be able to see it today.

*Natural Bridge.*

**Type of hike:** Out-and-back.
**Type of trip:** Day hike.
**Total distance:** 4.6 miles or 7.4 kilometers (round-trip).
**Difficulty:** Easy.
**Elevation gain:** Minimal.
**Maps:** Trails Illustrated (Yellowstone Lake);
Mount Sheridan USGS quad.
**Starting point:** Riddle Lake Trailhead (7K3).

**Finding the trailhead:** Drive 4.1 miles south of West Thumb and turn into the parking area on the east side of the road.

**The hike:** This ranks as one of the easiest hikes to a backcountry lake in the park. It's just over 2 miles and flat as a pool table—even though you hike over the Continental Divide!

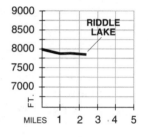

The trail is in great shape and passes through unburned forest and past several small meadows. Some of the meadows stay marshy until mid-July, so you might get your feet wet—although some of the small stream crossings have footbridges.

*Riddle Lake.*

# RIDDLE LAKE

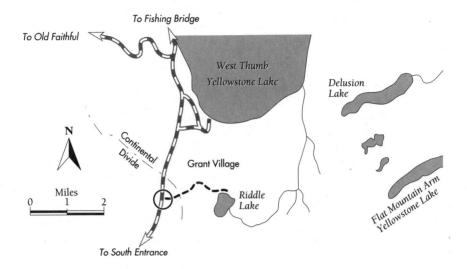

Watch for elk and moose in the meadows—and for bears. The area is a key bear management area, so it remains closed until July 15.

Riddle Lake gets its name because early on in the park's history, it was believed to be a "two-ocean lake" sitting right on the Continental Divide with outlets flowing both east and west. But this was only an early mapping error. The lake is actually about 2 miles east of the Divide, where the trailhead is located.

The huge, 274-acre lake also has a huge marshy meadow on its southwest corner, and in late summer lilypads float on the surface. The trail goes along the north edge of the lake to a small beach where it officially ends. You get a great view of the Red Mountains from the lake. Cutthroats come up Solution Creek from Yellowstone Lake to Riddle Lake.

## 97  ELEPHANT BACK MOUNTAIN

|                    |                                          |
|-------------------:|------------------------------------------|
| **Type of hike:**  | Out-and-back with a little loop at the end. |
| **Type of trip:**  | Day hike.                                |
| **Total distance:**| 4 miles or 6.4 kilometers (round-trip).  |
| **Difficulty:**    | Moderate.                                |
| **Elevation gain:**| 800 feet.                                |
| **Maps:**          | Trails Illustrated (Yellowstone Lake);   |
|                    | Lake USGS quad.                          |
| **Starting point:**| Elephant Back Trailhead.                 |

**Finding the trailhead:** Drive 0.7 mile south of Fishing Bridge or 0.5 mile north of Lake and park at the small parking area on the west side of the road.

*Stevensen Island and the "inland ocean," Yellowstone Lake.*

# ELEPHANT BACK MOUNTAIN
# • STORM POINT • NATURAL BRIDGE
# • PELICAN CREEK NATURE TRAIL

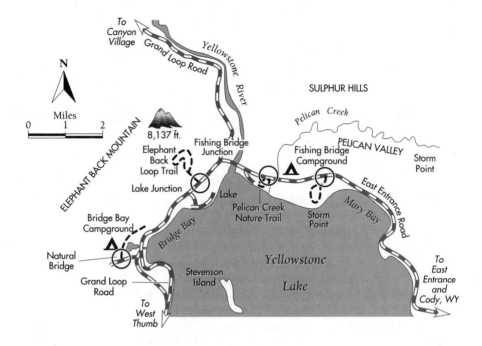

**The hike:** From some viewpoint, this forested ridge looked like an elephant's back to early explorers, but you'll have a hard time getting the same impression. Nonetheless, it's a nice day hike for anybody staying at Fishing Bridge or Lake, and because of its proximity to these areas, this trail receives heavy use. It also receives priority maintenance and is in excellent shape and double-wide most of the way.

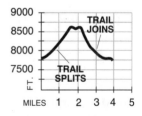

The trail goes through unburned timber the entire way. About halfway up the hill, go left or right on the loop trail. Go either way with no added difficulty and take the other route on the way down. The right fork is the most gradual, and longest route to the top, but well-designed switchbacks make the 800-foot, Category 3 climb seem fairly easy whichever fork you choose.

From the viewpoint on top, enjoy a panoramic view of "the inland ocean," Yellowstone Lake, and Stevenson Island and the massive Pelican Valley.

|  |  |
|---|---|
| **Type of hike:** | Out-and-back. |
| **Type of trip:** | Day hike. |
| **Total distance:** | 10 miles or 16.1 kilometers (round-trip). |
| **Difficulty:** | Moderate. |
| **Elevation gain:** | 440 feet. |
| **Maps:** | Trails Illustrated (Yellowstone Lake); |
|  | Lake Butte USGS quad. |
| **Starting point:** | Nine Mile Trailhead (5K5). |

**Finding the trailhead:** Drive 9 miles east of Fishing Bridge and park in the Nine Mile Trailhead parking area on the north side of the road. The NPS is constructing a new trailhead on the south side of the road, scheduled for completion in the fall of 1997.

**The hike:** Many maps and guidebooks show a trail going from the Pelican Valley to Turbid Lake, but this has been closed in recent years for bear management reasons. The best way to see Turbid Lake is to start from the East Entrance Road and go 3 miles north to the lake along an abandoned road.

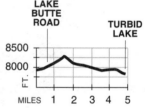

The trail starts out with a gradual, 400-foot climb along the east side of Lake Butte and then drops down to connect with an abandoned road that used to be paved. Make a mental note of this junction because it's easy to miss on the way back.

Follow the old road through forested terrain all the way—easy hiking the rest of the way, and flat, too, except for a small downhill stretch just before the lake. The trail is low priority for maintenance, so expect to climb over a few downed trees.

Turbid Lake is unlike any lake in the park. It obviously gets its name from its extreme turbidity. It's the color of sour milk, and smells like it, too. Instead of water, it seems to be filled with diluted sulfur-based liquid.

On the way back, make sure you don't miss the junction. When we did this hike, there was no sign, only one orange marker marking the junction. If you miss it, you'll follow the road to the East Entrance Highway about 1 mile east of the trailhead.

**Options:** You can make a shuttle trip out of Turbid Lake by continuing on the road into the Pelican Valley and hiking back to the Pelican Valley Trailhead. This means you'll probably get your feet wet crossing the outlet stream. At the north end of the lake, the road goes off to the west, but this road is

# TURBID LAKE

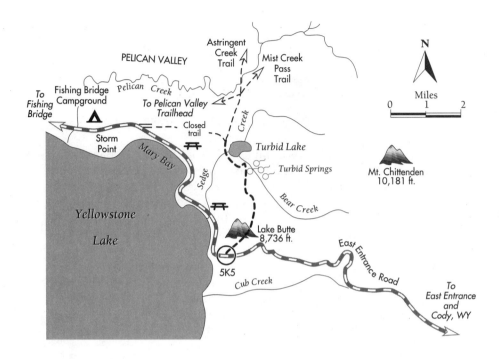

closed for bear management. You continue north on a lightly traveled, barely visible trail. However, the trail goes through open terrain, so it's fairly easy to continue on this route until you reach the well-defined Pelican Valley Trail near the Pelican Creek footbridge. From here, go left (west) and hike 3.4 miles back to the Pelican Valley Trailhead. The entire distance of the shuttle option is about 8 miles.

|  |  |
|---|---|
| **Type of hike:** | Out-and-back. |
| **Type of trip:** | Day hike. |
| **Total distance:** | 4 miles or 6.4 kilometers (round-trip). |
| **Difficulty:** | Moderate. |
| **Elevation gain:** | 2,100 feet. |
| **Maps:** | Trails Illustrated (Yellowstone Lake); |
|  | Sylvan Lake USGS quad. |
| **Starting point:** | The picnic area on the west end of Eleanor Lake. |

**Finding the trailhead:** Drive 19 miles east from Fishing Bridge or 8 miles west of the East Entrance to Eleanor Lake and park on the south side of the road in the picnic area on the west end of the lake.

**The hike:** For a truly spectacular view of the eastern part of Yellowstone and the North Absaroka Wilderness, take the short but steep hike up 10,566-foot Avalanche Peak. Looking south from the summit, you can marvel at the enormous expanse of real, hard-core wilderness stretching from Yellowstone Lake east over the park boundary into the Shoshone National Forest, a vast land without even a trail. From Avalanche Peak, you get about the best view possible of both America's first national forest (Shoshone) and first national park (Yellowstone).

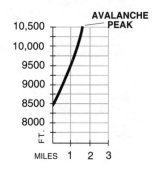

This trail starts on the right side of the stream, across the highway from the picnic area. You immediately start climbing through unburned forest, and it continues the steep incline the entire way. The trail isn't marked, but it's well-defined and easy to follow the entire way with rocky sections near the summit.

About a half mile up the trail, you cross the stream. Don't take the trail going directly up the drainage. This is an overly steep route that the NPS is trying to rehabilitate. From the stream, turn left (west) and follow the trail that traverses the slope for about a quarter mile out into an avalanche chute before continuing to climb. This is one of many avalanche chutes along the way, hence the name, Avalanche Peak.

At about the 1.2-mile mark, you reach the treeline, with great views the rest of the way. The last quarter mile or so is actually the easiest part of the hike.

# AVALANCHE PEAK

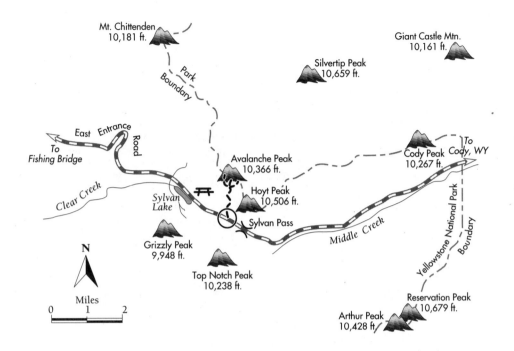

This is one of the few Category H climbs in the park, and it suffers from a shortage of switchbacks. This trail will definitely get the heart rate up and stretch out those calf muscles, but while you're relaxing on top, it's doubtful you'll resent the extra effort it took to get there.

Be sure to wait for good weather to try this hike, and if you go before mid-July, expect to be walking on snow. Also, take extra water. There are few water sources on this trail after the snow melts.

## 100 *FERN LAKE*

|  |  |
|---|---|
| **Type of hike:** | Loop. |
| **Type of trip:** | Base camp. |
| **Total distance:** | 26.1 miles or 42 kilometers. |
| **Difficulty:** | Difficult. |
| **Elevation gain:** | 420 feet. |
| **Maps:** | Trails Illustrated (Yellowstone Lake and Tower/Canyon); and Lake Butte, Mount Chittenden, Pelican Cone, and White Lake USGS quads. |
| **Starting point:** | Pelican Valley Trailhead (5K3). |

**Finding the trailhead:** Drive 3.5 miles east of the Fishing Bridge Junction and turn north on a gravel road. Follow it about a half mile until it ends at the trailhead.

### Key points:

| | | |
|---|---|---|
| 0.5 | (0.8) | Abandoned road and trail to Turbid Lake. |
| 3.4 | (5.4) | Junction with Astringent Creek Trail and Pelican Creek Bridge. |
| 5.0 | (8.0) | Ford Astringent Creek. |
| 5.2 | (8.3) | Junction with Tern Lake Trail. |
| 9.0 | (14.5) | White Lake. |
| 10.0 | (16.1) | Tern Lake. |
| 11.5 | (18.5) | Junction with cutoff trail to Pelican Creek Trail. |
| 12.1 | (19.5) | Junction with Fern Lake Trail and trail to 5B1 (5★) and 5B2 (5★). |
| 13.1 | (21.0) | Ford Pelican Creek. |
| 13.3 | (21.4) | Pelican Creek Trail. |
| 16.5 | (26.5) | Mudkettles and Mudpots. |
| 19.3 | (31.0) | Junction with Pelican Cone Trail. |
| 20.9 | (33.6) | Junction with Astringent Creek Trail. |
| 22.7 | (36.5) | Pelican Creek Bridge and junction with Mist Creek Pass Trail. |
| 26.1 | (42.0) | Pelican Valley Trailhead. |

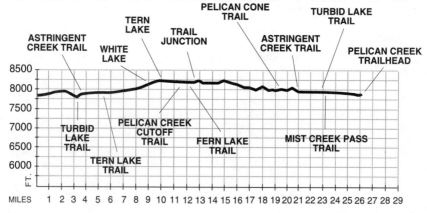

# FERN LAKE

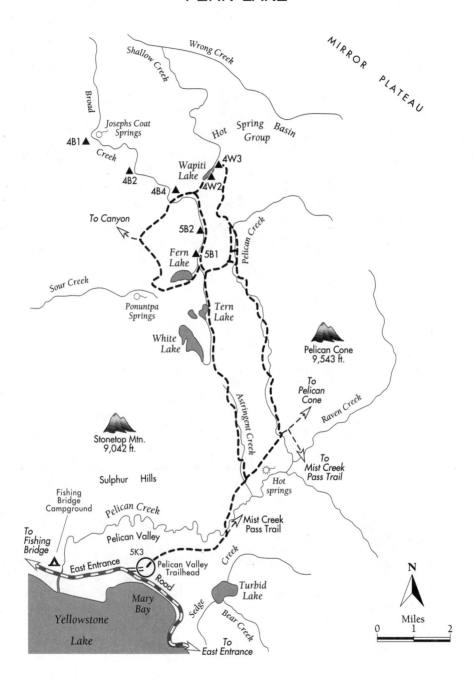

*The Pelican Valley.*

**Recommended itinerary:** I recommend hiking in along Astringent Creek all the way to 5B1 or 5B2, setting up a base camp, staying two or three nights, then hiking out Pelican Creek.

**The hike:** Pelican Valley is a favorite haunt of the grizzly, and the management priorities for the area are set accordingly. In some cases, what is good for the great bear is not so good for the backpacker. Because of the large distances between campsites and the restricted hours, this is a difficult area to hike. These regulations pretty much limit this area to serious, well-conditioned backpackers. If you can't carry an overnight pack 12 to 14 miles per day, you probably should choose a different hike. Those physically fit hikers who do try this hike, however, will be well rewarded.

You can't start hiking until 9 a.m. and you must be out of the Pelican Valley before 7 p.m. Plan on spending most of that 10-hour time span on your feet because it's at least 12.5 miles from the trailhead to any campsite, and on the way back, it's even farther, 14 miles, from base camp to the trailhead. That doesn't leave much time for relaxing, fishing, or side trips. In-between these two hard days, however, you can spend two or three days relaxing in the scenic, lake-filled valleys and take short side trips to fish or see the area's many hot springs and thermal areas.

The trail conditions are excellent the entire way, and unlike most long hikes in Yellowstone, there is minimal elevation gain.

The trail starts out on an abandoned road, but in about a half mile, you go left (north) at a junction where the road (now closed) goes straight to Turbid Lake and the also-abandoned Pelican Valley dump. The trail turns into a single-track, but it's an excellent trail through the open terrain of the Pelican Valley.

At the 3.4-mile mark, at the junction with the Mist Creek Pass Trail, turn left (north) and cross Pelican Creek on a footbridge. The bridge is closed to horses and might be dangerous for hikers, too, so be careful.

The trail continues through the incredible openness of the massive Pelican Valley until you reach the junction with the Astringent Creek Trail just after crossing it on a bridge. From the Pelican Bridge to this junction, the trail gets faint in a few places. At the junction go left (north), and follow Astringent Creek, crossing it two more times until you go over a small divide into the Broad Creek drainage and hike by White Lake, Tern Lake, and several unnamed ponds. This is an open, scenic stretch of trail.

The trail along Astingent Creek is in good shape, but gets faint in a few spots in the long grass by the lakes. Both White Lake and Tern Lake are big shallow lakes in huge meadows. Stay alert for members of the fairly large grizzly population inhabiting this area.

At the junction with the Fern Lake Trail, go straight (north) and set up your base camp at 5B1 or 5B2. (Your map might show another campsite, 4B5, just north of 5B2, but that site has been eliminated by the NPS.) Fern Lake is warm, and the stream leaving the lake is greenish with a heavy load of algae.

After spending a day or two relaxing, fishing, and day hiking, head back to the Fern Lake Trail junction and take a left (east). After 1 mile cross Pelican Creek to intersect with the Pelican Creek Trail. Most maps show the trail taking a jog to the north to cross the stream just south of the Tern Lake patrol cabin, but a well-defined unofficial trail crosses the creek about 1 mile south of the cabin, Going up to the cabin to cross would add 2 miles to your already-too-long 14-mile day.

After fording Pelican Creek, turn right (south) on the official trail and head down the Pelican Creek Trail, crossing Pelican Creek five times (no bridges) before getting back to the Pelican Creek Bridge. Along this leg of the trip, you hike through burned forest for about 1 mile before breaking out in a big open meadow. At this point, the trail disappears, so stay near the center of the valley until you get near a series of thermal features, where the trail reappears and angles off to the east side of the valley. Even though you'll be pressed for time, be sure to take short breaks to investigate the numerous and impressive hot springs and mud pots along this section of trail.

When you get to the junction with the Pelican Cone Trail, go right (west) at the Pelican Cone Junction and hike back into the expansive Pelican Valley to the Astringent Creek Trail junction.

You might be tempted to take the Pelican Cone side trip (8 miles round-trip), but you probably won't have the time or energy. (Bear management regulations make it extremely difficult to hike up Pelican Cone.) The trail between these junctions also gets faint in at least one spot. Go left (south) at the Astringent Creek junction and retrace your steps back to the trailhead.

**Options:** You could do the loop in reverse, but it would lengthen the time you spend the first day with your heaviest pack. This can also be a shuttle hike by hiking out the Wapiti Lake Trail to Canyon. You can also move your camp each night to other campsites in the Wapiti Lake/Broad Creek/Fern Lake area.

**Side trips:** Most people won't have enough time, but if you do, Pelican Cone makes a great side trip. It's a forested, Category 2 climb, and from the top you get a dramatic view of the Pelican Valley and the aftermath of the 1988 fires. If you try Pelican Cone, be sure to take water. You won't find any on the trail. And make lots of noise to warn bears of your approach.

Also, from the base camp, hike around the Fern Lake and Wapiti Lake loop trails and take off-trail jaunts up Broad Creek or to Wapiti Hot Springs to see a variety of thermal areas, or hike around sprawling Tern and White lakes.

# 101 *THE THOROFARE AND THE SOUTH BOUNDARY TRAIL*

| | |
|---|---|
| **Type of hike:** | Shuttle. |
| **Type of trip:** | A long backpacking trip. |
| **Total distance:** | 68.5 miles or 110.3 kilometers. |
| **Difficulty:** | Difficult. |
| **Elevation gain:** | 2,265 feet. |
| **Maps:** | Trails Illustrated (Yellowstone Lake); Lake Butte, Frank Island, Sylvan Lake, Trail Lake, Eagle Peak, The Trident, Badger Creek, Crooked Creek, Mount Hancock, Snake Hot Springs, and Lewis Canyon USGS quads. |
| **Starting point:** | Nine Mile Trailhead (5K5). |

**Finding the trailhead:** Drive 9 miles east of Fishing Bridge to the east shore of Yellowstone Lake and park at the Nine Mile Trailhead parking area on the north side of the road. The NPS is constructing a new trailhead on the south side of the road, due for completion in fall of 1997.

**Key points:**

| | | |
|---|---|---|
| 1.3 | (2.1) | Cub Creek. |
| 3.0 | (4.8) | Clear Creek. |
| 6.3 | (10.1) | Park Point and 5E9 (5★). |
| 6.5 | (10.4) | 5E7 (1★) and 5E8 (5★). |

**Key points (cont'd):**

| | | |
|---|---|---|
| 9.2 | (14.8) | 5E6 (4★) and 5E5 (4★). |
| 9.4 | (15.1) | Columbine Creek. |
| 12.3 | (19.8) | 5E4 (5★). |
| 14.7 | (23.6) | 5E3 (3★). |
| 15.5 | (24.9) | Terrace Point. |
| 17.3 | (27.8) | Beaverdam Creek and spur trail to 5E1 (4★). |
| 19.3 | (31.0) | Cabin Creek patrol cabin. |
| 19.7 | (31.6) | Trail Creek junction (lower ford). |
| 20.5 | (33.0) | Junction with Trail Creek Trail (upper ford). |
| 21.5 | (34.6) | 6C1 (1★). |
| 22.3 | (35.9) | Trail to 6C2 (5★). |
| 22.5 | (36.2) | Trail to 6C3 (3★). |
| 24.7 | (39.7) | Junction with Mountain Creek Trail (north). |
| 25.5 | (41.0) | Ford of Mountain Creek. |
| 25.6 | (41.2) | 6D2 (3★). |
| 26.2 | (42.2) | Junction with Mountain Creek Trail (south). |
| 26.3 | (42.3) | Trail to 6D1 (4★). |
| 28.5 | (45.8) | 6Y6 (4★). |
| 29.5 | (47.5) | Cliff Creek and trail to 6Y5 (3★). |
| 30.6 | (49.2) | Escarpment Creek. |
| 31.0 | (49.9) | Junction with trail to Thorofare Ranger Station and Bridger Lake and the South Boundary Trail. |
| 32.0 | (51.8) | Trail to 6Y4 (3★). |
| 32.2 | (51.8) | Junction with cutoff trail to Thorofare Ranger Station. |
| 32.5 | (52.3) | Trail to 6T2 (5★). |
| 32.6 | (52.4) | Ford of Thorofare Creek and 6T1 (4★). |
| 33.1 | (53.3) | Junction with trail to Bridger Lake. |
| 34.0 | (54.7) | 6Y2 (4★) and ford of Yellowstone River. |
| 35.2 | (56.6) | Lynx Creek. |
| 39.5 | (63.6) | Continental Divide on Two Ocean Plateau. |
| 41.0 | (66.0) | Mariposa Lake and 6B3 (2★). |
| 41.2 | (66.3) | 6M2 (4★). |
| 42.0 | (67.6) | Junction with Two Ocean Plateau Trail and 6M4 (3★). |
| 45.0 | (72.4) | 6M7 (3★) and Fox Creek patrol cabin. |
| 45.2 | (72.7) | Trail heading south out of park. |
| 45.6 | (73.4) | Ford Snake River. |
| 45.7 | (73.5) | Junction with Snake River Trail. |
| 49.0 | (78.9) | Big Game Ridge. |
| 56.5 | (90.9) | Harebell patrol cabin and trail heading north to Heart Lake. |
| 57.9 | (93.2) | Trail heading south out of park. |
| 59.0 | (94.9) | 8C2 (5★). |
| 59.5 | (95.8) | Junction with Snake River Cutoff Trail. |
| 62.0 | (99.8) | Junction with Heart Lake Trail. |
| 62.5 | (100.6) | Snake Hot Springs and 8C1 (3★). |
| 68.2 | (109.8) | Ford Snake River. |
| 68.5 | (110.3) | South Boundary Trailhead and Entrance Station. |

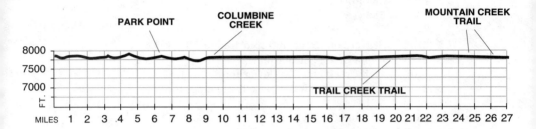

**Recommended itinerary:** This trip requires at least seven days, and you could spend as long as two weeks, but I recommend a nine-day trip averaging about 8.5 miles per day. This includes one rest day and extra time for fishing.

| | | |
|---|---|---|
| First night | — | Preferred— 5E9 or 5E8, alternate—5E7. |
| Second night | — | Preferred—5E1, alternate—5E3. |
| Third night | — | Preferred—6D2, alternate—6D1. |
| Fourth night | — | Preferred—6T2, alternate—6T1. |
| Fifth night | — | Rest day, same campsite |
| Sixth night | — | Preferred—6M2, alternate—6M4. |
| Seventh night | — | Outside park. |
| Eighth night | — | Preferred—8C2, alternate—8C1. |

**The hike:** Like the Gallatin Skyline hike, this hike offers hardy backpackers the opportunity to savor the wild essence of Yellowstone. Yet, these two major backpacking trips are strikingly different. The Gallatin Skyline transverses the highest ridgelines with easy escape routes, and this trip captures the uniqueness of Yellowstone Lake and the Thorofare with the added attractions of world-famous fishing and the allure of extreme remoteness with no easy way out.

Regardless of how you slice up this trip, it's still 68 miles long which means ultra-cautious and tedious preparation. Unlike most trips in Yellowstone, you really can't bail out if something goes wrong. When you get to the confluence of the Yellowstone River and Thorofare Creek, it's approximately 30 miles by trail in any direction to the nearest road. Therefore, more than any other trip in this book, make triple sure you're physically ready and packed as lightly as possible. Also, don't forget key equipment and carefully check all gear before leaving the trailhead. Plan for extreme weather, and take a backup stove and filter. Another essential piece of equipment is waterproof bags to keep the contents of your backpack dry during several serious fords. Before you leave on your trip, check with rangers at the Lake Ranger Station for current conditions of the fords. Because of the fords, don't try this trip until late-July.

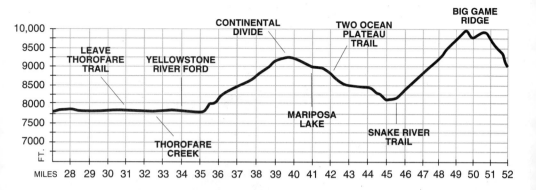

The scenery along this region rivals anything in the Rocky Mountains. You spend the first two days hiking along the "matchless mountain lake" of John Colter's journals. Yellowstone Lake, one of the world's largest freshwater lakes, is like an inland ocean. It covers 136 square miles (20 miles long, 14 miles wide) and is at least 320 feet deep in spots (139-foot average depth!). Regardless of how hot it gets on an August afternoon, the lake stays cold enough to bring on hypothermia in a few minutes. The level of the lake would probably drop several feet if the enormous population of cutthroat trout was removed. These native fish support the food chain in this area, so watch for all the fish-eaters—pelicans, cormorants, mergansers, otters, mink, eagles, ospreys, and of course, the-biggest-fish-eater-of-them-all, the grizzly.

After the lake, you go into the famous Thorofare, a wide, flat valley through which the upper Yellowstone River meanders. Because of its gentle terrain, trappers commonly used this route in and out of the Yellowstone Plateau and called it the "Throughfare," later shortened to Thorofare. The Two Ocean Plateau looms over the Thorofare from the west, and some of the highest peaks in the park (Colter Peak, Table Mountain, and the massive Trident) dominate the eastern horizon.

You also get to see a special jewel of the wildflower world, the Mariposa lily, which grows in the southern reaches of the Thorofare.

Anglers dream of this place, and if they take this hike, their dreams come true. The fishing in the lake, river, and several tributaries is fantastic. Most fish caught range in the 16 to 18 inch range, and it's actually hard to catch a legal-sized, 13-inch cutthroat.

You can hike four days on a perfectly flat trail, and then you get the rare experience of fording major rivers and climbing over the Continental Divide in the same day. You ford the Snake River, struggle up the precipitous Big Game Ridge, and then ford the Snake River again.

Simply put, this is a truly incredible trip. When you get to the South Boundary Trailhead, you'll want to give each other high-fives because you'll really have done something! And your jeans will definitely be easier to get on after this trip.

Since this is such a major backpacking trip, it only seems appropriate that it would have an especially difficult vehicle shuttle, and you won't be

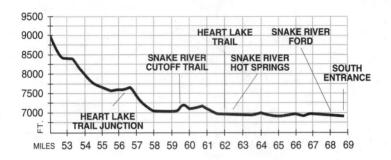

disappointed. If you can't arrange to be picked up at the end of the hike, plan on a half-day to shuffle vehicles around, leaving one at the South Boundary Trailhead just outside the park at the South Entrance Station. This makes it a wise decision to plan a fairly easy first day since you probably won't hit the trail until noon, and you don't want to wear yourself down on the first day when your pack is its heaviest.

Perhaps the only negative comment one could make about this trip is the condition of the trail. Although distinct and easy to follow, the trail suffers from extra-heavy horse traffic and has been pounded into dust. In some

*The north end of the Thorofare, where the Yellowstone River disappears into Yellowstone Lake.*

# THE THOROFARE AND
# THE SOUTH BOUNDARY TRAIL

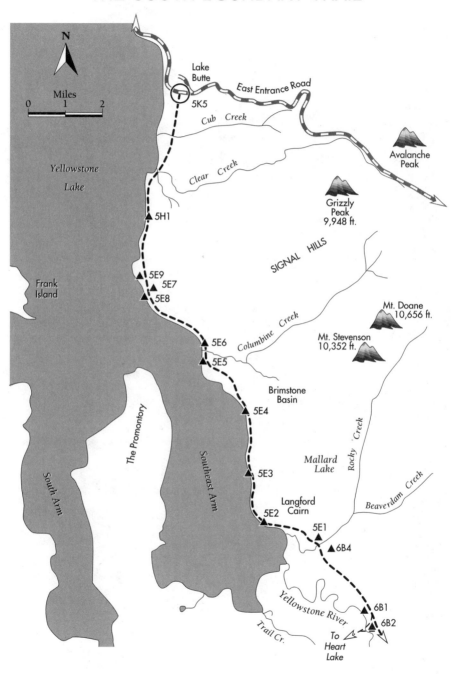

N

Miles
0   1   2

Lake
Butte

East Entrance Road

5K5

Cub   Creek

Avalanche
Peak

Yellowstone
Lake

Clear   Creek

Grizzly
Peak
9,948 ft.

5H1

SIGNAL   HILLS

Frank
Island

5E9
5E7
5E8

Mt. Doane
10,656 ft.

Columbine   Creek

Mt. Stevenson
10,352 ft.

5E6

5E5

Brimstone
Basin

The Promontory

Southeast Arm

5E4

Rocky   Creek

Mallard
Lake

5E3

South Arm

Langford
Cairn

5E2

5E1

Beaverdam   Creek

6B4

Yellowstone River

6B1

Trail Cr.

6B2

To
Heart
Lake

To Map 2

# THE THOROFARE AND
# THE SOUTH BOUNDARY TRAIL

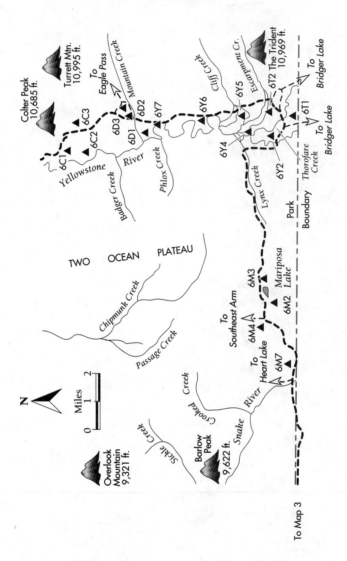

# THE THOROFARE AND
# THE SOUTH BOUNDARY TRAIL

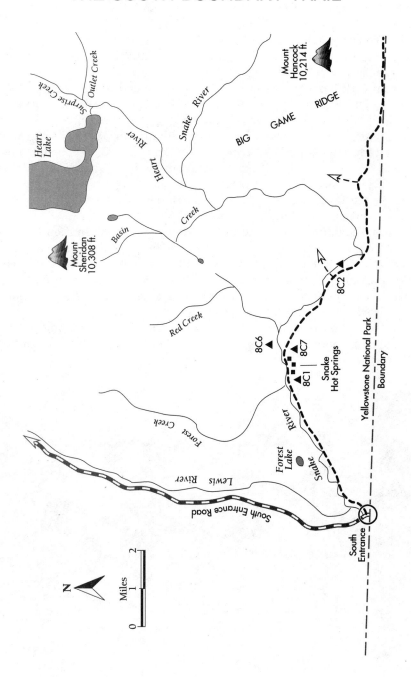

places, you have to hike 20 feet from each other to see through the dust cloud your partner kicks up.

The first 6-mile leg to Park Point is strikingly flat and somewhat monotonous as you hike over Cub and Clear creeks and through unburned lodgepole with no view of the lake until you reach Meadow Creek and Park Point, where you probably want to spend your first night out. The trail is wide and dusty, but the view from Park Point makes 5E9 and 5E8 two of the truly spectacular campsites in the park.

From Park Point to Beaverdam Creek at the end of the Southeast Arm, the trail opens up and passes through several open meadows, crosses Columbine Creek, and often goes right on the lakeshore with views of the Promontory. The meadows are carpeted with balsamroot and lupine in July.

After fording Beaverdam Creek, you go through the first section of burned trees. Even though most hikers prefer unburned forest, keep in mind that if you hiked through here 100 years ago, it would probably look similar, including the burned forest. Fire has been a vital part of the ecology of Yellowstone Park for hundreds of centuries.

The trail continues flat and dusty through open, intermittently burned forests and huge, marshy meadows (the trademark of the Thorofare) all the way to the South Boundary Trail. At Trail Creek, you'll see two trails going off to the right (west) to ford the Yellowstone River and continue on to Heart Lake. You go straight (south). Some older maps show three trail junctions at Trail Creek, but the middle ford has been abandoned.

At Mountain Creek, two trails head off to the left (east), joining and heading out of the park and up Eagle Pass in the South Absaroka Mountains. You

*Fishing Mountain Creek.*

*Mariposa Lake.*

ford Mountain Creek (a difficult ford early in the year) between the two junctions.

As you walk through and camp in the Thorofare, you discover that, along with all the great scenery, it has a huge wildlife population, including several bazillion mosquitoes. You commonly see elk, deer, and moose, but no bison. And it can be a noisy place with the incessant honking of Canada geese accompanied by the calls of sandhill cranes, coyotes howling, elk bugling, and squirrels chattering—all on the background buzzzzzz of mosquito clouds. It's a regular concerto, and a guy can't even get a good night's sleep!

When you reach the major junction with the South Boundary Trail, go right (west). The trail going straight (south) leads to the Thorofare Ranger Station (where you can usually find a ranger if you need one) and into Bridger Lake in the Bridger-Teton National Forest. About a quarter mile later, a cutoff trail goes east to the ranger station. You go right (west) to Thorofare Creek.

Most people would consider Thorofare Creek a river. It's a very large tributary of the Yellowstone and can be hazardous to ford early in the year. Depending on the place you choose to ford, it can be more difficult to cross than the Yellowstone. Shortly after this ford, another trail heads off to the left (south) to Bridger Lake. Go right (west) and in less than 1 mile, ford the Yellowstone River. Here, take a moment to look back into the Thorofare because you're leaving a very special place.

Both of these fords can be deep enough early in the year to get your adrenaline level up and backpack wet (especially for vertically challenged hikers), so be sure to pack your clothes and sleeping bag in waterproof bags.

After the Yellowstone ford, you hike along the river for about a half mile in mostly burned timber, crossing Lynx Creek and heading up this valley toward Two Ocean Pass. This is a Category 2 climb, and the trail worsens slightly from what you've hiked on so far. And don't be surprised by frequent downed trees over the trail. The forest opens up into high-altitude meadows just before the Continental Divide at about 9,400 feet in elevation and stays in the open terrain of the Two Ocean Plateau all the way to Mariposa Lake.

Not many people see Mariposa Lake, which is too bad for them. It's a charming but small (12 acres) mountain lake in a lush, greenish swale with a small population of hard-to-catch cutthroat-rainbow hybrids.

From the lake, the trail drops sharply down through unburned forest to the junction with the Two Ocean Plateau Trail. At this junction, go left (west) and hike along Plateau Creek to the Fox Creek patrol cabin. Just after the cabin, you might see a trail heading south out of the park and shortly thereafter the headwaters of the Snake River. The map may indicate that the junction with the trail up the Snake River to Heart Lake is on the east side of the river, but it's actually on the west side.

After hiking through the meadow on the west side of the Snake, head up the 2,000-foot, Category 1 climb to the top of Big Game Ridge. About halfway up the ridge, you'll see signs indicating the park boundary. For the next few miles, the trail goes in and out of the park. Unless you're up to 18 miles with a heavy pack (including this monster hill), you should spend the night in an undesignated site outside the park. There is no designated campsite in the park anywhere over this 18-mile stretch of trail.

Hope for a clear day when you go over Big Game Ridge (which was not the case when we did it). You should get some great views of the Grand Teton. Also, be alert for grizzly bears. We saw more bear sign on Big Game Ridge than anywhere in Yellowstone.

After enjoying a well-deserved rest on the ridge, drop into the headwaters of Harebell Creek where you stay all the way to the Harebell patrol cabin. This section of trail goes through burned forest most of the way, and if you're unlucky enough to get caught in a big rain (as we did) the trail gets extremely slick.

At the junction at the Harebell patrol cabin, the Snake River Trail goes off to the right (north). Go straight (west) and drop down into Wolverine Creek, where you go right (northwest) at the junction with the Wolverine Creek Trail, which goes left (south) out of the park.

Shortly thereafter, you see the Snake River again, although this is the real Snake River—swollen with the infusion of many tributaries and quite the departure from the little stream you waded across on the other side of Big Game Ridge. You might see the Snake River Cutoff Trail going off to the

*Fording the Snake River.*

right about 2 miles later. Even though the first part is marked, this trail is far down on the maintenance priority list and difficult to follow.

At the junction with the Heart Lake Trail, take a left (south) and continue to hike along the Snake River. Shortly after this junction, you see the Snake Hot Springs, several hot pools and streams over a half-mile stretch of river. Near Snake Hot Springs, you might think you see a small prairie dog town, but this is actually the burrows dug by yellow-bellied marmots. Interestingly, this local population tends to build burrows in the open meadow along the trail instead of the rocky hillsides. Also, they tend to delay hibernation later than usual because of the extra warmth the hot springs area provides.

After the hot springs, the trail goes through unburned forest with minimal views until a big meadow just before the trailhead. When you see the trail register, don't think you're done. It's still another mile to the trailhead. Also, watch for several unmarked spur trails. Right after the register, you see an unmarked split in the trail. Take the left fork. Later, at another unmarked split, take the right fork.

The trip finishes with a grand finale, a serious ford over the Snake River, swollen with the recent inclusion of the Lewis River. You can see the entrance station and the highway, but you still need to cross the river. After mid-July, this ford is safe, but earlier in the summer, or after a big thunderstorm, it can be dangerous. We forded just north of the marked ford and found it to be significantly easier than the designated route. (If the ford

291

looks too dangerous, you can follow an unofficial but well-maintained trail along the east side of the river for 3 miles to the Shelfield Creek Trailhead, which comes out at the highway just south of the Flagg Ranch.)

After the ford, it's less than a quarter mile and a small hill up to the bench above the river where you will find your vehicle—and where you can give each other those high-fives you richly deserve.

**Options:** You can do this trip in reverse with no significant difference in difficulty, but you start out with a big ford of the Snake River instead of finishing with it. Also, you can skip the first one or two days by getting a boat ride to Park Point or Beaverdam Creek.

**Side trips:** If you decide to spend more than eight days in this area, try side trips to Trail Lake or Bridger Lake.

# 102  *YELLOWSTONE LAKE TO HEART LAKE*

| | |
|---|---|
| **Type of hike:** | Shuttle. |
| **Type of trip:** | Long backpacking trip. |
| **Total distance:** | 49.6 miles or 79.8 kilometers. |
| **Difficulty:** | Difficult because of the distance, but otherwise, as easy as a 50-mile backpacking trip can be. |
| **Elevation gain:** | 270 feet. |
| **Maps:** | Trails Illustrated (Yellowstone Lake); Lake Butte, Frank Island, Trail Lake, Alder Lake, Heart Lake, and Mount Sheridan USGS quads. |
| **Starting point:** | Nine Mile Trailhead (5K5). |

**Finding the trailhead:** Drive 9 miles east of Fishing Bridge to the east shore of Yellowstone Lake and park at the Nine Mile Trailhead parking area on the north side of the road. The NPS is constructing a new trailhead on the south side of the road, due for completion in fall of 1997.

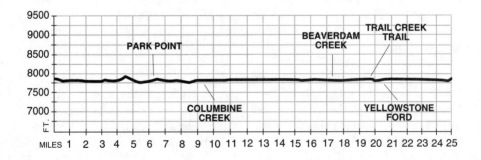

292

## Key points:

| | | |
|---|---|---|
| 1.3 | (2.1) | Cub Creek. |
| 3.0 | (4.8) | Clear Creek. |
| 6.3 | (10.1) | Park Point and 5E9 (5★). |
| 6.5 | (10.4) | 5E7 (1★) and 5E8 (5★). |
| 9.2 | (14.8) | 5E6 (4★) and 5E5 (4★). |
| 9.4 | (15.1) | Columbine Creek. |
| 12.3 | (19.8) | 5E4 (5★). |
| 14.7 | (23.6) | 5E3 (3★). |
| 15.5 | (24.9 | Terrace Point. |
| 17.3 | (27.8) | Beaverdam Creek and spur trail to 5E1 (4★). |
| 19.3 | (31.0) | Cabin Creek patrol cabin. |
| 19.7 | (31.6) | Trail Creek junction (lower ford). |
| 20.1 | (32.2) | Spur trail to 6B2 (4★). |
| 20.2 | (32.3) | Junction with upper ford cutoff trail. |
| 21.6 | (34.7) | Junction with off-trail route to Trail Lake. |
| 23.9 | (38.4) | Southeast Arm and 6A4 (4★). |
| 24.7 | (39.7) | Trail Creek cabin and spur trail to 6A3 (5★). |
| 25.3 | (40.7) | Spur trail to 6A2 (5★). |
| 26.2 | (42.1) | Junction with Two Ocean Plateau Trail. |
| 27.3 | (43.9) | Chipmunk Creek. |
| 28.7 | (46.2) | South Arm and second junction Two Ocean Plateau Trail. |
| 29.1 | (46.8) | 5L2 (3★). |
| 30.5 | (49.1) | 7G2 (4★). |
| 30.6 | (49.2) | Grouse Creek. |
| 30.8 | (49.6) | 7G1 (3★). |
| 34.7 | (55.8) | Outlet Lake and 8O2 (4★). |
| 37.4 | (60.2) | 8J3 (3★). |
| 37.7 | (60.7) | Junction with Heart River Trail and 8J4 (3★). |
| 38.0 | (61.1) | 8J6 (4★). |
| 40.2 | (64.7) | 8J1 (5★). |
| 41.6 | (66.9) | Junction with Heart Lake Trail. |
| 41.7 | (67.1) | Heart Lake patrol cabin. |
| 49.6 | (79.8) | Heart Lake Trailhead. |

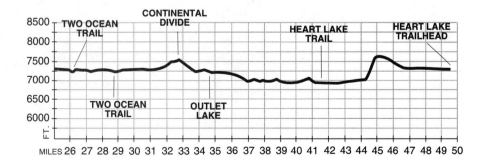

**Recommended itinerary:** This could easily be turned into a longer backpacking trip, but I recommend a six-day trip as follows:

| First night | — | Preferred—5E8 or 5E9, alternate—5E7. |
| Second night | — | Preferred—5E1, alternates—5E3 or 6B1. |
| Third night | — | Preferred—6A3, alternates—6A4 or 6A2. |
| Fourth night | — | Preferred—7G1 or 7G2, alternates—7N2 or 7N4. |
| Fifth night | — | Preferred—8J1, alternates—8J4 or 8J6. |

**The hike:** If you heard about a six-day backpacking trip in Yellowstone Park with no hills and only 270-foot elevation gain over the first 42 miles, which includes climbing over the Continental Divide, you probably wouldn't believe it. Right? But it's true, and here it is. You can hike from the Nine Mile Trailhead on the northeast corner of Yellowstone Lake around the south edge of the lake, over the "Great Divide," and to the west side of Heart Lake Trailhead without seeing anything that deserves to be called a hill. At the Heart Lake patrol cabin, you face a small climb up Witch Creek to the top of Paycheck Pass, but even this is easy compared to most hills in Yellowstone, and then it's flat the rest of the way to the trailhead.

This trip offers good fishing to go with the flat terrain, but you can't go until mid-July when most campsites in the area open. If you wait until late

# YELLOWSTONE LAKE TO HEART LAKE

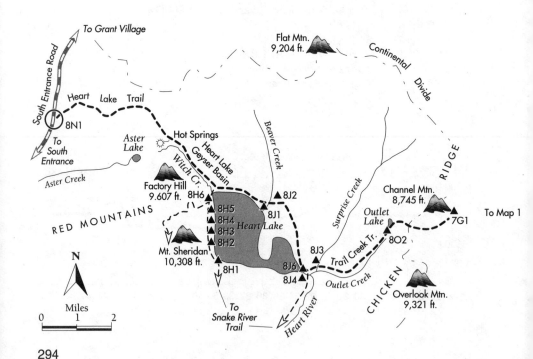

# YELLOWSTONE LAKE TO HEART LAKE

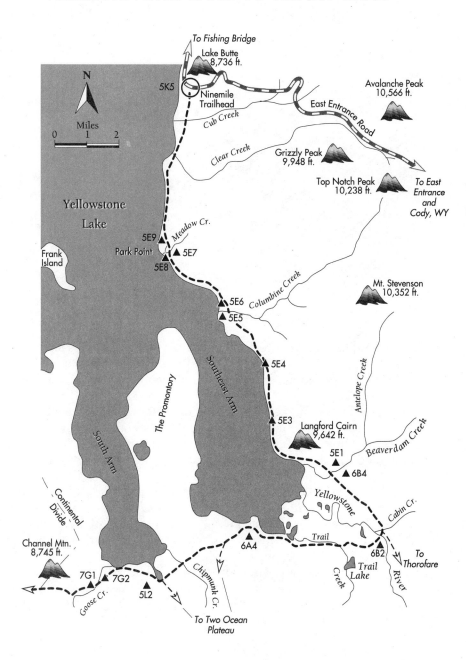

*To Fishing Bridge*

Lake Butte
8,736 ft.

5K5

Ninemile
Trailhead

Avalanche Peak
10,566 ft.

East Entrance Road

*Cub Creek*

*Clear Creek*

Grizzly Peak
9,948 ft.

Top Notch Peak
10,238 ft.

*To East
Entrance
and
Cody, WY*

N

Miles

0   1   2

Yellowstone

Lake

Frank
Island

5E9

*Meadow Cr.*

Park Point

▲ 5E7

5E8

5E6

*Columbine Creek*

Mt. Stevenson
10,352 ft.

5E5

5E4

*Southeast Arm*

*Antelope Creek*

The Promontory

5E3

Langford Cairn
9,642 ft.

*Beaverdam Creek*

5E1

▲ 6B4

*South Arm*

*Yellowstone*

*Cabin Cr.*

*Continental
Divide*

Channel Mtn.
8,745 ft.

*Trail*

6A4

7G1   ▲ 7G2

5L2

*Goose Cr.*

*Chipmunk Cr.*

*Trail
Lake*

6B2

*To
Thorofare*

*Creek*

*River*

To Map #2

*To Two Ocean
Plateau*

*Hiking along Southeast Arm.*

August or September, you might not need mosquito netting. This late season schedule also makes the ford of the Yellowstone River easier. (Be sure to check with the Lake Ranger Station on the conditions of the ford before taking this trip.)

The section between the lower ford of the Yellowstone and South Arm is the only section of this hike not already covered in other descriptions. The first section of this trip is covered in detail in the Thorofare and South Boundary hike and the last section is covered in the Heart Lake Loop and Heart Lake and Two Ocean Plateau hikes.

In brief, the trip along the lake is totally flat. The first leg to Park Point stays in the timber with no view, but the rest of the hike, along the east shore and Southeast Arm, is lined with postcard scenes. After the end of the Southeast Arm, you cross Beaverdam Creek and follow the river to the lower ford.

After the ford, the trail goes through an unburned forest for about 3 miles, before breaking out at the southernmost tip of the Southeast Arm and following the lakeshore to the Trail Creek patrol cabin. If you have time, hang your pack for a few hours and take the off-trail route to Trail Lake (55 acres, cutthroat trout).

From the Southeast Arm the trail goes through intermittently burned forest over the base of the Promontory and across Chipmunk Creek (on a bridge) over to the South Arm. At the junction with the Two Ocean Plateau Trail, go right (west).

At the South Arm, you reach the second junction with the Two Ocean Plateau Trail. Go right (west) again. From here, the trail circles around the end of the South Arm and heads up Grouse Creek.

All the way from the lower ford to this point, the trail remains in great shape and is easy to follow, with bridges over the streams. The only exception is where the trail goes through a few large meadows and gets faint. Watch for orange markers on the other side of the meadows.

Around Grouse Creek, however, the trail gets faint and boggy. Watch for trail markers and try to avoid getting diverted onto heavily used game trails. Between 7G2 and 7G1, ford Grouse Creek and head through burned forest over the Continental Divide (even though it doesn't seem like it) on Chicken Ridge and then past Outlet Lake and around Heart Lake to the patrol cabin. If you have enough time (and energy after 42 miles of backpacking) or want to stay an extra day, you should climb Mount Sheridan from here. This might seem more appealing after viewing the mountain across Heart Lake for the past 4 miles while hiking around enormous Heart Lake.

*Southeast Arm.*

From the patrol cabin, you face a minor upgrade over the next 3 miles to get to the top of the Witch Creek drainage before enjoying the last 8 miles to the Heart Lake Trailhead.

**Options:** Since the elevation rise is so minor, the trip can be done from either direction with no extra work. If you want to spend time fishing in Heart Lake, Yellowstone Lake, or in the Yellowstone River in the Thorofare, or prefer to have extra time for side trips, add two or three days to the trip. The trip can also be lengthened by several days by hiking the much longer south route around Heart Lake or by hiking down the Heart River and Heart Lake trails to the Snake River to the South Entrance Trailhead.

**Side trips:** The off-trail route to Trail Lake is rough, but a short side trip to some good fishing. If you have time and energy left upon reaching the Heart Lake Patrol Cabin, try the spectacular hike up to the top of Mount Sheridan. This might mean another day in the wilderness, but you can stay at one of the three campsites clumped close to where the spur trail to Mount Sheridan starts, and have an easy 8 miles on your last day.

# 103  *TWO OCEAN LOOP*

|  |  |
|---|---|
| **Type of hike:** | Loop requiring a boat ride to the trailhead. |
| **Type of trip:** | Long backpacking trip. |
| **Total distance:** | 40 miles or 64.4 kilometers. |
| **Difficulty:** | Difficult. |
| **Elevation gain:** | 1,680 feet. |
| **Maps:** | Trails Illustrated (Yellowstone Lake); Trail Lake, Alder Lake, Crooked Creek, Badger Creek, The Trident, and Eagle Peak USGS quads. |
| **Starting point:** | Start hiking the Trail Creek patrol cabin at the southernmost tip of the Southeast Arm after a boat ride across the lake. |

**Finding the trailhead:** This is the only hike in this book that requires a boat to reach the trailhead, which is at the southermost tip of Southeast Arm. Consult with rangers at the Lake Ranger Station for advice on the best routes and for special boating regulations in the Southeast Arm.

**Key points:**

| | | |
|---|---|---|
| 0.6 | (0.9) | Spur trail to 6A2 (5★). |
| 1.5 | (2.4) | Junction with Two Ocean Plateau Trail. |
| 4.0 | (6.4) | Junction with cutoff trail to Heart Lake. |
| 9.5 | (10.4) | 6M5 (3★). |
| 13.5 | (21.7) | 6M4 (3★) and junction with South Boundary Trail. |
| 14.5 | (23.3) | 6M3 (4★)and Mariposa Lake. |

# TWO OCEAN LOOP

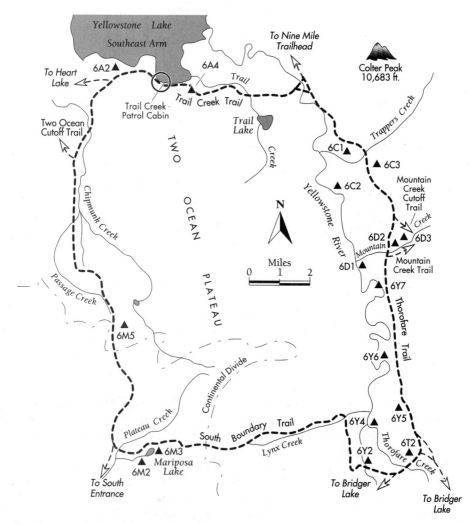

## Key points (cont'd):

| | |
|---|---|
| 14.8 (23.8) | 6M2 (2★). |
| 16.3 (26.2) | Continental Divide. |
| 21.8 (35.1) | Ford the Yellowstone River and 6Y2 (4★). |
| 22.7 (36.6) | Junction with trail to Bridger Lake. |
| 22.9 (36.8) | 6T1 (4★) and ford Thorofare Creek. |
| 23.0 (37.0) | Spur trail to 6T2 (5★). |
| 23.3 (37.5) | Junction with cutoff trail to Thorofare Ranger Station. |
| 23.5 (37.8) | Spur Trail to 6Y4 (3★). |
| 24.5 (39.4) | Junction with trail to Thorofare Ranger Station and Bridger Lake. |
| 26.0 (41.8) | Cliff Creek and 6Y5 (3★). |
| 27.0 (43.4) | 6Y6 (4★). |

**Key points (cont'd):**

29.2 (47.0)   Spur trail to 6D1 (4★).
29.3 (47.1)   First junction with trail to Eagle Pass.
29.9 (48.1)   6D2 (3★) and ford Mountain Creek.
30.8 (49.5)   Second junction with trail to Eagle Pass.
33.0 (53.1)   6C3 (3★).
33.2 (53.4)   Spur trail to 6C2 (5★).
34.0 (54.7)   6C1 (1★).
35.0 (56.3)   Junction with trail to upper ford.
35.4 (57.0)   Junction with trail to lower ford and 6B2 (4★).
36.9 (59.4)   Junction with off-trail route to Trail Lake.
39.2 (63.1)   Southeast Arm and 6A4 (4★).
40.0 (64.4)   Trail Creek patrol cabin.

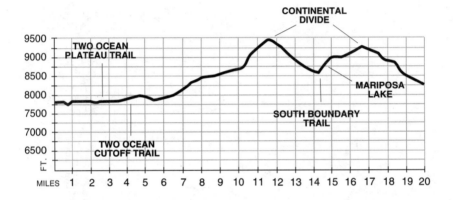

**Recommended itinerary:** If you take one day to paddle to the starting point (and another to return to your vehicle), this turns into a nine-day trip, including the two days spent paddling, with no rest day in the Thorofare.

| First night | — | Preferred—6A3, alternates—6A2 or 6A4. |
| Second night | — | Preferred—6M5. |
| Third night | — | Preferred—6M2, alternate—6M3. |
| Fourth night | — | Preferred—6T2, alternates—6T1 or 6Y2. |
| Fifth night | — | Preferred—6D2, alternate—6D1. |
| Sixth night | — | Preferred—6B2, alternate—6B1. |
| Seventh night | — | Preferred—6A3, alternates—6A4 or 6A2. |

**The hike:** This hike is like no other in Yellowstone. It combines the pleasures of paddling the shoreline of Yellowstone Lake with some of the best backpacking in the park. It skips the heavily used sections of trails near the highways by taking a 20-mile paddle across Yellowstone Lake, which leaves 40 miles of remote and scenic hiking. A ranger stays at Trail Creek Cabin for most of the summer, so this is a good place to safely store your canoe or kayak.

After spending your first night at one of the three campsites (6A2, 6A3, 6A4) on the shoreline of the Southeast Arm, start the loop by heading west toward the South Arm. When you reach the junction with the Two Ocean Plateau Trail, go left (south) and head for the highlands of the Two Ocean Plateau. This high-altitude ridge gets its name from Two Ocean Pass just south of the park where the waters of Pacific Creek and Atlantic Creek mingle before they start their long journeys to their respective oceans. This may be the only place where fish can actually swim over the Continental Divide.

You spend the first half of your first day hiking through mostly burned forest, as the trail goes along Chipmunk Creek and then Passage Creek, until you get up to the high country, which escaped the 1988 fires. The last pitches up to the plateau get steep. Most of the rest of the trip down to the

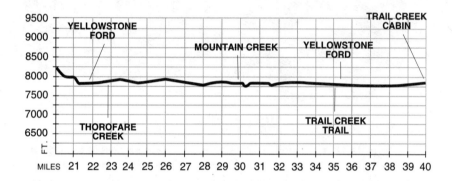

South Boundary Trail goes through open terrain with great scenery.

At the junction with the South Boundary Trail, turn left (east) and climb the mile-long hill up to Mariposa Lake. The lake sits in a gentle, lush meadow and hosts a small population of cutthroat-rainbow hybrids.

From the lake, it's a short 1.5 miles up to the Continental Divide through open terrain and more superb mountain scenery. After another mile of high-altitude hiking near treeline, you drop into Lynx Creek and go through burned forest most of the way to the Yellowstone River. Expect to climb over some downfall on this leg.

Before fording the river, make sure your sleeping bag and clothes are in waterproof bags. This ford can be deep enough to get your pack wet.

After the ford, the trail goes through a big meadow and past the junction with the trail to Bridger Lake where you go left (east). Immediately after the junction, you ford Thorofare Creek, which can be almost deep as the Yellowstone. After the ford, you pass by two trails going off to the right (east) to the Thorofare Ranger Station. If you need help, take the short trip over to see the ranger who stays there most of the summer.

*On the Continental Divide east of Mariposa Lake on the Two Ocean Plateau.*

From here, its a flat, dusty hike through the scenic openness of the Thorofare all the way to the upper ford where you cross the Yellowstone again. After the ford, follow the trail along the south edge of the Southeast Arm back to the patrol cabin where you stashed your boat. Spend the night at one of the nearby campsites before paddling back to your vehicle fresh with the memories of one of the classic backpacking vacations in the northern Rockies.

The trail is well-defined and in generally great shape the entire way with the exception of Lynx Creek (prone to heavy downfall) and a few stretches of the Thorofare, where extra-heavy horse traffic has pounded the trail into dust.

**Options:** If you take the counterclockwise route (as described here) you don't have to start the trip with a ford of the Yellowstone River. If you want to spend more time on the lake before hitting the trail, you can paddle over to the tip of the South Arm and start the loop there. You can also start at Beaverdam Creek in Southeast Arm, but this requires retracing your steps from the lower ford to Beaverdam Creek. You might want to extend your trip by one day by taking a rest day in the Thorofare. If you don't like paddling, you can arrange a motoboat ride to Columbine Creek on the east side of the Southeast Arm and start your hike from there.

**Side trips:** If you take a rest day in the Thorofare, you could use it for a nice loop around Bridger Lake. If you don't mind bushwhacking, take the short off-trail route to Trail Lake.

# 104  *HEART LAKE*

Type of hike:   Out and back.

Type of trip:   An overnighter that can be a long day hike.

See Map on Page 316

Total distance:   16 miles or 25.7 kilometers (round-trip).

Difficulty:   Moderate.

Elevation gain:   345 feet.

Maps:   Trails Illustrated (Yellowstone Lake); Mount Sheridan and Heart Lake USGS quads.

Starting point:   Heart Lake Trailhead (8N1).

**Finding the trailhead:** Drive 5.2 miles south of Grant Village Junction and park in the trailhead parking area on the east side of the road.

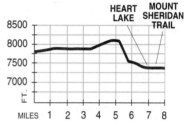

**Recommended itinerary:** Although a strong hiker can easily hike to Heart Lake and back in a day, it's a shame not to spend more time there. I recommend a three-day trip, staying two nights at the lake and climbing Mount Sheridan on the second day.

*On the way to Heart Lake.*

**The hike:** Heart Lake sort of looks like the big heart of Yellowstone, but it isn't named for its shape. Instead, it's named after Hart Humey, an old trapper who frequented the area before the park was created. Through the years, Hart Lake became Heart Lake.

Regardless of the name, however, this seems like the heart of the southeastern section of Yellowstone. It's a uniquely large and beautiful mountain lake in the shadow of stately Mount Sheridan. Anglers love the healthy population of large cutthroat and lake trout. Bald eagles and loons are there, too, looking for the same fish, and grizzlies roam the slopes of Mount Sheridan.

Heart Lake is a truly monstrous mountain lake. It spans 2,160 acres and gets down to 180 feet deep. It has also become a popular destination for hikers, so don't plan on having the lake or the trail to yourself. The trail is in great shape all the way with bridges over all streams. It goes through unburned forest interrupted here and there by small meadows for the first 5 miles. Then, the trail passes through a small burn from the 1988 fires to a great viewpoint of the lake, Factory Hill, and Witch Creek, probably named for the numerous hot springs and steam vents that line most of its course. At this viewpoint, it seems like you're closer to the lake because it's so large, but you actually have more than 2 miles to go.

From this point on, the trail goes through open terrain with great scenery as you drop down to the lake. If you stop to investigate thermal areas, be careful not to disturb delicate ecosystems or burn yourself. On a cold day, the thermal areas kick up so much steam that it clouds views of the lake. Factory Hill (named for the steam vents that resemble smoke stacks) partly blocks the view of Mount Sheridan.

Just before you reach the lake and the junction with the Trail Creek Trail, you'll see the Heart Lake patrol cabin off to the left. A ranger stays there most of the summer.

If you're staying overnight or climbing Mount Sheridan, turn right (south) at the junction. The trail follows the shoreline through the Witch Creek bottomlands and by the overflow of Rustic Geyser and several hot pools off to your right. Again, these thermal areas are fascinating to explore, but be cautious. At the first junction, the left fork goes to 8H6. You go right to the other campsites and to the Mount Sheridan spur trail, about 200 yards farther down the trail.

If you're staying overnight, you probably want one of the six campsites on the west side of the lake. If you're day hiking, don't spend too much time exploring thermal areas or fishing because it's another 8-mile hike (including a climb out of Witch Creek) back to the trailhead.

**Options:** Heart Lake can be part of several long backpacking trips in the southeastern section of the park.

**Side trips:** The obvious (and spectacular) side trip is the trail up Mount Sheridan. Refer to the Mount Sheridan hike for details.

# 105 *MOUNT SHERIDAN*

| | |
|---|---|
| **Type of hike:** | Out and back. |
| **Type of trip:** | Day hike. |
| **Total distance:** | 6 miles or 9.6 kilometers (round-trip). |
| **Difficulty:** | Difficult. |
| **Elevation gain:** | 2,700 feet. |
| **Maps:** | Trails Illustrated (Yellowstone Lake); Mount Sheridan USGS quad. |
| **Starting point:** | Where the spur trails leaves the Heart Lake Trail on the west shore of Heart Lake. |

See Map on Page 316

**Finding the trailhead:** The spur trail takes off from the Heart Lake Trail 0.7 mile south of the Trail Creek Junction.

**The hike:** The hike up to the lookout on 10,308-foot Mount Sheridan may be the most scenic mountain top hike in the park. It definitely rivals the climbs up Mount Washburn and Mount Holmes for scenery. It might seem better, and it takes more effort to get here. It's a 22-mile round-trip from the South Entrance Road to the summit and back.

The trail starts out through some large meadows before going into burned lodgepole and a series of large switchbacks. The switchbacks soon give way to a steeper, winding trail up the north ridge of the mountain. This is the steepest part of the climb. At the 2-mile mark, the

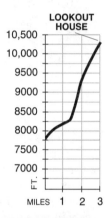

*Taking a deserved break on the top of Mount Sheridan.*

*Heart Lake still looks big, even from the top of Mount Sheridan.*

trail breaks out above the treeline, and the slope gets more gradual as the trail loops around to the west side of the mountain. But "more gradual" does not imply "gradual." This is a tough Category H climb, covering 2,700 feet in only 3 miles.

Be sure to bring water because you won't find any on the mountain unless you go early enough to catch a few snowbanks before they disappear. Don't try this hike until mid-July to avoid deep snow.

Plan on spending an hour or so at the lookout at the summit to identify all the mountains and lakes you can see, such as the nice look at the Grand Teton to the south and the seldom-seen Delusion Lake to the north. Even from up here, Heart Lake looks big, and you can look way down at the Continental Divide, which comes through the area just north and east of Heart Lake.

| | |
|---|---|
| **Type of hike:** | Loop. |
| **Type of trip:** | Backpacking trip. |
| **Total distance:** | 33.9 miles or 54.5 kilometers. |
| **Difficulty:** | Moderate. |
| **Elevation gain:** | Minimal. |
| **Maps:** | Trails Illustrated (Yellowstone Lake); |
| | Mount Sheridan and Heart Lake USGS quads. |
| **Starting point:** | Heart Lake Trailhead (8N1). |

See Map on Page 316

**Finding the trailhead:** Drive 5.2 miles south of Grant Village Junction and park in the trailhead parking area on the east side of the road.

**Key points:**

| | |
|---|---|
| 5.0   (8.0) | Viewpoint down Witch Creek to Heart Lake. |
| 7.8  (12.5) | Heart Lake patrol cabin. |
| 8.0  (12.8) | Trail Creek Trail junction. |
| 8.2  (13.2) | Rustic Geyser. |
| 8.3  (13.3) | Trail to 8H6 (4★). |
| 8.7  (14.0) | Trail to 8H5 (4★) and spur trail to Mount Sheridan. |
| 9.0  (14.5) | Trail to 8H4 (4★). |
| 9.5  (15.3) | Spur trails to 8H3 (4★) and 8H2 (4★). |
| 10.5  (16.9) | 8H1 (2★). |
| 11.5  (18.5) | Sheridan Lake. |
| 13.0  (20.9) | 8B1 (4★). |
| 13.5  (21.7) | Basin Creek Trail junction. |
| 15.6  (25.1) | 8B5 (3★). |
| 16.0  (25.7) | Junction with Snake River Trail. |
| 16.9  (27.2) | Ford Snake River. |
| 18.2  (27.3) | Ford Snake River. |
| 18.3  (29.4) | 8C5 (4★). |
| 18.4  (29.6) | Junction with Heart River Trail. |
| 19.0  (30.5) | Ford Heart River. |
| 21.5  (34.6) | Ford Heart River and Outlet Creek. |
| 21.7  (34.9) | Junction with Trail Creek Trail and 8J4 (3★). |
| 22.0  (35.4) | 8J6 (4★). |
| 24.2  (38.9) | 8J1 (5★). |
| 25.7  (41.3) | Junction with Heart Lake Trail. |
| 25.9  (41.6) | Heart Lake patrol cabin. |
| 33.9  (54.5) | Heart Lake Trailhead. |

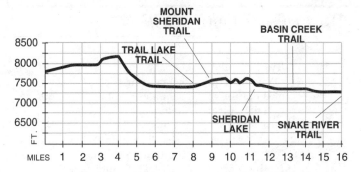

**Recommended itinerary:** I recommend a five-day trip with two nights on the west shore of Heart Lake (using the extra day to climb Mount Sheridan), the third night at 8B2, 8B5, or 8C5, and the last night at 8J4, 8J6, or 8J1.

**The hike:** This is a superb, moderately difficult backpacking trip especially suited for anglers—and one of the few major backpacking trips in Yellowstone that doesn't require an annoying vehicle shuttle.

The first section (8 miles) is a pleasant, mostly level walk into Heart Lake, as described in the Heart Lake hike.

If you're taking the counterclockwise route for the loop around the lake, turn right (south) at the junction just past the patrol cabin and stay at one of the six campsites on the west side of the lake. If you plan on hiking up to the summit of Mount Sheridan (and you'll be sorry if you don't), reserve the campsite for two nights.

*Exploring the Rustic Geyser area with Heart Lake in background.*

308

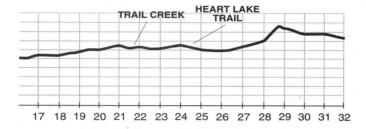

```
17  18  19  20  21  22  23  24  25  26  27  28  29  30  31  32
```

TRAIL CREEK        HEART LAKE
                     TRAIL

The hike along the west side of the lake climbs slightly away from the lakeshore after 8H6 and then drops back to the shoreline before 8H1. You climb a little hill when leaving the lake before dropping into Sheridan Lake, a small, marsh-lined lake off to your right (west). In the spring, the trail gets boggy in spots near the lake.

The trail continues through mostly open terrain and meadows along Basin Creek. At the junction with the Basin Creek Trail, go left (southeast) and continue following Basin Creek through mostly burned timber until you see the Snake River and the junction with the Heart River Trail. The trail through this section is well-defined with frequent stream crossings.

Here, turn left (northeast) and hike along the Snake River through a big meadow for about 1 mile until you reach the ford. The trail is a little rocky, but in fair shape. Early in the season, the ford might be hazardous, but after mid-July, it's usually knee-deep.

*Almost there! Climbing Mount Sheridan.*

*Heart Lake with Mount Sheridan as a scenic backdrop.*

After fording the Snake, the trail angles away from the river into a heavily burned area until you reach the junction with the trail going south to the headwaters of the Snake. Turn left (north) and head toward Heart Lake on the Heart River Trail. You ford the Snake River again just before the junction, but it's an even smaller stream because the Heart River hasn't joined yet.

This section of trail is in good shape as it closely follows the Heart River and passes through lightly burned forest most of the way to Heart Lake. About halfway to the lake you ford this river and then again, as well as Outlet Creek just before reaching Heart Lake. All of these fords are easier than the Snake River ford.

When you reach the Trail Creek Trail, go left (west) and finish your circle of Heart Lake back to the junction at the patrol cabin. The trail is in great shape through this section. It stays in the timber much of the way, but a few openings in the trees provide for some great views of the lake with its incredible backdrop, Mount Sheridan.

From here, retrace your steps to the Heart Lake Trailhead.

**Options:** You can take the loop in either direction with no increased difficulty.

**Side trips:** The Mount Sheridan hike is almost a must-do side trip, but you can also take short hikes to Basin Creek Lake and Outlet Lake.

## 107  *HEART LAKE AND THE SNAKE RIVER*

| | |
|---|---|
| **Type of hike:** | Shuttle. |
| **Type of trip:** | Short backpacking trip. |
| **Total distance:** | 24 miles or 38.6 kilometers. |
| **Difficulty:** | Moderate. |
| **Elevation loss:** | 902 feet. |
| **Maps:** | Trails Illustrated (Yellowstone Lake); Mount Sheridan, Heart Lake, Snake Hot Springs, and Lewis Canyon USGS quads. |
| **Starting point:** | Heart Lake Trailhead (8N1). |

*See Map on Page 316*

**Finding the trailhead:** Drive 5.2 miles south of Grant Village Junction and park in the trailhead parking area on the east side of the road.

**Key points:**

| | | |
|---|---|---|
| 5.0 | (8.0) | Viewpoint down Witch Creek to Heart Lake. |
| 7.8 | (12.5) | Heart Lake patrol cabin. |
| 8.0 | (12.8) | Trail Creek Trail Junction. |
| 8.2 | (13.2) | Rustic Geyser. |
| 8.3 | (13.3) | Trail to 8H6 (4★). |
| 8.7 | (14.0) | Trail to 8H5 (4★) and spur trail to Mount Sheridan. |
| 9.0 | (14.5) | Trail to 8H4 (4★). |
| 9.5 | (15.3) | Spur trails to 8H3 (4★) and 8H2 (4★). |
| 10.5 | (16.9) | 8I1 (2★). |
| 11.5 | (18.5) | Sheridan Lake. |
| 13.0 | (20.9) | 8B1 (4★). |
| 13.5 | (21.7) | Basin Creek Trail junction. |

**Key points (cont'd):**

| | | |
|---|---|---|
| 14.3 | (23.0) | 8B2 (3★). |
| 14.4 | (23.1) | Basin Creek Lake. |
| 18.0 | (28.9) | 8C6 (3★). |
| 18.5 | (29.9) | Snake River ford and junction. |
| 19.0 | (30.6) | Snake Hot Springs and 8C1 (3★). |
| 24.0 | (38.6) | Snake River Trailhead and South Entrance. |

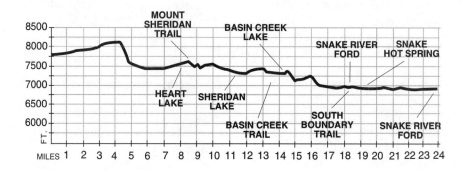

**Recommended itinerary:** This trip can easily be done in three days, but I recommend five days with two nights at Heart Lake, one at Basin Creek Lake, and one at Snake Hot Springs. This leaves a day for climbing Mount Sheridan, time for fishing Heart Lake, and two moderately easy days to get out to the South Entrance Trailhead.

*Basin Creek Lake.*

*Hiking through Red Creek, one of the many open valleys in Yellowstone.*

**The hike:** For details on the first part of the hike to Heart Lake refer to the description for that hike.

From the Trail Creek Trail junction, the Heart Lake Trail follows the shoreline for almost 2 miles to the southern tip of the lake. Here, it climbs a small hill and drops into marshy Sheridan Lake, going through partially burned timber. From here, the trail drops into Basin Creek and stays in mostly open terrain as it follows the stream past the Basin Creek Trail junction to Basin Creek Lake. Go straight (south) at the junction. The trail gets faint in a few meadows, but orange markers show the way.

Basin Creek Lake is small (8 acres), surrounded by wet meadows and has a small cutthroat population. Don't go wading or swimming in the lake unless you like picking leaches off your legs—you'll have a dozen attached in a few minutes.

After Basin Creek Lake, the trail goes into Red Creek drainage and continues to alternate between unburned timber and open meadows. Just before reaching the Snake River Trail, you ford the river. This ford can be difficult before mid-July, but usually not a problem in August.

The last 5.5 miles goes through unburned timber with minimal views, with the exception of the first half mile, which goes through a big meadow containing the Snake Hot Springs. When you get to the trail register, you still have about 1 mile to go. Take a left at the first fork in the trail right after the register, and go right at the next fork near a small pond.

*Fording the Snake River.*

At the end of the hike you face another ford of the Snake River, which has experienced surprising growth in the last 5 miles, mainly because the Lewis River joined in just upstream from the South Entrance. You can usually cross safely after mid-July as long as you're careful, but water conditions can make this ford dangerous later in the season than most. We crossed just upstream from the official ford and found it significantly easier. To avoid this ford, follow an unofficial but well-maintained trail along the east side of the river for about 3 miles where it comes to the highway just south of the Flagg Ranch at the Shelfield Creek Trailhead.

**Options:** You can hike this shuttle trip from the south, but this means a gradual uphill instead of downhill hike.

**Side trips:** Hopefully, you left time for a side trip to the top of Mount Sheridan. Refer to that hike for details.

|                    |                                                          |
|--------------------|----------------------------------------------------------|
| **Type of hike:**  | Loop.                                                    |
| **Type of trip:**  | Long backpacking trip.                                   |
| **Total distance:**| 62.3 miles or 100.3 kilometers.                          |
| **Difficulty:**    | Difficult.                                               |
| **Elevation gain:**| 1,498 feet.                                              |
| **Maps:**          | Trails Illustrated (Yellowstone Lake); Mount Sheridan, Heart Lake, Mount Hancock, Snake Hot Springs, Alder Lake, Trail Lake, Crooked Creek, and Badger Creek USGS quads. |
| **Starting point:**| Heart Lake Trailhead (8N1).                              |

**Finding the trailhead:** Drive 5.2 miles south of Grant Village Junction and park in the trailhead parking area on the east side of the road.

## Key points:

|            |                                                              |
|------------|--------------------------------------------------------------|
| 5.0  (8.0) | Viewpoint down Witch Creek to Heart Lake.                    |
| 7.8 (12.5) | Heart Lake patrol cabin.                                     |
| 8.0 (12.8) | Trail Creek Trail junction.                                  |
| 9.5 (15.3) | 8J1 (5★)                                                     |
| 11.7 (18.8)| 8J6 (4★)                                                     |
| 12.0 (19.3)| 8J4 (3★) and junction with the Heart River Trail.            |
| 12.3 (19.8)| 8J3 (3★).                                                    |
| 15.0 (24.1)| 8O2 (4★) and Outlet Lake.                                     |
| 17.8 (28.6)| 7G1 (3★).                                                    |
| 18.2 (29.3)| 7G2 (4★).                                                    |
| 18.4  29.6)| Bushwhack to 7N4 and 7N2.                                    |
| 20.9 (33.6)| 5L2 (3★).                                                    |
| 21.3 (34.2)| Junction with Two Ocean Plateau Trail.                       |
| 22.7 (36.5)| Junction with cutoff trail to Trail Creek Trail.             |
| 28.0 (45.1)| 6M5 (3★).                                                    |
| 32.3 (52.0)| 6M4 (3★), junction with South Boundary/Mariposa Lake Trail.  |
| 35.8 (57.6)| 6M7 (3★) and the Fox Creek patrol cabin.                     |
| 36.0 (57.9)| Trail going south out of park.                               |
| 36.4 (58.6)| Ford the Snake River.                                        |
| 36.5 (58.7)| Junction with Snake River Trail.                             |
| 38.5 (61.9)| 8C9 (3★).                                                    |
| 47.0 (75.6)| Junction with Heart River Trail to 8C5 (4★).                 |
| 50.3 (80.9)| 8J4 (3★) and junction with the Trail Creek Trail.            |
| 50.6 (81.4)| 8J6 (4★).                                                    |
| 52.8 (86.0)| 8J1 (5★).                                                    |
| 54.3 (87.4)| Junction with Heart Lake Trail.                              |
| 54.5 (87.7)| Heart Lake patrol cabin.                                     |
| 62.3(100.3)| Heart Lake Trailhead.                                        |

# HEART LAKE AND THE TWO OCEAN PLATEAU
## • HEART LAKE • HEART LAKE LOOP
## • HEART LAKE AND THE SNAKE RIVER
## • SNAKE RIVER LOOP • MOUNT SHERIDAN

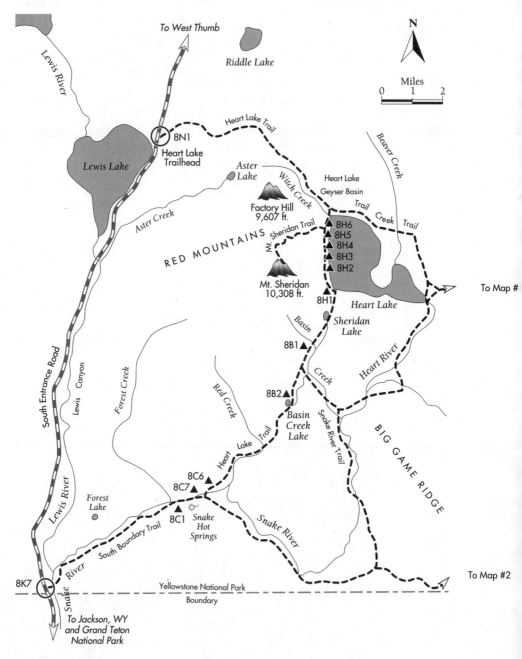

# HEART LAKE AND THE TWO OCEAN PLATEAU

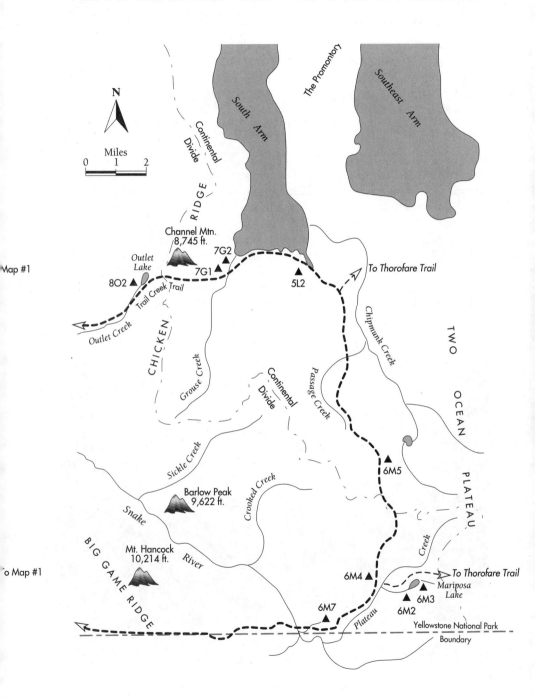

N

Miles
0   1   2

Continental Divide

The Promontory

South Arm

Southeast Arm

RIDGE

Map #1

Channel Mtn.
8,745 ft.

Outlet
Lake

7G2

7G1

8O2

5L2

To Thorofare Trail

Trail Creek Trail

Outlet Creek

CHICKEN

Grouse Creek

Continental
Divide

Passage Creek

Chipmunk Creek

TWO

OCEAN

Sickle Creek

Crooked Creek

Barlow Peak
9,622 ft.

6M5

PLATEAU

Snake

Mt. Hancock
10,214 ft.

River

Creek

To Map #1

BIG GAME RIDGE

6M4

6M7

6M2

6M3

Mariposa
Lake

To Thorofare Trail

Plateau

Yellowstone National Park
Boundary

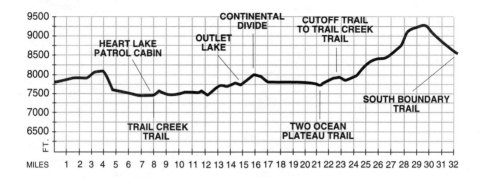

**Recommended itinerary:** The distance between campsites makes this loop trip most suitable for serious hikers who can cover up to 12 to14 miles in a day. I recommend a six-day trip as follows:

| | | |
|---|---|---|
| First night | — | Preferred—8J1, alternates—8J6 or 8J4. |
| Second night | — | Preferred—5L2, alternates—7G1, 7G2, 7N4 or 7N2. |
| Third night | — | Preferred —6M2, alternates—6M5 or 6M4. |
| Fourth night | — | Preferred— 8C9, alternate—6M7. |
| Fifth night | — | Preferred—8C5, alternates—8J4 or 8J6. |

*On the Continental Divide between Southeast Arm and Mariposa Lake.*

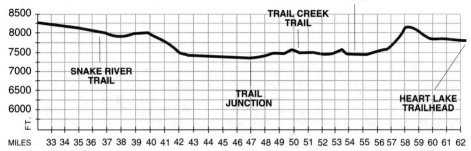

**The hike:** This trip goes through some of the most remote and infrequently visited parts of Yellowstone—for well-prepared and self-reliant hikers only. It's also one of the most difficult sections of the park because the campsites are farther apart, which often means 3 to 5 miles more per day. Also, because of high water at the fords and bear management regulations, most campsites don't open until July.

Refer to the Heart Lake and Heart Lake Loop hikes for more details, but the first leg of the trip to Heart Lake is an easy hike on a great trail with a nice view of Heart Lake, Factory Hill, and the thermal features of Witch Creek along the last 3 miles. The junction with the Trail Creek Trail is right on the shoreline of Heart Lake just past the patrol cabin (where you can usually find a ranger).

If you've chosen the clockwise route (as described here), take a left at this junction and circle around the north side of the lake where you probably want to spend your first night out. This section of trail offers a terrific view of the lake with massive Mount Sheridan as the backdrop. (If you started early enough and have time for a hike up Mount Sheridan, hang your packs near this junction and enjoy this ultra-scenic side trip.)

On the east side of Heart Lake, turn left (east) at the junction with the Heart River Trail going south (from whence you will return four days later). From here to South Arm, the trail goes through mostly burned forest. Trail conditions worsen from the heavily used trail around Heart Lake, especially one seriously boggy section about 1 mile after leaving the lake. You follow Outlet Creek, subliminally climbing up to Outlet Lake just before crossing the Continental Divide on Chicken Ridge (most likely named for the high grouse population in the area). Outlet Lake is a beautiful nugget in the forest with open shoreline, but no fish.

After leaving Outlet Lake, it's a short hill up to a gentle pass over the Continental Divide (only about 7,900 feet here) where the forest opens up into a huge meadow. From the Divide to the South Arm, the trail isn't well marked and gets faint in places, especially near Grouse Creek. The trail generally follows the creek and crosses it near 7G1.

Around the South Arm, the trail improves. At the junction with the Two Ocean Plateau Trail, go right (south). About 1 mile later, take another right

*Two Ocean Plateau near the Continental Divide.*

(south) at the cutoff trail to the Southeast Arm. From here, the trail follows the Chipmunk Creek bottomlands for about 1 mile before going over a small divide into Passage Creek. Then, the trail climbs more steeply up to the Continental Divide. Crossing the Divide here takes much more work than the crossing back on Chicken Ridge, especially a precipitous last half mile or so.

The trail from the Divide down toward the South Boundary Trail goes through open terrain with the outstanding scenery of the Two Ocean Plateau country. The trail gets inconspicuous in several places on both sides of the Divide, so watch carefully for trail markers—which you might not be able to see because of the clouds of particularly nasty mosquitoes.

The section of trail from South Arm to the South Boundary Trail is a long day, so you might not have the energy to take the side trip up to Mariposa Lake. It's only 1 mile to the lake, but it's steep. If you stay at 6M4, you can hike it after dinner or early in the next morning.

From this junction, the trail follows Plateau Creek through unburned timber past the Harebell patrol cabin to the headwaters of the Snake River. Some maps indicate that the junction is on the east side of the river, but it's on the west side. Fording the Snake at this point is usually easy because it's smaller than many creeks in Yellowstone.

At this junction, go right (northwest) and hike through the meadows lining the river. Be extra alert not to get diverted onto one of the many game trails in this area. Lots of elk go through here, and in many cases, their trails are better than ours. Mud slides have also taken out a few sections of trail. Ford the Snake just past 8C9. It's an easy crossing after mid-July.

At the junction with the Heart River Trail, go right (north) unless you're staying at 8C5 or taking the long route back to Heart Lake. You face two easy fords of the Heart River before reaching the Trail Creek Trail. From this junction, retrace your steps back to the trailhead.

**Options:** The loop can be done in reverse with no extra work. You can extend the trip and make a larger loop by going west on the Heart Lake Trail to the Basin Creek Trail, and then north along the west side of Heart Lake to hook up with the Trail Creek Trail at the Heart Lake patrol cabin. This avoids retracing your steps around the north side of Heart Lake, but it adds 6.5 miles to your trip.

**Side trips:** If you get an early start on the first or last day of your trip (and haven't had enough exercise yet), take the 8-mile (round-trip) climb up to the summit of Mount Sheridan. If you don't camp at Mariposa Lake (6M2), you would be rewarded by taking the 2-mile (round-trip) side trip to this scenic, high-altitude lake.

# 109 SNAKE RIVER LOOP

| | |
|---|---|
| **Type of hike:** | Loop. |
| **Type of trip:** | Backpacking trip. |
| **Total distance:** | 32 miles or 51.5 kilometers. |
| **Difficulty:** | Difficult. |
| **Elevation gain:** | 800 feet. |
| **Maps:** | Trails Illustrated (Yellowstone Lake); Lewis Canyon, Snake Hot Springs, and Mount Hancock USGS quads. |
| **Starting point:** | South Boundary Trailhead (8K7). |

*See Map on Page 316*

**Finding the trailhead:** The trailhead is about 100 yards south of the South Entrance Station.

**Key points:**
|  |  |  |
|---|---|---|
| 5.0 | (8.0) | 8C1 (3★) and Snake Hot Springs. |
| 5.5 | (8.8) | Junction with Heart Lake Trail. |
| 8.0 | (12.8) | Snake River Cutoff Trail. |
| 8.5 | (13.6) | 8C2 (5★). |
| 9.6 | (15.4) | Junction with Wolverine Creek Trail. |
| 11.0 | (17.7) | Harebell patrol cabin and junction with Snake River Trail. |

**Key points (cont'd):**

| | |
|---|---|
| 13.4 (21.5) | Ford of the Snake River. |
| 13.5 (20.9) | Junction with Snake River Cutoff Trail. |
| 13.9 (22.3) | 8C4 (4★). |
| 19.0 (30.6) | Junction with Basin Creek Trail. |
| 19.4 (31.2) | 8B5 (3★). |
| 21.5 (34.6) | Junction with Heart Lake Trail. |
| 22.4 (36.0) | 8B2 (3★) and Basin Creek Lake. |
| 26.0 (41.8) | 8C6 (3★). |
| 26.5 (42.6) | Junction with South Boundary Trail. |
| 27.0 (43.4) | Snake Hot Springs and 8C1 (3★). |
| 32.0 (51.5) | South Entrance Trailhead. |

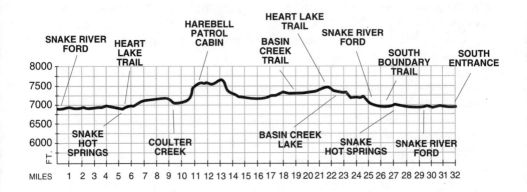

**Recommended itinerary:** This mileage might be slightly ambitious for some hikers, but I made this a four-day trip, staying the first night at 8C2, the second at 8B5, and the third at 8C6 or 8C1 while hiking the counter-clockwise route. This trip means about 11 miles with a big pack (but no big hills) on the second day.

**The hike:** This hike avoids the problematic shuttles of most long backpacking trips in Yellowstone. You start and finish at the South Boundary Trailhead, but it's not a true loop. You retrace your steps over the 5.5 miles to the Snake River Trail junction.

You start this hike with a big ford of a big river, the Snake. It's usually easy to cross after mid-July, but to play it safe check river conditions at the South Entrance Ranger Station before you leave. If the river is too high, you can start your hike 3 miles south of the park at the Shelfield Creek Trailhead (trail not shown on most maps), just south of the Flagg Ranch.

The first leg of the hike to the meadow by Snake Hot Springs is somewhat monotonous. The trail stays in the unburned timber along (but out of sight of) the Snake River. You can't really get a good view until you break out of the forest into the meadow by the hot springs. For the next half mile or so, the trail passes several hot springs and pools.

Near Snake Hot Springs, you might think you see a small prairie dog town, but this is actually the burrows dug by yellow-bellied marmots. Interestingly, this local population tends to build burrows in the open meadow along the trail instead of the rocky hillsides. Also, they tend to delay hibernation later than usual because of the extra warmth the hot springs area provides.

At the junction with the Snake River Trail, turn right (southeast) and follow the Snake River as it makes a big loop to the south. The trail climbs away from the river and stays out of sight most of the next 3 miles with the exception of where it goes through a big meadow in the last mile before coming to the junction with the Wolverine Creek Trail heading south out of the park.

Just before you reach the meadow, you might see the Snake River Cutoff Trail going off to your left (east). It's tempting to take this trail to trim some distance off the trip, but resist the temptation. This trail is low on the priority list for maintenance and is often difficult to follow. You'll save time by staying on the South Boundary Trail.

Take a left (east) at the Wolverine Creek junction and hike through an open, unburned forest to the Harebell patrol cabin, where you'll find the junction with the trail going north up the Snake River. From here, you drop into the Snake River Valley again, fording the river just before you reach the cutoff trail and 8C4. The ford is easier than the one you did at the beginning of the hike. After the ford, the trail continues through meadows and unburned timber to the junction with the Basin Creek Trail, where you turn left (northwest) and hike through intermittently burned timber to the Heart Lake Trail junction.

At this junction, go left (south) and hike about 1 mile through a big meadow to Basin Creek Lake. On a hot day, you might feel like jumping in the lake, but I'd advise against it. My kids tried it, and they had a dozen leaches on their legs in a few minutes.

From Basin Creek Lake, you drop into Red Creek and follow it through meadows and open forest until you reach the Snake River Trail junction, where you turned two days earlier. Here, you ford the Snake River again just before the junction. From here, retrace your steps to the South Entrance Trailhead.

**Options:** Since this trip lacks any big hills to wear you down, you probably can cover the same distance in three days. It can be done just as easily in the clockwise route.

**Side trips:** If you have enough time, hang your pack and day hike to Heart Lake (6 miles round-trip) on the Heart Lake Trail.

# BACKCOUNTRY CAMPSITES

These campsites serve backpacking trips in southeast section of the park and are on the Yellowstone Lake Trails Illustrated map. Stock-party or boater-only campsites are not covered.

Please keep in mind that the rating serves as a general guide only. We only visited these campsites once, and it might have been an especially good or especially bad day. For example, campsites clounded with bugs in July may be bug-free in September, and campsites without a view on a rainy day might have a good view on a clear day.

All campsites in Yellowstone allow campfires unless otherwise indicated. Likewise, all campsites are supposed to have bear poles, but just in case, be prepared to improvise.

As this book goes to print, the NPS is in the process of moving campsites previously located along the trail. Bears use the trails as travel corridors, which increases the chance of an encounter.

**Yellowstone Lake:** All three campsites closed until July 15 and use of a pit toilet along the trail.

5E7 (1★) is a mixed site right along Meadow Creek. In a swampy area close to the trail with a minimal view over a small meadow. Poor tent sites.

Both 5E8 (5★) and 5E9 (5★) rank among the best campsites in the park with postcard views of Yellowstone Lake and Frank Island from the food areas. Both hiker-only campsites have good tent sites, and the lake serves as

*Camping along Southeast Arm.*

an easy water source. 5E8 is more difficult to reach (not a good access trail), but it's more private than 5E9.

**Southeast Arm:** All Southeast Arm campsites closed until July 15.

6A2 (5★) is a secluded, hiker-only site on a little point in the Southeast Arm, about a third-mile off the main trail. Great view, good water source, but limited tent sites. Also used by boaters.

6A3 (5★) is a secluded, hiker-only site requiring a half-mile off-trail bushwhack from the main trail. Hard to get to but worth the effort. Most often used by boaters (non-motorized only). Located on Trail Point, which juts out into the Southeast Arm providing a terrific view from camp. Good water source and tent sites.

6A4 (4★) is a hiker-only site right along the trail and on the lakeshore near the Trail Creek Cabin. Great view of the Yellowstone River. Good tent sites and water source. Stays mildly boggy until late in the year. This site has a history of bear problems.

5E3 (3★) is similar to 5E4, a hiker-only site about 200 yards off the trail for privacy. Again, a great view from camp of the lake with Chicken Ridge, Channel Mountain, and the Two Ocean Plateau as a backdrop.

5E4 (5★) is a private, hiker-only site right on the lakeshore about 200 yards from the trail. Great view of the Promontory from the food area.

5E5 (4★) is not on most maps, but you might be able to stay there if you ask about it. It's about 200 yards south of 5E6, and has the same amenities. Great view and adequate tent sites. More private than 5E6. Use pit toilet at 5E6.

5E6 (4★) is a semi-private, mixed site near the start of the Southeast Arm with a great view of the Promontory from the food area. Good tent sites and pit toilet.

**Thorofare:** 5E1 (4★) would be an ideal campsite (especially for anglers) if it weren't so difficult to get water. The hiker-only campsite is on a high bench above Beaverdam Creek, and it's difficult to get up the steep trail with water. It's private (about a quarter mile east of the main trail) and has a great view across Beaverdam Creek and of Colter Peak. Closed until July 15.

6B2 (4★) is a rarely used, hiker-only site on the Yellowstone River near the upper ford. Good view and water source and plenty of tent sites. Closed until July 15.

6C1 (1★) is a mixed site right along the trail with a poor water supply and a minimal view, but lots of good tent sites.

6C2 (5★) is a very private, mixed site on the bank of the Yellowstone River. It's about 1 mile west of the main trail, but it's worth the walk and would be a good destination camp for a two- or three-day stay.

6C3 (3★) is a hiker-only site about 150 yards east of the main trail on the edge of a big meadow below Turret Mountain. It's private and has a decent view, but you need to hike about 75 yards to water.

6D1 (4★) is a private, mixed site at the confluence of Mountain Creek and the Yellowstone River. A fair view of Mountain Creek. Good water source and tent sites. A mile-long bushwhack (something you might not want at the end of a hard day) to the site. On the way back, we hiked along the stream instead of the "trail" and found it easier. This would be a good destination camp where you could stay two or three days. It's interesting to note from this site how the river stopped the advance of the 1988 fires.

6D2 (3★) is a not-so-private, hiker-only site on your left (east) just after you ford Mountain Creek. It has room for lots of tents, a good view over the stream wash of Mountain Creek and Turret Mountain, and an easily accessible water source.

6Y4 (3★) is a private, mixed site near the confluence of Thorofare Creek and the Yellowstone River. The food area is regrettably located in a stand of live timber which blocks the view. Lots of good tent sites and a good water source. When coming from the north, it's tempting to look at the topo map and bushwhack across the marshy meadow to the site. But it's better to wait until you get past the South Boundary Trail junction, where you find a good trail leading to this campsite.

6Y5 (3★) is a private, hiker-only site about 150 yards west (on a marginal trail) of the main trail. Watch for the sign just after you cross Cliff Creek. Good water source and a fair view out into the meadows along the river.

6Y6 (4★) is a semi-private, mixed site on the Three Mile Bend of the Yellowstone River. A good view of the meadows south down the Thorofare and Hawks Rest, which overlooks Bridger Lake. Good water source and tent sites.

6T1 (4★) is a not-so-private, mixed site on the left just west of Thorofare Creek. Good tent sites and water source, but exposed to the weather. Both 6T1 and 6T2 make good destination sites and are both close to the ranger station if you need help.

6T2 (5★) is an ideal campsite on the banks of Thorofare Creek just north of the ford on the east side of the stream. This private, hiker-only site has a great view, good tent sites, and an easy water source.

6Y2 (4★) is a not-so-private, hiker-only site right along the trail and just east of the ford of the Yellowstone River. Good water source and a great view.

You can also camp south of the park around Bridger Lake.

**Mariposa Lake:** 6M2 (4★) is a private, mixed site at the west end of the lake. It's nicer than 6M3 with a better view and tent sites and a good water source. You have to cross the outlet stream to get to the campsite. Off-trail travel between July 15 and August 21 by permit only.

6M3 (2★) is a lightly used, mixed site on the east end of Mariposa Lake. Private and so infrequently used that it's difficult to find. Good location and a nice view, but only one tent site (and a marginal one at that). No trailside sign when we were there. Off trail travel between July 15 and August 21 by permit only.

**Two Ocean Plateau:** 6M5 (3★) is a private, mixed site on the Two Ocean Plateau. Good tent sites and water source. Off-trail travel allowed between July 15 and August 21 by permit only.

**South Boundary Trail:** 6M4 (3★) is a semi-private, mixed site at the junction of the South Boundary and Two Ocean Plateau trails. Good tent sites and water source. Decent view out into a big meadow. Off trail travel between July 15 and August 21 by permit only.

6M7 (3★) is a hiker-only site about 300 yards off the trail just before reaching the Fox Creek patrol cabin. Rarely used campsite. Marginal tent sites and a minimal view, but a good water source.

You can also camp outside the park up Wolverine Creek, on Big Game Ridge, and near the Harebell patrol cabin.

**Snake River:** 8C1 (3★) is not-so-private, hiker-only site right along the trail near the Snake Hot Springs. Limited tent sites, but a good water source (the river) and a terrific view up the Snake River Valley.

8C2 (5★) is a private, mixed site on the banks of the Snake River. Great view of the Snake River, plenty of excellent tent sites, an easy water source, and the spur trail is easy to follow. Firewood is sparse.

8C4 (4★) is a mixed, private site right on the Snake River about 60 yards off the trail. Easy access to water and a decent view

8C5 (4★) is a mixed site along the trail, just west of the junction with the Heart River Trail. Great view, good tent sites and water source. Closed until July.

8C6 (3★) is a semi-private, mixed site on the west of the ford of the Snake River about 50 yards from the trail. Exposed site with lots of good tent sites and a good view of the Snake River. Far enough to water to be inconvenient.

8C9 (3★) is a mixed site near the confluence of Crooked Creek and the Snake River. Heavily used by stock parties. Limited view, good tent site, and water source.

**Heart Lake:** All six campsites on the west side of the lake are hiker-only and closed until July. Only 8H2 and 8H3 allow campfires, but this regulation might change because the 1988 fires burned some of the shoreline leaving lots of firewood. With the exception of 8H1, these campsites are close to the lake. All sites have their own toilets or share with a nearby site. All six campsites are suited for small groups only with no more than two tents.

8H4 (4★), 8H5 (4★) and 8H6 (4★) are clumped together near the Mount Sheridan Trail with limited privacy. Avoid old tent sites too close to the bear poles. 8H2 (4★) and 8H3 (4★) have the best views and are the most private, but each has a marshy trail leading to it. 8H2 and 8H3 are close together— a good choice for two parties who know each other. 8H1 (2★) is at the far end of the lake located 200 yards from the lake in a narrow gully with no view and marginal tent sites. All sites closed until July.

8J1 (5★) is a private, hiker-only site on the lakeshore with a great view and pit toilet. Closed until July.

8J3 (3★) is a hiker-only site right along the trail less than a half mile from the Heart River Trail junction. Good water source. Minimal view and marginal tent sites. Closed until July.

8J4 (3★) is a not-so-private, hiker-only site at the junction with the Trail Lake Trail and the confluence of the Heart River and Outlet Creek. Limited tent sites, marginal view, but good water source. Closed until July.

8J6 (4★) is a private, hiker-only site about a quarter mile from the trail on the shore of Heart Lake with a super view of the lake and Mount Sheridan. Good water source, but limited tent sites. Pit toilet. Closed until July.

**Basin Creek:** 8B1(3★) is a semi-private, hiker-only site on your right (west) along a small tributary to Basin Creek. Good water source and a fair view out into a big meadow along Basin Creek. Watch for the sign immediately south of the stream. Closed until July.

8B2 (3★) is a mixed site on your right (west) just north of Basin Creek Lake. If the signs are down (as they were when I was there), it's difficult to find. It's in a grove of trees about 150 yards from the lake (the water source). It's private with decent tent sites, but has no view. Closed until July.

8B5 (3★) is a hiker-only site right along the trail, but still fairly private since very few people use this trail. Good water source, plenty of good tent sites, but no view. Closed until July.

**Outlet Lake:** 8O2 (4★) is a mixed, private site about 200 yards off the main trail. Good view of the lake and southwest toward Mount Sheridan. Good water source and adequate tent sites. Closed until June. No off-trail travel east of campsite before July 15.

**Grouse Creek:** 7G1 (3★) is a private, mixed site on Grouse Creek which is a handy water source. Plenty of tent sites and a fair view. A quarter mile off trail. Closed until July 15.

7G2 (4Y) is a mixed, private site along Grouse Creek and within sight of the South Arm. Great view and about 100 yards to water. Closed until July 15.

**South Arm:** 5L2 (2★) a difficult-to-find, mixed site at the terminus of the South Arm of Yellowstone Lake. Fair view, but you have to haul water a quarter mile from the lake. Closed until July 15.

# AFTERWORD: A BAD IDEA?

It has been whispered here and there, usually by "locals," that books like this are a bad idea.

The theory goes something like this: Guidebooks bring more people into the wilderness; more people cause more environmental damage; and the wildness we all seek gradually evaporates.

I used to think like that, too. And here's why I changed my mind.

When I wrote and published my first guidebook in 1979 (*Hiking Montana*), some of my hiking buddies disapproved. Since then, I've published more than fifty hiking guides, and I'm proud of it. I also hope these books have increased wilderness use.

Experienced hikers tend to have a lofty attitude toward the inexperienced masses. They think anybody who wants to backpack can buy a topo map and compass and find their own way through the wilderness. But the fact is, most people want a guide. Sometimes inexperienced hikers prefer a real, live person to show them the way and help them build confidence, but most of the time, they can get by with a trail guide like this one.

All guidebooks published by Falcon (and most published by other publishers) invite wilderness users to respect and support the protection of wild country. Sometimes, this is direct editorializing. Sometimes, this invitation takes the more subtle form of simply helping people experience wilderness. And it's a rare person who leaves the wilderness without a firmly planted passion for wild country—and waiting for a chance to vote for more of it.

In classes on backpacking taught for the Yellowstone Institute, I have taken hundreds of people into the wilderness. Many of them had on a backpack for the first time. Many of them were not convinced that we need more wilderness, but they were all convinced when they arrived back at the trailhead. Many, many times, I've seen it happen without saying a single word about wilderness.

It doesn't take preaching. Instead, we just need to get people out into the wilderness where the essence of wildness sort of sneaks up on them and takes root, and before you know it, the ranks of those who support wilderness has grown.

But what about overcrowding? Yes, it's a problem in many places and probably will be Yellowstone. The answer to overcrowded, overused wilderness is not limiting use of wilderness and restrictive regulations. The answer is more wilderness.

How can we convince people to support more wilderness when they have never experienced wilderness? In my opinion, we can't. Without the support of people who experience wilderness, there will be no more wilderness.

That's why we need guidebooks. And that's why I changed my mind. I believe guidebooks have done as much to build support for wilderness as pro-wilderness organizations have ever done through political and public relations efforts.

And if that's not enough, here's another reason. All FalconGuides (and most guidebooks from other publishers) contain sections on no-trace camping and wilderness safety. Guidebooks provide an ideal medium for communicating such vital information.

In thirty years of backpacking, I have seen dramatic changes in how backpackers care for wilderness. I've seen it go from appalling to exceptional. Today, almost everybody walks softly in the wilderness. And I believe the information contained in guidebooks has been partly responsible for this change.

Having said all that, I hope many thousands of people use this book to enjoy a fun-filled vacation hiking in Yellowstone—and then, of course, vote for wilderness preservation the rest of their lives.

*Bill Schneider*, Publisher

# PRESERVING YELLOWSTONE

The Yellowstone Association is a non-profit organization founded in 1933 to assist with educational, historical, and scientific programs for the benefit of Yellowstone National Park and its visitors. Through the years, the Association has raised millions of dollars to help preserve Yellowstone and supplement the park's educational programs.

The Association operates bookstores in all park visitor centers and information stations with the proceeds from sales of books, maps, and videos going to fund interpretive programs and exhibits for visitors, as well as research projects and equipment. The Association also publishes books, pamphlets, and leaflets about the park and maintains the park research library.

The Yellowstone Institute, an in-depth educational program for the public, is also sponsored by The Yellowstone Association. The Institute offers about 80 courses and is based at the Buffalo Ranch in the Lamar Valley. If you're interested in taking an Institute course or getting a free catalog, call (307) 344-2294 or write Yellowstone Institute, P.O. Box 117, Yellowstone National Park, WY 82190.

You can help preserve Yellowstone by becoming a member of The Yellowstone Association. Besides contributing to the protection of the park, membership benefits include a newsletter, a subscription to the park newspaper, *Yellowstone Today*, a 15 percent discount on books, maps, and videos sold at visitor centers, and discounts on Yellowstone Institute class tuition. All memberships or donations are tax-deductible.

To become a member or get more information on The Yellowstone Association, write The Yellowstone Association, P.O. Box 117, Yellowstone National Park, WY 82190 or call (307) 344-2296. To order books, maps, or videos, call (307) 344-2293 or stop at any visitor center.

# HIKER'S CHECKLIST

**Hiking Equipment:** Equipment does not have to be new or fancy (or expensive), but make sure you test everything before you leave home.

## Equipment Checklist for Day Hiking:

- ☐ Day pack or fanny pack
- ☐ Water bottles
- ☐ First-aid kit
- ☐ Survival kit
- ☐ Compass
- ☐ Maps
- ☐ Toilet trowel

- ☐ Toilet paper
- ☐ Sun screen and lip lotion
- ☐ Binoculars*
- ☐ Camera and extra film*
- ☐ Flashlight and extra batteries
- ☐ Pocket knife
- ☐ Sunglasses

## Added Equipment for Overnight Trips:

- ☐ Tent and waterproof fly
- ☐ Sleeping bag (20 degrees F. or warmer) and stuff sack
- ☐ Sleeping pad
- ☐ Cooking pots and pot holder
- ☐ More water bottles
- ☐ Full-size backpack
- ☐ Cup, bowl, and eating utensils
- ☐ Lightweight camp stove and adequate fuel

- ☐ Garbage sacks
- ☐ Zip-locked bags
- ☐ Stuff sacks*
- ☐ Paper towels*
- ☐ Nylon cord (50 ft.)
- ☐ Small towel
- ☐ Personal toilet kit
- ☐ Notebook and pencil*

**Clothing:** In general, strive for natural fibers such as cotton and wool, and "earth tones" instead of bright colors. Dig around in the closet for something "dull." Your wilderness partners will appreciate it. Try out the clothing before leaving home to make sure everything fits loosely with no chafing. In particular, make sure your boots are broken in, lest they break you on the first day of the hike.

## Clothing for Day Hiking:

- ☐ Large-brimmed hat or cap
- ☐ Sturdy hiking boots
- ☐ Light, natural fiber socks
- ☐ Lightweight, hiking shorts or long pants

- ☐ Long-sleeve shirt
- ☐ Lightweight, windproof coat
- ☐ Raingear
- ☐ Mittens or gloves

---

\* = optional.

## Additional Clothing for Overnight Trips:

- ☐ Warm hat (i.e. stocking cap)
- ☐ Long underwear
- ☐ Water-resistant, windproof wilderness coat
- ☐ Sweater and/or insulated vest
- ☐ Long pants
- ☐ One pair of socks for each day, plus one extra pair
- ☐ Underwear
- ☐ Extra shirts
- ☐ Sandals or lightweight shoes for wearing in camp

**Food:** For day hiking, bring high-energy snacks for lunching along the way. For overnight trips, bring enough food, including high-energy snacks for lunching during the day, but don't overburden yourself with too much food. Plan meals carefully, bringing just enough food, plus some emergency rations. Freeze-dried foods are the lightest and safest in bear country, but expensive and not really necessary. Don't forget hot and cold drinks.

*Derek Sonderegger, Greg Schneider, Carrie Bowen (left to right) on the South Boundary Trail.*

*Bill Schneider on Electric Pass.*

*Russ Schneider in Nez Perce Creek.*

---

# THE TEAM APPROACH

---

Yellowstone National Park is a big place—actually too big for one person to hike all the trails in one year. So to research this book, we employed the team approach. In the summer of 1996, five of us hiked about 850 miles of trails in Yellowstone.

The primary author and editor is Bill Schnieder who has spent more than thirty years hiking trails all across America and written six other hiking guides.

During college in the mid-1960s, he worked on a trail crew in Glacier National Park. He then spent the 1970s publishing the *Montana Outdoors* magazine for the Montana Department of Fish, Wildlife & Parks and covering as many miles of trails as possible on weekends and holidays.

In 1979, Bill and his partner, Mike Sample, created Falcon Press Publishing Company and released two guidebooks that first year. Bill wrote one of them, *Hiking Montana*, which is still popular. Since then, he has written eleven more books and many magazine articles on wildlife, outdoor recreation, and environmental issues. Along the way, on a part-time basis over a span of 12 years, Bill has taught classes on bicycling, backpacking, no-trace camping, and hiking in bear country for the Yellowstone Institute, a nonprofit educational organization in Yellowstone National Park.

Today, Bill still serves as publisher of Falcon Press Publishing, which is now established as a premier national publisher of recreational guidebooks with more than 300 titles in print.

Russ Schneider (Bill's son) works part-time at Falcon as an acquisitions editor and at Glacier Wilderness Guides as a hiking and fishing guide. Russ is author of *Hiking the Columbia River Gorge* and soon-to-be-published *Fishing Glacier National Park.*

Carrie Bowen, Derek Sonderegger, and Greg Schneider (also Bill's son) are students at Montana State University in Bozeman, Montana.

Falcon employees Randall Green and Ric Bourie hiked and provided information for the Mallard Lake hike.

# BOOKS BY THE AUTHOR

*Where the Grizzly Walks*
*The Dakota Image*
*Hiking Montana*
*The Yellowstone River*
*The Tree Giants*
*The Flight of the Nez Perce*
*Hiking the Beartooths*
*Hiking Carlsbad & Guadalupe Mountains National Parks*
*Bear Aware*
*Exploring Canyonlands & Arches National Parks*
*Best Easy Day Hikes Canyonlands & Arches*
*Best Easy Day Hikes Yellowstone*

get
**FALCON** GUIDED

# Hiking the National Parks

The national parks have some of the very best hiking in the world, and just because it's in a national park doesn't mean it's crowded. In many parks, the roads are clogged with traffic, but the trails are nearly devoid of people.

As part of the **FALCON** GUIDES® series, Falcon plans to publish a complete set of hiking guides to every national park with a substantial trail system. If your favorite park isn't on the following list of books currently available, you can plan on it being available soon. Each book comprehensively covers the trails in the parks and includes the necessary trip planning information on access, regulations, weather, etc., to help you put together a memorable adventure.

AVAILABLE NOW:

*Hiking Big Bend National Park*
*Hiking California's Desert Parks* (includes Death Valley and Joshua Tree National parks,
    Mojave National Preserve, and Anza-Borrego State Park)
*Exploring Canyonlands & Arches National Parks*
*Hiking Carlsbad Caverns & Guadalupe Mountains National Parks*
*Hiking Glacier & Waterton Lakes National Parks*
*Hiking Grand Canyon National Park*
*Hiking Great Basin National Park*
*Hiking Olympic National Park*
*Hiking Shenandoah National Park*
*Hiking South Dakota's Black Hills Country* (includes Wind Cave, Badlands and
    Mount Rushmore national parks, and Custer State Park)
*Hiking Yellowstone National Park*
*Hiking Zion & Bryce Canyon National Parks*

ALSO AVAILABLE:
42 state-wide, wilderness area, and regional hiking guides

TO ORDER:
Check with your local bookseller or
call Falcon at **1-800-582-2665**
www.falconguide.com

FALCON®

# get FALCON GUIDED

## BIRDING GUIDES
Birding Minnesota
Birding Montana
Birding Texas
Birding Utah

## FIELD GUIDES
Bitterroot: Montana State Flower
Canyon Country Wildflowers
Great Lakes Berry Book
New England Berry Book
Pacific Northwest Berry Book
Plants of Arizona
Rare Plants of Colorado
Rocky Mountain Berry Book
Scats & Tracks of the Rocky Mtns.
Tallgrass Prairie Wildflowers
Western Trees
Wildflowers of Southwestern Utah
Willow Bark and Rosehips

## FISHING GUIDES
Fishing Alaska
Fishing the Beartooths
Fishing Florida
Fishing Glacier National Park
Fishing Maine
Fishing Montana
Fishing Wyoming

## PADDLING GUIDES
Floater's Guide to Colorado
Paddling Montana
Paddling Okeefenokee
Paddling Oregon
Paddling Yellowstone & Grand
　　Teton National Parks

## ROCKHOUNDING GUIDES
Rockhounding Arizona
Rockhound's Guide to California
Rockhound's Guide to Colorado
Rockhounding Montana
Rockhounding Nevada
Rockhound's Guide to New Mexico
Rockhounding Texas
Rockhounding Utah
Rockhounding Wyoming

## WALKING
Walking Colorado Springs
Walking Denver
Walking Portland
Walking St. Louis

## HOW-TO GUIDES
Avalanche Aware
Backpacking Tips
Bear Aware
Leave No Trace
Mountain Lion Alert
Reading Weather
Wilderness First Aid
Wilderness Survival

## MORE GUIDEBOOKS
Backcountry Horseman's
　　Guide to Washington
Camping California's
　　National Forests
Exploring Canyonlands &
　　Arches National Parks
Exploring Hawaii's Parklands
Exploring Mount Helena
Recreation Guide to WA
　　National Forests
Touring California & Nevada
　　Hot Springs
Trail Riding Western
　　Montana
Wild Country Companion
Wild Montana

■ *To order any of these books, check with your local bookseller
or call FALCON® at **1-800-582-2665**.*

*Visit us on the world wide web at:*
www.falconguide.com

FALCON®

get
**FALCON** GUIDED

**HIKING GUIDES**

Hiking Alaska
Hiking Alberta
Hiking Arizona
Hiking Arizona's Cactus Country
Hiking the Beartooths
Hiking Big Bend National Park
Hiking Bob Marshall Country
Hiking California
Hiking California's Desert Parks
Hiking Carlsbad Caverns
   and Guadalupe Mtns. National Parks
Hiking Colorado
Hiking the Columbia River Gorge
Hiking Florida
Hiking Georgia
Hiking Glacier & Waterton Lakes National Parks
Hiking Grand Canyon National Park
Hiking Grand Staircase-Escalante/Glen Canyon
Hiking Great Basin National Park
Hiking Hot Springs in the Pacific Northwest
Hiking Idaho
Hiking Maine
Hiking Michigan
Hiking Minnesota
Hiking Montana
Hiker's Guide to Nevada
Hiking New Hampshire

Hiking New Mexico
Hiking New York
Hiking North Cascades
Hiking Northern Arizona
Hiking Olympic National Park
Hiking Oregon
Hiking Oregon's Eagle Cap Wilderness
Hiking Oregon's Mount Hood/Badger Creek
Hiking Oregon's Three Sisters Country
Hiking Pennsylvania
Hiking Shenandoah
Hiking South Carolina
Hiking South Dakota's Black Hills Country
Hiking Southern New England
Hiking Tennessee
Hiking Texas
Hiking Utah
Hiking Utah's Summits
Hiking Vermont
Hiking Virginia
Hiking Washington
Hiking Wisconsin
Hiking Wyoming
Hiking Wyoming's Wind River Range
Hiking Yellowstone National Park
Hiking Zion & Bryce Canyon National Parks
The Trail Guide to Bob Marshall Country

■ *To order any of these books, check with your local bookseller*
*or call FALCON® at* **1-800-582-2665** .

*Visit us on the world wide web at:*
www.falconguide.com

FALCON®

# Discover the Thrill of Watching Wildlife.

 The Watchable Wildlife® Series

Published in cooperation with Defenders of Wildlife, these high-quality, full color guidebooks feature detailed descriptions, side trips, viewing tips, and easy-to-follow maps. Wildlife viewing guides for the following states are now available with more on the way.

| | | |
|---|---|---|
| Alaska | Massachusetts | Ohio |
| Arizona | Montana | Oregon |
| California | Nebraska | Tennessee |
| Colorado | Nevada | Texas |
| Florida | New Hampshire | Utah |
| Idaho | New Jersey | Vermont |
| Indiana | New Mexico | Virginia |
| Iowa | New York | Washington |
| Kentucky | North Carolina | West Virginia |
| | North Dakota | Wisconsin |

*Watch for this sign along roadways. It's the official sign indicating wildlife viewing areas included in the Watchable Wildlife® Series.*

WILDLIFE VIEWING AREA

■ *To order any of these books, check with your local bookseller or call FALCON at 1-800-582-2665.*

www.falconguide.com

FALCON®

The TwoDot line features classic western literature and history. Each book celebrates and interprets the vast spaces and rich culture of the American West.

# TWODOT
*An Imprint of Falcon Publishing*

*Bozeman and the Gallatin Valley: A History*
*Charlie's Trail: The Life and Art of C.M. Russell*
*Flight of the Dove: The Story of Jeannette Rankin*
*Jeannette Rankin: Bright Star in the Big Sky*
*Men with Sand: Great Explorers of the American West*
*Montana Campfire Tales: Fourteen Historical Essays*
*More Than Petticoats: Remarkable Montana Women*
*The Only Good Bear is a Dead Bear*
*Today I Baled Some Hay to Feed the Sheep the Coyotes Eat*

## It Happened in Series

Entertaining and informative, each book is written in a lively, easy-to-read style, and features 31-34 stories about events that helped shape each state's history.

*It Happened in Arizona*
*It Happened in Colorado*
*It Happened in Montana*
*It Happened in New Mexico*
*It Happened in Oregon*
*It Happened in Southern California*
*It Happened in Texas*
*It Happened in Utah*
*It Happened in Washington*

## Four-Legged Legends Series

Young adult readers will be enthralled and inspired by these true tales of animal bravery, loyalty, and ferocity.

*Four-Legged Legends of Colorado*
*Four-Legged Legends of Montana*
*Four-Legged Legends of Oregon*

FALCON®

To order check with your local bookseller or call Falcon at
# 1-800-582-2665.

Ask for a FREE catalog featuring a complete list of titles on nature, outdoor recreation, travel, and the West.